PUBLIC FINANCE
IN DEMOCRATIC PROCESS

PUBLIC FINANCE
IN
DEMOCRATIC PROCESS

Fiscal Institutions and Individual Choice

JAMES M. BUCHANAN

THE UNIVERSITY OF NORTH CAROLINA PRESS · CHAPEL HILL

Preface

Fiscal theory is normally discussed in a frame of reference wholly different from that adopted in this book. This dramatic shift of emphasis plays havoc with disciplinary orthodoxy, and few guideposts remain to indicate whether or not the bounds of reasoned argument have been overextended. By necessity the approach taken here requires that I consider the processes through which individual choices are transmitted, combined, and transformed into collective outcomes. Careful research and scholarship in this area is in its infancy, and the necessary reliance on crude, unsophisticated models underscores the exploratory nature of the work.

My best critics have been my graduate students, and the theme most recurrent in their comments concerns the unreality of the individualist-democracy models of political order on which the analysis is based. In the real world, individuals, as such, do not seem to make fiscal choices. They seem limited to choosing "leaders," who will, in turn, make fiscal decisions. This idea, that, in modern political structures, individuals are satisfied when they "choose the choosers," is sufficiently pervasive to justify some discussion, even at this early stage. In certain aspects of life, it is, of course, meaningful and efficient for the individual to choose "experts" who will, in turn, be empowered to make the necessary ultimate decisions. The case of medical care is perhaps the most familiar. In selecting a doctor, the individual is choosing someone that he considers more qualified than he to make decisions on his behalf. The individual does so, however, only because the ultimate criterion, good health, is understood by both parties and is capable of reasonably definite objective measurement.

Is politics like medicine? Are we willing to choose "experts" who will decide for us? Are we prepared to allow government "for the people" but not "by the people"? It is apparent that there is a fundamental difference here, and that it is summarized by the absence of agreed-on and objective criteria. We are not normally willing to allow chosen political "leaders" to decide for us, save within very restricted limits, because we disagree sharply among ourselves concerning what should be chosen. In one sense, the departure from standard democratic procedures during periods of war emergency confirms the basic hypothesis of democracy. For only in such periods are collective goals or objectives shared sufficiently by the populace to make genuine delegation of decision making to experts acceptable. In the absence of such emergency, the delegation of ultimate decision power to experts, or presumed experts, is inconsistent with our notions of a free society. Individuals do not agree on criteria, and the range for collective action is wide. Why should the individual be willing to delegate to a presumed expert his power of public choice when he is unwilling to so delegate his power of private choice?

The delegation of choice discussed here is not the same thing as *representative* government. To an extent, of course, elected representatives choose for their constituents in any large democracy. So long as their choices are, however, constrained and guided by the ultimate wishes of their constituents, the democratic models retain relevance.

The central criticism of the individualist-democracy models is in part introspective, and it stems from each person's feeling that he is alienated from "the State." The primary psychological relation of the single individual to government is one of coercion, and, recognizing this, the individual is reluctant to discuss, or even to think about, voluntaristic aspects of the process. This reaction mechanism need not be damaging, so long as the alienation is kept within appropriate limits. Effective democratic process, and useful theorizing, does not require that each and every citizen feels himself to be a participant in a continuous referendum. The individual may, and does, recognize that many of the complex political-governmental institutions are beyond his own range of control or influence. He must, nonetheless, recognize that some power of ultimate choice rests with him and his fellows. To the extent that personal alienation from the state extends beyond this point, to the extent that the individual loses all sense of influence in determining the limits on political action, effective democratic process is eliminated, and the models developed in this book are admittedly inapplicable.

In this case, the analysis should properly shift from the behavior of the voter-citizen-taxpayer-beneficiary to that of the decision maker, who secures benefits without suffering costs, and of the decision taker, who suffers costs and secures benefits only at the suffrage of his rulers. The political-fiscal process factors down into a two-class model, and the behavior of two groups must be examined. Developments in American democracy may suggest to some observers a shifting toward such a model. Descriptive realism is often deceptive, however, and, hopefully, the individualist-democracy models retain predictive relevance. If they do not, we should at least be willing to examine the alternative.

Is it not possible, indeed probable, that our conceptual analysis of social-political institutions is basically analogous to our visual reaction to the familiar staircase figure below? We can view the

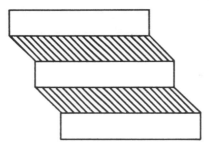

figure in either one of two ways, but it is impossible to view it in both ways simultaneously. One must, somehow, shift his vision, itself an interesting mental process, in order to change the steps into risers and vice versa.

Our conception of fiscal process seems much the same. It may be consistently interpreted and analyzed in a ruling-class, "establishment," or force model of political order. And, as I hope this book suggests, the process can also be consistently interpreted through an individualist-democracy framework. In any relevant modern setting that is broadly described as "democratic" in the Western sense, each of the two conceptions possesses some explanatory potential. The relative efficacy of the two models need not be

Preface

discussed, and the normative implications can also be left out of account. Orthodox discussion in public finance reflects an uncertain mixture of the two approaches, along with a liberal dosage of idealist-democracy norms. The resulting inconsistencies are not surprising. If this book does little else than call attention to the importance of the political decision process in public finance theory, its lesser purpose will have been achieved.

* * * * *

The basic draft of this book was written during the summers of 1962, 1963, and 1964. The manuscript was thoroughly revised during the period, February-August, 1965, and final changes were made in early 1966. I am indebted to the National Committee on Government Finance, Brookings Institution, for research support and assistance. Helpful clerical assistance has also been provided by the Thomas Jefferson Center for Political Economy, University of Virginia, and especially through the services of Mrs. Betty Tillman. Emilio Giardina, Charles Goetz, W. C. Stubblebine, and Gordon Tullock provided helpful comments on early drafts. Among editorial readers who were identified James S. Coleman, Anthony Downs, Roland N. McKean, and William N. Riker contributed useful advice for revision. Mark Pauly deserves especial thanks for his assistance with the index.

Charlottesville
March, 1966

Contents

Contents

PART I

THE EFFECTS OF INSTITUTIONS ON FISCAL CHOICE

I am ready to admit that much of my discussion may be classified as arm-chair speculation. I accept the title gladly, for this is, in fact, the manner in which everything may be taken into account, and an inclusive, internally consistent system constructed. For this reason, I never worry about the external consequences of carrying out my theory. How much of it—or whether any at all—may be practically applied in the near future, practical men may decide. I become the same as they if I try to take into account every conceivable practical criticism.

Knut Wicksell, in the Preface to
Finanztheoretische Untersuchungen
(Jena: Gustav Fischer, 1896).

1. *Introduction*

Individuals, separately and in groups, make decisions concerning the use of economic resources. They do so in at least two capacities: first, as purchasers (sellers) of goods and services in organized markets, and, secondly, as "purchasers" ("sellers") of goods and services through organized political processes. Economic theory has been developed largely to explain the workings of organized markets, and the trained economist understands how decentralized decisions are mutually co-ordinated so as to produce allocative results that are internally consistent. Economists, especially English and American, have devoted little time and effort to an explanation of individual behavior in the second decision process.[1] Individual participation in collective decision-making has not been thoroughly analyzed, and the means through which the separate private choices are combined to produce "social" or "collective" outcomes have not been subject to careful and critical research. This relative emphasis on the interaction process in private markets was, to some degree, justifiable so long as organized markets retained overwhelming allocative importance. But when more than one-fourth of all products, even in those economies that are presumably noncollectivist, is destined to be used for collective rather than for private purposes, some modification in the emphasis seems in order.

There exists no "theory of collective choice," no "theory of demand for collective goods," that is analogous to the familiar

1. "The application of income to the payment of taxes is a particular case of the general law of the division of income." The recognition of this point was characterized as a major Italian contribution to the theory of public finance by Gino Borgatta in his summary preface to a volume of translations. (Gino Borgatta, "Prefazione," *Nuova Collana di Economisti*, Vol. IX, *Finanza* [Torino: Unione Tipografico Editrice Torinese, 1934], p. xxxi.)

theorems and propositions in neoclassical economics. We know little about how individuals behave as they participate in collective choice. In societies that are organized democratically, even in the broadest sense of this highly ambiguous term, individuals must be assumed to participate in the formation of "public" decisions. They may, of course, do so indirectly and at several stages removed from specific allocative choices. They may be motivated by group rather than individual interest, and they may remain indifferent over wide margins of public choices. The complexities of modern politics and bureaucracy should not, however, conceal the underlying realities, and gross misunderstanding can result if individual participation in, and reaction to, public decisions is either neglected or assumed away. The omniscient and benevolent despot does not exist, despite the genuine love for him sometimes espoused, and, scientifically, he is not a noble construction. To assume that he does exist, for the purpose of making analysis agreeable, serves to confound the issues and to guarantee frustration for the scientist who seeks to understand and to explain.

Political decision-making is a complex and intricate process, much more complicated than is the nonpolitical decision-making in market institutions. The rules constraining individual choice are necessarily different in the two cases, and because of the nature, both of these rules and the underlying objectives, simple correspondence between private cost and benefit, a basic feature of market choice, cannot exist in politics. Nevertheless, at some ultimate stage or level, the individual must, somehow, "choose" how his resources are to be used collectively as well as privately. In the final analysis, the individual must "decide" on the appropriate size of the government budget, and on the breakdown of this budget among component items. Despite his acknowledged ignorance, the individual citizen must, ultimately, choose the size of outlay on public education as well as number of veterans' hospitals.

This is not to suggest that the individual makes collective choices only, or even primarily, in his role as a voter in elective processes. He exerts influences on public choices through professional organizations to which he belongs, through the publications that he supports, through the public and private bureaucracies that employ his talents. Collective outcomes emerge out of the utility-maximizing behavior of many persons acting in many separate capacities.

These outcomes are not independent of or divorced from the activities of individuals even if there is little consciousness on the part of any particular person that he is choosing *for* the community, save in specific and isolated cases. Even here, he is perhaps conscious of opting for or against a highly uncertain package; rarely is he given the opportunity to make specific indications of preference for or against tax or expenditure proposals. Nonetheless, analysis that cuts through the maze and examines the cost and benefit calculus of the individual *as if* he makes specific choices seems necessary as a starting point.

How can the private "costs" that the individual takes into account in such decisions be isolated and identified? How can the private "benefits" that are expected to balance off these costs be determined? Even to raise such questions as these suggests that research objectives here must be modest. Common sense indicates that the institutions through which costs and benefits are presented to the private citizen may influence his decision. The direct costs of governmental services appear to the citizen as *taxes,* and the manner in which these are levied may significantly affect his attitudes toward the extension or the contraction of such services. This study has as its purpose the development of some rudimentary predictions concerning the effects of the various fiscal institutions on the decision calculus of the individual, as citizen-voter-taxpayer-beneficiary. The limitations of this purpose should be stressed. When the study is completed, we shall remain a long way from an integrated "theory of fiscal choice." But some of the essential elements will, hopefully, have been provided, some crude hypotheses will have been tested, and some normative implications for reform in the existing fiscal structure may have emerged in the process.

THE TRADITIONAL APPROACH TO PUBLIC FINANCE

Public finance, as a subdiscipline of classical, neo-classical, and even Keynesian political economy, has consisted primarily in the analysis of the effects of alternative fiscal institutions on individual and group behavior in the private economy. Taxes and expenditures, separately or in the aggregate, have been studied, both analytically and empirically, with a view toward determining their effects on the activities of persons, families, firms, and other voluntary organizations. The influence of income taxation on the individual's

5

choice between work and leisure, the effects of business taxation on managerial efficiency, the effects of agricultural subsidies on output, the impact of highway spending programs on transportation development, the effects of budget deficits or surpluses on income, employment, and prices: all these, and many more similar topics, are familiar chapters in the treatise written in the traditional framework.

These subjects are important, and past research has yielded fruitful results. Current and future research promises to add still more to our analytical capital stock. The absence of an important aspect of public finance must be noted nonetheless. The individual does choose how to allocate his income-earning power between earning and not-earning, and he is surely influenced in this choice by fiscal institutions. But he also chooses, as a citizen in a democratically organized political community, how to allocate his potential income between private uses and public or collective uses. The structure of fiscal institutions must also affect this choice, and in important ways, even if participation in such choice by the individual seems remote and indirect. Public finance, as traditionally developed, studies individual behavior in the *private* sphere of his activity. It has not, sufficiently, examined behavior in the *public* sphere of activity, although here, too, the choices must remain *individual* in the final analysis, regardless of the decision-making rules.

SPECIFIC PURPOSE

This study is not aimed at developing a comprehensive "theory of fiscal choice," even at the level of individual participation. Its primary purpose is that of analyzing the effects of designated fiscal institutions on individual behavior in collective choice situations. Attempts will be made to predict the effects of such institutions as the income tax on the individual's behavior as he confronts decisions on the public usage of economic resources.

There are two parts to the study. In the first, Part I, we shall assume that the various fiscal institutions are exogenously imposed on the individual. That is to say, he is assumed to adjust his behavior under a set of institutions that he considers to be beyond his power to alter or to modify. In this initial stage of inquiry, we leave aside the more difficult and complex problems that arise when the individual is allowed some power of selection among these institutions themselves. Part II is devoted to this extension.

6

ANALOGUES FROM ECONOMIC THEORY

There are no readily applicable analogues that can be drawn from orthodox economic theory. In the latter, the one-to-one or direct correspondence between cost and benefit for the choosing individual is normally considered to be sufficiently in evidence to allow the assumption that choice is made on the full knowledge of alternatives. Institutional variations in the manner of implementing ordinary market transactions are not held to be significant in affecting choice behavior. To the chooser, price reflects private cost, and price is price and that is that. In a certain broad, and usefully conceptual, sense any tax is also a "price" paid by an individual or by the community of individuals for the public services that are provided collectively. Quite apart from the difficulties of disaggregating a community total into "individual or private prices," however, the forms of taxation affect choice behavior. And, also differently from market choice, the individual is not allowed to choose his most preferred means of payment. Normally he must meet his fiscal obligations through the means laid down for everyone.

It is as if we should ask, in our analysis of consumer behavior, how the *institution of payment* itself modifies choice patterns. Suppose that an individual may purchase commodity A in unlimited amounts for cash but that access to credit is denied by law. Now compare his behavior with that which would emerge when he is confronted with an alternative institution of payment that requires him to purchase the commodity only on credit. The "price" computed in present value terms is, we may assume, identical, and the same physical commodity is available. However, the behavior of the average or representative consumer may be quite different in the two cases, as has been empirically demonstrated by the effects of legally imposed constraints on the installment purchase of consumer durables.

When we begin to look at the fiscal structure within this frame of reference, it seems evident that the institutions through which the costs and the benefits of collective action are presented to the individual can significantly influence his evaluation of, and his own reactions to, the flow of such costs and benefits.

INDIVIDUAL RATIONALITY IN FISCAL CHOICE

To what extent shall individual behavior in fiscal choice processes be assumed "rational"? Clearly, terms must be defined here. We might, at the one extreme, conceive of some omniscient individual who is able, without cost, to determine precisely and immediately the costs and the benefits of any proposed collective decision, both for himself and for all other members of the collective group. Accepting this as a sort of benchmark, it would then be possible to define behavior arising out of such a calculus as ideally "rational" and all departures from such behavior as "irrational." Individuals are not, of course, omniscient, even those who think themselves to be. The securing of information about the predicted effects of alternatives is a costly process, even in a world with reasonable certainty. Recognizing this, individual utility-maximizing behavior remains "rational" when choices are made on the basis of less-than-perfect information. There is some "optimal" investment in fact-finding and analysis for the deciding individual at each stage of his deliberation.

The institutions of payment may modify this "optimal" level of investment in information gathering and analyzing; "rational" behavior under one set of institutions may require that the individual accept a greater degree of ignorance than he does under some other set. Fiscal choice is constrained in the sense that, normally, the individual is allowed to reach decisions only under one set of institutions. He cannot, therefore, choose the particular means of payment that seems most convenient or most efficient.

Behavior based on "rational ignorance" is not, of course, "irrational," except in the rarified comparison with the sort of benchmark noted above, that of "costlessly computed rationality" of the omniscient. But behavior that is based on such ignorance and uncertainty as may be rationally accepted cannot be readily distinguished from behavior that arises because of the presence of illusions and false conceptions of the actual alternatives existing. It will be necessary, therefore, to examine institutions, not only in terms of the degree of information presented to the ultimate individual participant in collective choice, but also in terms of their predicted ability to foster illusion or false beliefs. The "fiscal illusion," a concept that has been stressed by certain Italian scholars in public finance, becomes highly relevant to the analysis.

Despite these acknowledged difficulties, it will be convenient, in the initial stages of inquiry, to make the assumption that illusion is absent. That is to say, the individual will be assumed able to measure costs and benefits accurately within the limits of the uncertainty inherent in the choice that he confronts. He will be assumed "rational" in the sense that his behavior will be directed toward maximizing his own utility.

AN OUTLINE OF THE STUDY

The approach will become clear only after the discussion of the model developed in Chapter 2 where the demand for public goods is considered. Following this preliminary model, abstracted models of actual tax institutions are examined in Chapters 3 and 4, divided, roughly, as between direct and indirect tax instruments. Chapter 5 introduces the temporal aspects of fiscal institutions, and the familiar adage "an old tax is a good tax" is examined. The decision process of the individual is obviously affected by the degree to which the tax choice is tied to the spending choice. This is treated in Chapter 6, which includes a formal analysis of earmarked taxes.

This fragmentation of the fiscal decision into tax choices and expenditure choices and the institutional means by which these apparently isolated sides may be reconciled is discussed in Chapter 7. There is a direct relationship between taxing decisions and spending decisions only in a regime that requires strict budget balance. Since such balance need not characterize the fiscal structure, it becomes helpful to examine the effects of potential unbalance on the type of decisions that emerge. This is attempted in Chapter 8.

For the most part, public services are aimed at providing "general" benefits to all members of the collective group. Individualized shares in these benefits are difficult to isolate. To what extent does this very generality, this indivisibility, make the individual reluctant to give up private goods for public goods? To what extent does the "free rider" problem inhibit the reaching of rational fiscal choices? This is examined in some detail in Chapter 9.

The tendency of fiscal institutions to generate illusions for the individual taxpayer-beneficiary is discussed in Chapter 10. This chapter presents the most extensive summary to be found in English of the major Italian contributions on this topic.

The individual participates, directly or indirectly, in the formation of collective decisions. But he does not, individually, determine the outcome of the decision process. The analysis remains incomplete, therefore, until and unless some discussion of decision rules is introduced. This opens up a different area of analysis, one that cannot be thoroughly explored. At best, certain very simple decision models can be presented; this is done in Chapter 11.

Chapter 12 provides a methodological discussion of some of the problems encountered in any attempts to move from theory to the real world. Chapter 13 summarizes the research results that seem to be relevant to the approach to fiscal institutions developed.

The second part of the book opens up a second-level choice problem. Here the individual is assumed able to select the institutions that characterize the whole fiscal structure. He is presumed to decide, with his fellows, on the "fiscal constitution." Chapter 14 discusses the setting of this sort of choice problem. Chapters 15, 16, 17, and 18 discuss some of the familiar fiscal institutions in the institutional-choice setting, with interesting results. This area of analysis has scarcely been explored, and the discussion is speculative. The approach itself, however, points toward the development of a set of norms for fiscal reform that may require fewer ethical value statements than those required in the traditional approach.

Chapter 19, the final chapter in the book, outlines this set of norms and suggests the way in which these may be further refined and elaborated.

2. *Individual Demand for Public Goods*

The analysis is designed to contribute to the derivation of a "theory of demand for public goods and services." Difficulties arise at the very outset, however, when we begin to think about public goods and services in such terms. How are public goods demanded by individuals? What are public goods?

For our purposes, *any* good or service that the group or the community of individuals decides, for any reason, to provide through *collective* organization will be defined as *public*. The inclusive category may include some goods that Samuelson and others have designated as "purely collective," but it may also include other goods and services, with the degree of "publicness" ranging from zero to 100 per cent. The inclusive definition is suitable because our purpose is that of analyzing the *organization* of public goods provision, and not that of determining the proper classification of particular goods and services independently of organization. Our purpose is not that of answering the question: What goods should be public?

PURELY COLLECTIVE GOODS

It is, however, precisely because goods and services that are provided governmentally are rarely, if ever, wholly collective that problems arise in discussing demand. Recall the initial Samuelson definition of a purely public good;[1] one that must be consumed equally by all members of the collective group. If a unit is available to any one member of the collectivity, a unit must be, by definition,

1. Paul A. Samuelson, "The Pure Theory of Public Expenditure," *Review of Economics and Statistics,* XXXVI (November, 1954), 387-89; "Diagrammatic Exposition of a Theory of Public Expenditure," *Review of Economics and Statistics,* XXXVII (November, 1955), 350-56.

also available to each other member of the group. The benefits are wholly indivisible with respect to the shares of the separate individuals. Only in such a polar case can the "quantity" of a public good be defined unambiguously. In this polar model, the individual compares potential costs and benefits of a public good which he knows to be available equally to all. It is possible to discuss the demand of the individual in this case without introducing the complexities that are involved when partial divisibility of benefits among separate individuals is present.

To facilitate analysis, think of public expenditure decisions as being made marginally or incrementally. The group decides on the number of units to be provided one at a time, and serially. The choice is not all-or-none. It is now possible to construct, conceptually, for each individual in the community a schedule or curve of marginal evaluation. Assume that only one public good is considered. If we neglect income effects, this schedule or curve is fully analogous to the demand schedule or curve for an ordinary private good or service. Figure 2.1 illustrates. On the vertical axis is

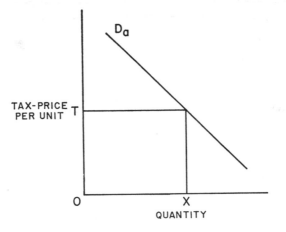

FIGURE 2.1

measured the individual's marginal evaluation of the public good in dollars. On the horizontal axis is measured the quantity of the good, per time period, potentially available to the individual, and equally available to each other individual in the group.

In this simple construction, which wholly neglects income effects, we can think of this demand or marginal evaluation curve as indicating the quantities of the public good that would be optimally desired by the reference individual at each of a series of different "tax prices per unit" confronting him. For simplicity, we may assume that the "tax price per unit" in each case remains constant over quantity. In other words, the "marginal tax" remains equal to the "average tax," per unit, as these are faced by the choosing individual. Through this convention, we may think of the individual as being confronted with a series of horizontal "supply curves" for the public good analogous to the standard derivation of demand curves for private goods. For most of the analysis of this chapter more complex models need not be introduced. For those who are concerned about the neglect of income effects, however, it should be noted that, through specifying a single schedule of tax-prices, that is, through fixing a single "supply curve" for the public good, as faced by the individual, we may fix a unique curve of marginal evaluation. The circularities in this procedure need not be damaging at this stage.

In Figure 2.1, D_a represents the single person's demand for the single public good under one specifically designated institution of payment, that which is identical to payment in the private economy. At a tax-price per unit of OT, the individual would, if his own private desires are fulfilled, "purchase" an amount, OX, of the public good. There is, of course, no assurance that the individual can be at or even near to his own preferred position, his private "equilibrium," in public goods purchases. The final quantity of goods provided must be chosen by the whole community, acting through complex institutional processes. The demand curve for a single public good allows us to think more clearly about the individual's participation in such decision processes, even though we recognize that he will not normally confront fiscal alternatives in such an abstracted setting.

Assume that the individual knows that the public good, to be made equally available to all persons, will be financed by a specific tax institution that will be expected to impose upon him, personally and privately, a per-unit charge shown at OT. The individual will tend to approve all spending proposals for extending the provision of the good up to an amount OX. Similarly, he will tend to "vote against" all proposals for providing more than OX, keeping in mind our assumption that all-or-none choices are not presented. It should be noted that the individual calculus depicted in this demand-curve construction is straightforward. The individual has no incentive to "conceal" his true preferences for the public good or service. This aspect of behavior is absent because we have postulated that a specific tax scheme is pre-selected, externally to the chooser, and that his own action cannot modify the tax-price-per unit at which the public good is made available to him. The methodological defense of this approach is postponed until Chapter 9.

Suppose that the collective good is Polaris submarine defense, and that the quantity is measured by the number of submarines in commission. The same number of submarines is available to each and every citizen. Suppose further that the provision of this particular defense is to be financed through the imposition of an equal-per-head tax and that the marginal cost of supplying additional submarines is equal to average cost. The individual taxpayer-beneficiary can, in this abstracted model, estimate his own "private" or "individualized" share in the collective benefits provided at each level of submarine defense and also his own "private" share in the tax cost that this defense embodies. Now assume that the decision on quantity to be supplied is made by a referendum process, where the individual is allowed to vote on successive spending proposals, commencing with one unit and increasing until some group decision is attained. He will tend to vote in favor of proposals for spending up to a level of OX submarines, and he will vote against all proposals for extensions beyond this quantity. As emphasized, the individual person will not be allowed to make an independent quantity adjustment; he cannot, by definition, consume a quantity different from anyone else. For this reason alone, and even in this highly abstract referendum model, it will be unlikely that his preferences will be fully reflected in the group-decision outcome. But this outcome, both in simple and complex models, can only be determined through some analysis of the choices of the individuals who participate.

We seek now to examine the effects on an individual's choice behavior that might be exerted by the institutions of taxation, by the methods through which the individual is required to meet his financial obligations for the public good. Suppose that the position shown in Figure 2.1 reflects the individual's predicted response under a head tax. Let us now modify the taxing institution. Assume that the same collective good, submarine defense, is to be financed, not through the levy of a head tax, but through a tax on the net income of corporate enterprises. How will this change in the institution of

14

payment affect the private decision of the single voter-taxpayer-beneficiary? Three possible effects may be distinguished. First of all, the new means of payment may be more or less "convenient" to the individual, quite apart from considerations of uncertainty or ignorance about shares in the aggregate tax liability. In other words, any individual will have some preference ranking for the various means of meeting financial obligations to government, even if he must pay the same net tax in each case. This scale of preference is rarely noted in connection with ordinary market choices because the individual is considered to be free to make payments in any manner that he chooses. He is not required to discharge obligations in any particular way, as he normally is in the fiscal process.

To isolate this first effect on individual choice behavior, suppose that, as an owner of a specific number of corporate stocks and as a consumer of a specific quantity of commodities produced in the corporate sector, the individual estimates his own personal tax liability to be the same as that predicted under the head tax scheme depicted in Figure 2.1. Suppose, however, that he would "prefer" to pay this sum under the corporate tax arrangement rather than through the head tax. For purposes of his decision calculus, this would have the effect of shifting the supply curve, or tax-price line, downwards, even though the net tax paid is the same in the two cases. Due to the nonpecuniary advantages and disadvantages of the various methods of payment, the individual may act differently in separate institutional situations, even with equivalent net taxes. The effects on his choices will be identical to those stemming from a tax-price reduction. This nonpecuniary or convenience effect does not seem likely to be of major importance in influencing the individual's behavior in demanding public goods. It is introduced briefly here primarily for analytical completeness.

The second, and much more important, effect of the suggested shift in institutions arises, not out of preferences for or against particular means of payment, but out of the differential effects on the uncertainty and ignorance concerning the individual's own share in the aggregate tax liability. The taxpayer may know that he owns a specified number of corporate shares and he may also know how many commodities he purchases from the corporate sector. But he may have no idea at all about how much his own share in the cost of an additional Polaris submarine will be under the institution of the corporation income tax. The contrast in this respect with the head tax, under which we have assumed the individual able to predict his own tax liability with reasonable accuracy, seems dramatic. His estimate of the "private opportunity cost" of the public good is likely to be grossly in error. This introductory example indicates that the influences of fiscal institutions on the information pattern of the individual warrant careful examination.

The third possible effect of the change in fiscal institutions on the behavior of the individual stems from the fact that he is able, under most tax schemes, to influence the tax-price, the terms-of-trade, with the fisc. The individual may, through modifying his pattern of private earning or spending, or through participating in collective decisions, change the net tax-price per unit of public good that he confronts. This third influence is not present under the equal-per-head tax, used here as a benchmark. But it will be present under most other institutions. If the rate structure of the tax is chosen independently of the decision on the amount of the public good supplied, we may still think of the individual as being faced with a horizontal "supply" curve. His behavior as a direct participant in the collective choosing process cannot modify the tax-price per unit, although it can, of course, modify the total tax bill. However, if the tax base involves any relationship to his behavior in the private economy, he will be able, by changing this behavior, to modify this tax base, and, through this, the tax-price per unit at which he, along with others, may "purchase" the public good. For example, under the personal income tax, the individual, through not earning taxable income, may slightly increase the tax-price at which units of public good are made available to every other member of the community while at the same time lowering the tax-price for himself. His own estimate of the tax-price that he faces will depend, therefore, on some prediction as to the private behavior of others as well as his own. Clearly, additional uncertainty is introduced in an individual's decision calculus.

How do these separate effects combine in influencing the behavior of an individual in demanding a single public good? Figure 2.2 illustrates. Instead of a uniquely determinate "equilibrium" position, depicting the most preferred position of the individual, we get, at best, a whole range of indeterminacy. As we allow the "tastes" of the individual to vary over a relatively narrow range we can think of minor shifts in the effective supply curve. But as the information pattern of the individual is modified under the various

16

fiscal institutions, we can think of this shifting taking on major pro-
portions. The supply curve, upon which the individual actually
makes a choice, may fall anywhere within the shaded range drawn
in Figure 2.2 as the tax institutions change. Clearly, the behavior of
the individual as he participates in collective decision processes will
depend, and significantly so, on the way in which his tax bill is
presented to him.

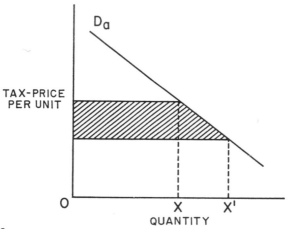

FIGURE 2.2

As shown in Figure 2.2, the range of choice is wide, even in
this highly rarified model. The individual would approve all spending programs, regardless of the tax institution, up to OX. He would
disapprove all programs beyond OX'. Within the broad range,
OX-OX', he might approve or reject proposals to finance extensions
or contractions, depending on the particular institution of payment.

This preliminary discussion is designed to make one elementary
point. The effects of the institutions of payment on individual choice
behavior are more important in fiscal choice than they are in market
choice. Part I of this study may be summarized as an attempt to
make some rudimentary predictions concerning these effects. Will
the individual choose to spend more publicly under income taxation
or expenditure taxation? Before this question can be directly answered, what variables must we analyze?

17

QUASI-COLLECTIVE GOODS

The analysis of an individual's demand for public goods is relatively simple only in the polar case of the purely collective good. We know, of course, that such goods rarely exist, in any descriptively realistic sense, and that governmental units privide goods and services with widely varying degrees of benefit divisibility among separate persons. Individual shares cannot normally be treated as equal, and units of the public good available to one individual need not be equally available to all others. Insofar as *any* divisibility of benefits among separate persons is introduced, the consumption of units by one person must decrease the availability of units for others in the group. To use Musgrave's terminology,[2] exclusion rather than nonexclusion applies, at least to a degree, for most publicly supplied goods and services.

This fact of partial divisibility makes it necessary to introduce, for almost all publicly provided goods and services, *two* distinct demand elements. The first is the private demand for the good or service, as this is exhaustively treated in basic economic theory. The demand for divisible components of the good is an inverse function of the direct user price that is charged, other things equal. The familiar propositions in the standard theory of consumer's choice apply; the fact that the supplier happens to be the collectivity has little relevance. The individual is a quantity-adjuster, or potentially so, and different individuals may consume different amounts.

This individual or private demand for excludable or divisible components of goods provided collectively is not, however, the individual demand with which this study is concerned. By definition, divisibility implies that separate units may be demanded and consumed, individually and privately. This behavior is outside our field of reference, however, since we are concentrating attention on individual choice and behavior in *collective* decisions to purchase and to consume public goods. The demand for "private" or divisible components is absent from individual behavior here. Individual responses in demanding quantities of a public good as a participant in political choice processes, and as related to tax-prices, not user prices, become the relevant behavioral elements.

An illustration will prove helpful. Consider a good that is

2. Cf. R. A. Musgrave, *The Theory of Public Finance* (New York: McGraw-Hill, 1959).

18

characterized by both "collective" and "private" components, say, the services of a municipal park. Decisions as to the amount and quality of park services must be taken collectively through some set of institutional rules for reaching political-administrative decisions. Individuals participate in these decisions, and it is this participation that is the object of our researches. Behavior in this process may, however, depend upon the *private* demand for the services of the park, and this demand may, in turn, be functionally related to the direct user charge that is to be placed on usage of the facility. However, insofar as the collectivity, in making decisions, does not respond directly and automatically to privately-expressed demands and nothing more, that is, insofar as pure market criteria are not utilized, other demand considerations enter into the individual's decision calculus. These reflect, or should reflect, the genuinely indivisible components that the facility embodies, and the demand for these collective elements can be treated in the same manner as in the analysis of the purely collective good, discussed above.

Let us say that a decision is made to charge direct users twenty-five cents for each visit to the park. This privilege of strolling or sitting in the park, at twenty-five cents per visit, is equally available to all citizens, or rather it is considered to be potentially available at the moment of collective decision. The individual, as a member of the municipal community, considers the availability of park services, at twenty-five cents, to be genuinely collective in the polar sense. Through this convention of incorporating direct user pricing into the institution itself, we convert, as it were, all quasi-collective goods and services into purely collective goods for purposes of the analysis. In effect, the procedure amounts to breaking down the mixed public-private good into its two component elements. Once we have specified a user price for divisible components, we may proceed to construct a demand schedule or curve for the collective components. The fact that a person knows that he will be charged a user price of twenty-five cents will, of course, affect his estimate of the tax-price that incremental additions to the facility will involve. While he may value collective components of a zero-user price facility, at the same level of usage, higher than he would value components of a positive-price facility, he will also recognize that the revenues from user pricing in the latter case will reduce the share of the facility that must be financed from tax-prices. Direct user prices will be treated as a partial substitute for tax prices.

19

We may illustrate this in Figure 2.3. D_a represents the individual's demand for the park services, *as a collective good,* on the assumption that these services are to be made available at zero user prices. D_b represents the same person's demand curve for services on the assumption that a twenty-five cents user charge will be levied. As drawn, this curve lies below D_a throughout the range. This relationship need not hold universally. If congestion is sufficiently serious, the individual may value park services higher with than without user prices. The estimated tax-price that he will be required to pay is clearly lower in the second case than in the first. If OT is the predicted tax-price when park services are made avail-

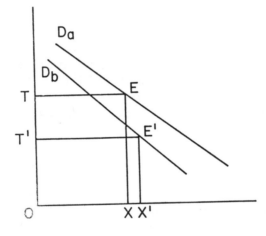

FIGURE 2.3

able free of direct user charges, the position of private "equilibrium" will be at E, with the most preferred quantity (size of facility) at OX. At the lower estimated tax-price, OT', which accompanies the demand curve, D_b, the equilibrium position is shifted to E', with preferred quantity OX'. The geometry of Figure 2.3 shows that the position of individual "equilibrium" may move in either direction along the abscissa with the introduction of direct user charges. Even without undue congestion, collective decision processes may well generate more total investment in public facilities that provide quasi-collective services with the charging of direct user prices than without. Public parks may be larger in municipalities that charge user prices than in those that do not.

This analysis may be generalized for any degree of "publicness,"

20

from pure collective goods to pure private goods. Consider a good that is supplied through ordinary market institutions, or through a public enterprise that operates solely in accordance with profitability criteria. Even in this case, it is possible to conceive of an individual demand for the good, as a collective, not a private, good, quite apart from demand for the specifically divisible components. Under market institutions, the tax-price that the individual expects to pay is, of course, zero since direct user charges, market prices, are expected to finance the whole supply. Nevertheless, an individual demand schedule for the good, as a collective good, may exist, and this schedule may be employed to indicate various tax-prices, over and above market prices, that the individual would be prepared to pay for the availability of the good, *at market prices*. The right to purchase unlimited quantities at going market rates becomes, in this model, a purely collective good for the purposes of the analysis. Since the "supply" curve facing the individual is, however, expected to be that reflecting zero tax-price, the individually preferred quantities are those generated through the institutions of the market.

The point is that the elements of demand for any good, whether this be classified as wholly, partially, or not at all "public" by the standard criteria, may be factored down into *private* and *collective* aspects.[3] Recognizing this, it is possible to analyze individual demand for collective benefits provided by any good or service in terms of the Samuelson polar model. We can ask the same questions posed in the preceding section. How do the institutions of payment, the form in which taxes are imposed, affect the demand of the individual for those components of goods and services supplied publicly that must be equally available to all members of the group?

3. This is noted, in a somewhat different way, by Burton A. Weisbrod in his article, "Collective-Consumption Services of Individual-Consumption Goods," *Quarterly Journal of Economics,* LXXVIII (August, 1964), 471-77.

3. *Tax Institutions and Individual Fiscal Choice: Direct Taxation*

INTRODUCTION

In this chapter and those following, various *tax institutions* will be examined. The objective is to determine effects on individual behavior in demanding public services through participation in political decision processes. The discussion may be facilitated by certain simplifying assumptions, which are for the most part analytically helpful rather than essential. We consider a single collective good or service, and all benefits are assumed to be indivisible as among separate persons. We assume that the collectivity makes no attempt to provide this good or service "efficiently"; that is to say, no attempt is made, in the taxing-pricing process, to satisfy the necessary marginal conditions for Pareto optimality.[1] We assume, more realistically, that the public good or service is financed through some specific institution of taxation that exists independently of the particular public expenditure decisions taken. Such an institution requires the sharing of the total costs among taxpayers in some way that is *not* directly tied to the separate marginal evaluations, except as the latter are reflected in the participation of the individual in collective decisions on total spending. In this setting, the individual is able to estimate his own tax cost for each anticipated quantity of public goods that may be supplied. As one additional assumption,

1. This assumption means only that the marginal conditions are not directly utilized as allocative criteria for the fiscal process. To satisfy such conditions, different individuals must pay differing marginal tax-prices depending on their separate marginal evaluations of the good. It is difficult to conceive of any real-world taxing scheme that might lead to this solution.

the cost-price of the public good is assumed invariant over quantity. That is, the good can be supplied at constant marginal (average) cost.

Under these assumptions, several familiar tax institutions will be analyzed for possible relationships between the payments imposed on the individual and the benefits that he expects to receive. The tax consciousness of the individual, as this may be influenced by the fiscal structure, is the point of primary emphasis.

INVARIANT TAX-PRICE

The number of variables that is embodied in any tax institution, real or imagined, makes it essential that specific description be provided, even at the expense of tedious detail. The first institution to be analyzed is described as follows:

1. the tax is newly imposed;
2. the revenues from the tax are clearly earmarked for the financing of a single public service;
3. the benefits from this public good or service are enjoyed currently;
4. the amount of the tax, per unit of public good or service, to the individual, is independent of his own, or other persons' behavior in collective choice;
5. the amount of the tax, per unit of public good or service, to the individual, is independent of his own and others' behavior in market choice;
6. the amount of the individual's total tax bill depends strictly on the quantity of collective good that the community chooses to supply.

An institution meeting this description is rarely, if ever, encountered in real-world fiscal structures. It is useful, nonetheless, in providing a starting point for analysis. Only a payment scheme that embodies the descriptive characteristics noted would allow the individual to confront the financing of the public good in a manner that is roughly analogous to his position as a prospective purchaser of a private good in the marketplace. With this comparison in mind, it may be helpful to examine each characteristic of the initial model in some detail.

When a person finds himself in a market for private goods and services, as a potential purchaser-consumer, he is aware of the fact that, to secure the benefits promised from the consumption of the good, he must initiate action. He must "give up" or "sacrifice" units of generalized purchasing power. But nothing in the institution of payment restricts him in his choice among alternative uses of this purchasing power as potential sources for financing the purchase of the single good under consideration. There is a direct and observable one-to-one correspondence between the transfer of general purchasing power to the seller and the receipt of the good or service that is purchased. In fully competitive markets, the individual cannot alter the terms upon which the private good is made available to him. No change in his behavior can modify the price that he confronts; he is a price taker.

The individual who confronts a fiscal situation in the role of a taxpayer cannot, of course, be placed in a wholly similar position. The nature of the public good, and, derivative from this in part, the nature of the political process, make his position inherently different in the two cases. Under the initial model of invariant tax-price, however, several characteristics of the market-choice situation remain. We have specified that the individual considers the imposition of a *new* tax. Action must be initiated by the group before benefits are available to any member of the group. The single individual cannot, of course, initiate action on his own. But he can behave, in collective choosing processes, on the basis of a more or less well defined preference scale. As a second characteristic, we specified that the institution involves the financing of a single and specifically designated public good or service, not a whole budgetary bundle. The taxpayer chooses on the knowledge that there exists a one-to-one correspondence between some general community decision to raise the tax revenues and the supplying of the good or service to the whole community. Again, of course, it is impossible to secure a personal or individualized one-to-one correspondence in the market sense. The individual can never be insured that his own agreement to pay taxes will secure additional quantities of the public good. At best, he knows only that, if his preferences coincide with a sufficient number of his fellow citizens (the precise number and form of agreement being determined by the rules for group decision-making), his tax payment will be accompanied by an increase in the supply of the public good.

The third characteristic of this initial tax institution is the *current* enjoyment of benefits from the good or service. Both in private market processes and in political processes current payments may be utilized to purchase goods that yield services, and are thus "consumed," in future as well as current periods of time. Conversely, current payments may be necessary to cover costs of services consumed in past periods. This temporal restriction is imposed largely for simplification purposes.

The fourth characteristic requires that there be no influence of the individual's own behavior or of the behavior of others in the collective choice process on the tax-price-per-unit of the public good that he confronts. The "tax-price" represents the terms of trade between the individual and the fisc, and it is specified that his own behavior as a participant in public choice cannot modify this tax-price. The individual cannot, by "voting" for or against a proposal to expand or to contract the rate of expenditure on the public good, change the tax-price per unit of the good that he confronts. This feature must be present to insure that the individual behave non-strategically when he participates in collective choices. Similarly, the behavior of others should not influence the tax-price that the individual confronts. The collective decision on the quantities of the public good to be supplied should not affect the tax-price facing the individual.

The fifth characteristic extents this relationship to behavior in market choice. It is specified that there is no influence on the tax-price confronting the individual exerted by possible modifications of his behavior in the private market economy. The terms of trade between the individual and the fisc cannot be changed by any change in behavior in earning or spending income. This suggests that our initial model, the invariant tax-price institution, is similar to the familiar benchmark of the welfare analysis of taxation, *the lump-sum tax*. To avoid confusion, however, the differences as well as the similarities must be noted. The traditional lump-sum tax is normally defined so that the individual's *total* tax liability remains unchanged regardless of his own behavior. Under our model, only the *tax-price per unit* is set independently of the individual's behavior. As the sixth characteristic explicitly sets out, the total tax liability of the individual depends upon the quantity of the public good that the community chooses to supply, and, insofar as the individual exerts some influence on this collective outcome, he may exert some, even if slight, effect on his own total liability.

Note that the fourth and fifth characteristics refer to two separate types of individual behavior, that which takes place in collective decision processes and that which takes place in market processes. The invariant tax-price institution does not allow the individual to modify the terms of trade with the fisc through changing his behavior in either of these two processes. He has no incentive to behave strategically in "voting," and he has no incentive to change his income earning or spending habits.

Our reference institution resembles that which the individual confronts in ordinary market pricing, where perfectly-working markets are present. In this latter case, the individual cannot directly influence the terms on which he purchases goods and services. He can, of course, determine the total expenditure on a commodity by varying quantity purchased, as we allow the action of the community to do in the public-goods case.

The purpose of this initial model should be clear. Given the framework assumptions, this model allows the individual voter-taxpayer-beneficiary to "sense" or to be conscious of a more direct relationship between his own tax payment and the benefits that he expects to receive than any other institution that could be conceptually described. As we modify each of the particular characteristics noted in the model, this connection between individual tax-cost and the individual collective-goods benefit must become more and more indirect. Full and complete knowledge of alternatives becomes more and more costly for the individual to obtain as the tax institution becomes more complex. Utility-maximizing behavior must include reactions to, and adjustments for, the cost of securing information and of making the required computations. As the institutions of political-fiscal choice become more complicated, information about alternatives will be deliberately sacrificed because of cost considerations. In addition, elements of genuine uncertainty enter to affect individual behavior in unpredictable ways.

This procedure of commencing the analysis with that fiscal model or institution that allows the most direct connection between individual cost and individual benefit should not be interpreted to imply that the individual, either in his private market choices or in the political process, necessarily or even normally behaves in the full knowledge of the alternatives that are open to him. He obviously does not, and he makes errors for many reasons. Private-goods markets are rarely, if ever, perfect, and few approach the models of economic theory. The consumer should not, and could not, make the personal investment that would be necessary to insure that he commands full knowledge about alternatives. Among other things, pressures of competitive selling through the media of modern advertising and sales promotion tend to make accurate knowledge difficult to secure. All of this must be acknowledged. Nevertheless, the fact remains that such choice embodies a direct correspondence between private cost and private benefit, the characteristic that is stressed here, and the one that is absent, in varying degree, from individual choice in collective decision processes. This central feature of market choice, rather than any implied assumption of rationality, makes individual behavior in organized markets useful as a benchmark from which we begin to assess collective choice institutions.

There is, of course, no presumption that the individual behaves "rationally" in the highly restricted fiscal model that has been initially discussed. "Optimal rationality" need not be assumed in order to justify our using this model as the starting place for comparative analysis. Unless it could be shown that, systematically, there exists some feature of this initial model that offsets the predicted effects of the changes to be introduced, we can plausibly think of this initial institution as the one that will, *ceteris paribus,* minimize uncertainty in individual fiscal choice. From this base, we can proceed to discuss various fiscal structures in terms of departures from some "ideal." We may do this without implying that other institutions to be examined are either "better" or "worse." The analysis in this respect is strictly positive, and no normative implications need be drawn concerning ultimate fiscal reforms. Normative judgments may be made only if specific value standards are introduced, and these may include some minimization of distortion in individual choice. In this manner, the analysis may contain relevance for policy, but the exercise, as such, contains no normative extensions.

THE TAXATION OF WEALTH

We propose now to analyze a tax institution that resembles the invariant tax-price model in most of its essential features, but one that might be found in real-world fiscal structures. The imposition of proportional taxes on individuals on the basis of net wealth, or capital value, fits this description. The other restrictions are retained. The characteristics are as follows:

27

1. the tax is newly imposed;
2. the revenues from the tax are clearly earmarked for the financing of the single public service;
3. the benefits from this good or service are enjoyed currently;
4. the amount of the tax, per unit of public good or service, to the individual, is independent of his own, or other persons' behavior, in collective choice;
5. the amount of the tax, per unit of public good or service, to the individual, *is dependent, to a degree, on his own and others' behavior in market choice;*
6. the amount of the individual's total tax bill depends upon the quantity of collective goods that the community chooses to supply, and on the tax-price per unit that he is required to pay.

Note that the first four characteristics are identical with those used in describing the invariant tax-price institution. Change is introduced only in the fifth characteristic, as italicized, and, of course, the sixth feature is changed because of the change in the fifth. The tax-price per unit of public good imposed on the individual is not fully independent of his behavior. There is a tax base other than the individual's mere existence as a person. It follows that by behaving in such a way that he becomes a different person, the individual can modify the tax-price that he confronts. In examining the individual's demand for the public good, we are no longer able to treat him simply as a conceptual quantity-adjustor responding to a fixed tax-price, analogous to the purchaser of private goods in the market. He retains some control, slight though this may be here, over the tax-price that he must pay.

It is evident, however, that the tax on net wealth ranks high on the scale of tax-price invariance. The individual can, of course, change the tax-price that he faces by modifying the size of his own net wealth, or asset value. This value is estimated by capitalizing anticipated income streams over future time periods, and since accretions to the stock of wealth take place over time, any change in current behavior affects the tax base relatively little. As an illustrative example, consider an individual whose net wealth is measured at ten times his annual income. Assume that, prior to the levy of the tax, he saves one-half of his income each year. Suppose that a tax is imposed on net wealth, and that the individual desires to reduce the tax-price to the maximum extent possible without actually "eating up" capital. He can reduce his saving to zero in the current income period, but his tax base will be reduced only by some 5 per cent as a maximum. Dramatic changes in the tax-price that he faces can be produced only if he is willing to consume his wealth currently. Few individuals will be predicted to respond so drastically to the imposition of the tax. For this reason, any one individual can measure, with a relatively high degree of accuracy, the tax-price that he will confront if he can measure the net wealth of the whole community, the total tax base. The genuine tax on net wealth must stand quite high on the "cost certainty" scale implicit in this whole analysis.

If the tax should be limited to nonhuman wealth, as would normally be expected in any real-world system, this feature is reduced to an extent. The individual would have available an additional means of changing his behavior in response to the tax, and in reducing the tax-price of the public good by so doing. He may shift investment from nonhuman to human capital without changing the rate of accumulation or decumulation. Since he will recognize this possibility, both for himself and for his fellow taxpayers, the individual faces greater uncertainty in any attempt to estimate the true tax-price that he will confront from the imposition of a given levy.

Under either form of wealth taxation, the individual may, of course, modify the tax base substantially over a long period of time. This does not affect the comparative place of this institution in the analysis here, however, since consideration has been limited specifically to short-run decisions, involving the financing of some current-benefit public good from a currently-collected tax. The fact that, over time, individuals may adjust their net wealth in response to the tax is not directly relevant. The question concerns only their ability to adjust the tax base within the decision period considered.

This point introduces a major qualification that must be mentioned, even in this brief treatment of asset or wealth taxation. The restrictions of the model require that we examine only a new tax, and one that will remain in being for only the single period. In other words, the tax on wealth is a once-and-for-all capital tax, not a recurrent levy. This restriction allows us to eliminate from discussion the whole complex of issues involving tax capitalization.

It must also be noted that the analysis is limited to proportional taxation of wealth. The introduction of a progressive rate structure involves further distortions; the discussion of these is delayed until progressive income taxation is analyzed.

PERSONAL INCOME TAXATION

In this section the most familiar fiscal institution, personal income taxation, is analyzed. We remain within the restrictions of the overall model, and the characteristics of this tax are identical to those listed above for wealth or capital taxation. The difference between these two institutions lies solely in the degree of individual response that is possible within the given decision period. Under the personal income tax, the individual is able to modify the tax-price that he confronts more than under wealth taxation. We shall first consider the levy of a one-period personal tax that employs in-period measured income as the base with a single standard rate: in other words, proportional income taxation.

Proportional income taxes. The total payment that the individual must make under this tax is determined by two things. First, there is a collective decision on the quantity of the public good to be provided, a decision in which the individual is presumed to participate, directly or indirectly. Secondly, tax liability is determined by the size of the personal income that he receives, as this is defined and measured by the tax authorities. If these two variables are known, we can compute both total tax liability for the individual and tax-price per unit of the public good. Recall that, under the invariant tax-price institution, the tax-price is known to the individual independently of his total tax liability, which, there as here, is determined by the collective decision on total goods supply.

The interdependence introduced even in this reasonably general tax must be emphasized. It is not possible, as it was with the invariant tax-price, to assign to the individual a specific share of the cost of each unit of public good, and, at the same time, allow him to adjust to a specific rate of tax on his income. If the tax-price should be fixed in advance, the rate of tax on his income must be residually determined by the size of the total tax base. On the other hand, if the rate of tax is fixed in advance, the tax-price per unit of the public good must be residually determined by the size of the total tax base. The potential variability in the tax base, in the aggregate, modifies the rate of tax on income necessary to finance any quantity of public good, or, conversely, the potential variability modifies the quantity of public good that can be financed from any given rate of tax.

Consider the problem that the individual faces in this fiscal setting. If he is influenced by the tax in his behavior in earning taxable income, he must make decisions on the basis of some prediction as to the rate of tax. If, however, he predicts, and adjusts to, a specific rate of tax on his income, he is internally inconsistent if, at the same time, he predicts, and adjusts to, a specific tax-price per unit of public good. Since he, along with fellow taxpayers, retains power to change the tax base, the revenue yield from any specific rate of tax is indeterminate. Hence, the quantity of public good that may be purchased from this yield is indeterminate. Conversely, if a specific quantity of public good is predicted, the rate of tax that will be required to produce revenues sufficient to finance this quantity is indeterminate so long as the fiscal structure allows individuals to modify the base of the tax by their own market behavior.

It will be helpful to discuss this in terms of a simplified example. Suppose an island community of fishermen are considering the construction of a lighthouse. This is, of course, the standard collective-goods illustration. Assume that some prior agreement or rule dictates that taxes are to be imposed proportionately on personal incomes, with income being measured in some agreed-on manner. We examine the choice calculus of a single fisherman as he participates in the formation of some final community decision concerning the amount of revenue to be collected in taxes and expended in the construction of the lighthouse, which we shall assume can be quantified in terms of height, which can be produced at constant cost. There will exist an individual demand schedule for lighthouse services, which can be derived in the usual manner as previously shown. But how will the single fisherman determine the "supply price," the "tax-price" per unit of the public good that he must take into account as he tries to reach a decision in some voting process? If we could assume that the *rate* of tax on his income is set *independently* from the collective decision on the amount of public good to be supplied, the problem would be greatly simplified. Here we could think of the fisherman making the two decisions in isolation, one from the other, the decision as to the earning of income in response to the tax and the decision as to the appropriate amount of the public good to be collectively supplied. It is relatively easy for us to think of the individual making a decision as to how much income he should earn, at least marginally, if for no other reason than that this sort of choice behavior has been much discussed in economic theory. It is not easy for us to think of the individual making the second choice. He cannot decide on a most preferred or "equilibrium" quantity of collective good without making some sort of estimate of the tax-price that he must, privately and individually, pay. At one extreme, he may act as if this cost is zero, in which case he will approve all spending programs so long as incremental benefits remain positive. Such behavior does not seem likely to occur, however, since the individual is surely aware of some bridge between the tax costs and the benefits.

Ideally these two decisions must be made simultaneously. The individual must try to estimate the tax-price that he will be required to pay, in terms of some rate per cent on his income for each level of public spending, and then decide how much income he will earn and how much public spending he will approve in the political choice process. He cannot separate the two sides of the decision, since his choice between earning taxable income and enjoying leisure or other nontaxable income must depend upon the marginal price at which additional income can be secured (which is determined by the rate of tax) and on the total level of income.

In the one-man group, this simultaneity of choice is recognized as a feature of rational decision-making. The individual acts so as to equate the utility per dollar's worth of potential income spent for each available alternative. He will purchase leisure and "public" goods simultaneously, and his choices will be interdependent. The costs of the "public" good could, in this extension, be translated into rates of tax on earned income without modifying the simple theorems of consumer behavior. And, of course, "public" goods and "private" goods are the same in a one-man group.

We are not interested here in the individual as a one-man group. The individual purchases leisure, along with other private goods, privately and he consumes these privately. He "purchases" collective goods and consumes these jointly with other members of the political community. The theorems of consumer choice no longer apply directly. We are required to construct a new and considerably different calculus of individual decision. We cannot make any simple translation of the costs of supplying the public good, in either total or per unit terms, into private tax-prices that the individual confronts. The public goods "purchaser" cannot be in a position analogous to that of the purchaser of market goods, even to the comparable degree that the invariant tax-price allows.

If we allow any one individual to vary his own liability to the tax by changing his behavior so as to modify the tax base, we must also allow other members of the group to do likewise. The tax liability of any single person or family is, therefore, dependent on the responses of all others in the group. The "terms of trade" between the individual and the fisc, the terms at which he can "purchase" public goods, cannot be predicted accurately in advance, even if he decides not to change his own behavior so as to change the tax base. In other words, even if the individual's own income should be exogenously fixed, there will remain tax-price variability due to the tax-base variability stemming from the behavior of other members of the group. The fiscal choices of separate individuals are necessarily interdependent, quite apart from the necessity of joint participation in the collective decision and joint enjoyment of the benefits of public goods.

Despite this interdependence, however, it should be noted that one element of behavior sometimes stressed remains outside this model, especially in large-number groups. The individual has no incentive to behave strategically, vis-à-vis his fellow citizens. He will make no attempt to conceal or to hide his true preferences for the public good or service in his collective-decision activity or in his private-market responses to the tax. This aspect of behavior arises only when the individual considers his own behavior to be influential in modifying the behavior of others in the group. This possibility does not exist in large-number groups because the individual taxpayer-beneficiary has no power to determine, at least directly, the distribution of the tax load among members of the group. This distribution is set by the tax institution itself, which we have assumed to be selected in advance, through some quasi-constitutional process. The individual can, of course, modify the tax-price that he confronts by not earning taxable income. His behavior in reducing the tax base will, even if slightly, increase the tax-price to all others. He will not, however, explicitly recognize this indirect influence to be significant enough to warrant overt "strategy." He behaves simply in direct response to the situation that he finds himself in, and no bargaining elements enter.[2]

Table 3.1 may be helpful. We shall simplify by assuming that the rate of tax is residually determined, rather than the amount of public goods supplied. This concentrates the uncertainty on the tax-price side. Once a quantity of the public good is selected by the community, the individual knows that he will have access to that quantity. He will not know what rate of tax he will have to pay. The example assumes a ten-man group, with each person having available to him the same income-earning possibilities. Each person may, through changing his own behavior, earn between $100 and $150 for the relevant period under consideration. The public good is available to the group at constant marginal (average) cost of $100 per unit. All public activity is financed through the levy of a proportional tax on measured income. Since each member of the community can vary his income-earning similarly, the taxable income of others than the reference individual varies potentially between $900 and $1350.

TABLE 3.1

Units of Public Good	Total Cost Public Good $	Taxable Income of Individual $	Taxable Income Others $	Rate of Tax %
1	$100	$100-$150	$900-$1350	10- 6.7
2	200	100- 150	900- 1350	20-13.3
3	300	100- 150	900- 1350	30-20
4	400	100- 150	900- 1350	40-26.7
5	500	100- 150	900- 1350	50-33
6	600	100- 150	900- 1350	60-40

In this hypothetical example, the effective range over which the rate of the proportional income tax may settle, for any person, is shown in the fifth column of the Table. If the group decides, through the political process, to supply only one unit of the public good, and

2. The individual's behavior in reducing the tax base in response to this, or any other, institution as if the tax side is wholly independent from the spending side of the fiscal account is fully analogous, in fact is one aspect of, the "free rider" behavior that has been much discussed in the theory of public goods. This problem, generally, will be analyzed in Chapter 9.

if all members of the group choose to earn the maximum taxable income, the rate of proportional tax can be as low as 6.7 per cent. At the other extreme, if the individual whose calculus we are examining along with all others chooses to earn the minimum income of $100, then the rate would be 10 per cent. The actual rate can vary within these limits as the various members of the group adjust their income earning behavior. In terms of rate of tax, different rate ranges must, of course, be derived for each possible level of public goods supply. This complexity is avoided through the use of tax-price per unit of the public good. Regardless of the response to the imposition of the tax, so long as all individuals in the group behave identically, the tax-price will remain unchanged at $10. If all persons earn $150, this implies a tax rate of 6.67 per cent to finance one unit of the public good. If all persons earn $100, this implies a tax rate of 10 per cent.

If, however, we now allow the individuals in the group to respond differently to the tax in terms of their income-earning decisions this tax-price invariance no longer holds. Suppose that the reference individual chooses to earn the minimum income of $100 while all of his fellows continue to earn $150, or a total others' income of $1350. The total community income is now $1450, necessitating a proportional tax rate of 6.9 per cent. This rate generates a tax-price of $6.90 for the reference individual, and a tax-price of $10.35 for all other persons. Through his own behavior in choosing to earn less income, the individual has, in this extreme case, reduced his own tax-price from $10.00 to $6.90 and at the same time increased the tax-price on everyone else in the group from $10.00 to $10.35.

To take the other extreme, consider the effect on the tax-price that the individual faces when all others reduce their earned incomes to the lowest possible level while he chooses to remain at the maximum. He continues to earn $150, while others earn $100. Community income is $1050, and the rate of proportional tax required to finance one unit of public good is 9.5 per cent. The tax-price to all other persons is reduced from $10.00 to $9.50, whereas the tax-price to the individual who continues to earn maximum income is $14.25. In this case, the individual will find that by going along with others he can reduce the tax-price that he confronts by more than $4.00.

This extreme and oversimplified arithmetical example demonstrates the essential interdependence between the behavior of the individual and that of his fellow citizens in responding to fiscal instruments, even to those that stand as high in the scale of generality as the familiar proportional income tax. The limits to which the individual can, through his own behavior, modify the tax-price that he confronts are, of course, exaggerated in the example. Insofar as the institutions of earning income, such as length of working week, prohibit adjustments, the effects traced here do not follow, and the proportional tax on income moves closer to the invariant tax-price. Also, to the extent that the demand for leisure, or more generally, for nontaxable income, is relatively inelastic with respect to price, the opportunity costs of taking advantage of the potentially lowered tax-price by changing behavior are increased. The example in one sense demonstrates the obvious; the individual taxpayers who can vary the amount of taxable income within wide limits and who can, without great losses in utility, substitute nontaxable income for taxable income, secure "bargains" at the public-goods counters. There are obvious testable implications of this proposition. We should expect individuals and groups with these characteristics to be relatively favorable toward extensions in public spending programs.

How will the individual decide when asked to approve or disapprove proposals for expansions or contractions in the amount of public spending? This central question has not been met, even in the simplified example. Will the reference individual vote for or against a proposal, say, to supply four rather than three units of the public good, thereby increasing the budgetary spending from $300 to $400 per period? Refer again to Table 3.1. Let us suppose that the rate of spending has previously settled at $300 for several periods, and that each individual in the group has fully adjusted his income earning behavior to the rate of proportional tax that this quantity of public spending implies. For simplicity, we may assume that each person in the group has, as a result of this adjustment, reduced taxable income from the maximum of $150, which he would presumably earn without the tax, to a level of $145, which implies a proportional tax rate of 20.7 per cent. Assume further that all individuals have responded identically. The tax-price per unit of the public good facing each person is, of course, $10, under these circumstances.

The proposal is now made to increase the rate of spending to

$400, in order to supply one additional unit of the public good. If the individual whose calculus we examine is in private "equilibrium" at the $10 tax-price, should he not oppose any such proposed extension in public-goods supply? He should do so only if he predicts that others in the group will respond to the implied tax-rate increase in the same manner or to some greater extent than himself. The arithmetical example makes this clear. If, in response to the required higher tax rate, all individuals act identically, the tax-price remains at $10, and would, by construction, exceed the individual's marginal evaluation of the additional unit of public good under our assumption that he was in "equilibrium" at the previous position. Suppose, however, than an individual predicts that he will, personally, be able to respond more than his fellows to the incremental tax which the new financing requires. Suppose that he predicts that he can reduce taxable income further to, say $140, whereas his fellows will continue to earn $145. In this case, the required rate of tax is increased to 27.66 per cent, but the tax-price to the reference individual actually falls to $9.68. If a sufficiently large number of individuals make predictions in this direction, a collective-community decision may well be made to expand spending.

This case seems analogous in reverse to the more familiar "free rider" behavior that causes individuals to contribute below-optimal amounts to the voluntary financing of commonly-shared goods and services. Given the institutional setting postulated here, each individual may be led to vote for a level of total public outlay in excess of that which he might "optimally" choose. He will do so if he considers the behavior of all others in the group as being exogenously determined but considers his own behavior to be subject to change in response to the incremental tax increase. And it should be noted that, for purposes of the individual's choice calculus, it does not matter that his predictions should turn out to be wrong, except in so far as the experience provides learning for future choices.

In part the response of an individual to a proposal to modify the rate of public spending, with the required change in the rate of revenue collection, will depend on the means through which he translates the whole fiscal process into terms relevant for his own behavior. Further research is surely needed here, but it seems intuitively plausible that many, perhaps most, persons adopt extremely crude conventions or rules-of-thumb. The most likely of these conventions may be simple proportionality; that is, the individual may translate a 10 per cent increase in the rate of public outlay into a 10 per cent increase in his own tax bill. To the extent that this proportionality rule is followed, the individual will act as if tax-price is invariant over varying quantities of public good, even if it should vary. To the extent that individuals follow such a rule in making fiscal choices, elements of uncertainty that might arise from attempts to predict differential responses to tax rate changes are not present.

This consideration restores somewhat more definitiveness to the model than the arithmetical example, or the subsequent discussions, makes apparent. There must remain, however, the central difficulty that the individual confronts in estimating tax-price. He may well ignore possibly differential responses, but he must predict some aggregative response before he can properly figure his own share in the cost of a proposed public outlay. In one sense, his problem is solved when he does make an estimate for tax-price. Broad uncertainties remain, but these should not be exaggerated. The individual learns through trial and error, through continual adjustment. If the taxing-spending institutions are in existence over a succession of periods, initial mistakes in estimates can be corrected. At the level of aggregate estimates, also, the individual has recourse to professionally competent advice. Estimates for total revenue collections under varying rates of tax are made professionally, and these exhibit a high degree of accuracy. The individual may, if he desires, call directly on such estimates.[3] All things finally considered, proportional income taxation, as an institution, must stand high on any ranking of tax schemes arrayed in terms of the potential "rationality" of the fiscal process.

Progressive Income Taxation. The analysis of proportional income taxation can be extended to progression with predictable results. The difference in rate structures between these two institutions must modify the uncertainty that the individual confronts in assessing his own cost-benefit situation. And progression must also increase the costs of making any reasonably accurate estimate for tax-price, even within the limits of such uncertainty. The differential

3. For a discussion of professional estimating procedures, in the context of their importance for individual fiscal choice, see Charles J. Goetz, "Tax Preferences in a Collective Decision-Making Context," Unpublished Ph.D. dissertation, Alderman Library, University of Virginia, 1964.

effect of progression arises, of course, from the variation in the "marginal price" of not earning taxable income over the range of income prospects.

Under progression, the individual is able, through changing his own base of tax, to modify more than proportionately the aggregate real base of tax, and through this, the effective rate on others than himself. This may be illustrated by a variation on the arithmetical example used earlier. Suppose that in our ten-man community each person is earning the maximum income of $150, which is taxed at 20 per cent. Total revenue is $300, and three units of the public good are being supplied. Suppose further that the rate structure dictates that, if income falls to $100, the rate of tax falls to 10 per cent. Now consider the effects of one individual's reducing his earnings from $150 to $100. Total income in the community falls from $1500 to 1450, or by 3.33 per cent. Tax revenues fall by $20, or by 6.67 per cent. Either the quantity of public good must fall more than proportionately, or the tax bills for remaining citizens must rise more than proportionately.

Note also that, under progression, differential responses to tax changes must normally be taken into account. The taxpayer cannot rely so rapidly on simple proportionality rules in computing his own changes in tax-price. If he could, in some way, be insured that constant-share progression would hold over different budgetary levels, the simple proportionality rule would be sensible. There is little basis on which the individual can assume constant-share progression, however. A specific rate structure, under progressive taxation, normally indicates only the respective shares in aggregate community liability at a series of different taxable income levels. Once the individual knows this rate schedule, he can, after a fashion, adjust his own income-earning behavior as his appropriate trade-off ratios indicate. Insofar as estimates for aggregate revenue yields are available to him, he may also make some crude estimate of the tax-price per unit of the public good that he pays, given all of the limitations previously discussed. He may find himself below, near-to, or beyond his private "equilibrium" position as concerns his "purchase" of the public good. What we want to examine is his behavior in "voting" for more or less outlay.

Let us suppose that the taxpayer's estimates indicate to him that, at the tax-price he is paying, he should prefer a sizable increase in budgetary expenditure on the public good. If he could proceed on the assumption that tax-price would remain invariant over larger quantities, he would tend to "vote for" spendings increases. The existing rate structure will not, however, tell him anything at all about the pattern of progression at different, and higher, budgetary levels. His own share in the costs of public goods may be significantly modified by a change in public-goods quantity. In our same arithmetical example, assume that a given person is earning $150 which is taxed at 20 per cent, or a total tax bill of $30. Assume that four of his fellows earn $150 each, while the remaining five men earn $100 each, and are taxed at 10 per cent. The tax collections finance an outlay of $200, which purchases two units of the public good. The reference individual must now decide whether or not he should vote for or against a proposal to double the rate of spending. If he could be insured that the tax-price he confronts would remain invariant at $15, he would, let us say, vote for the proposal. However, in the shift from a $200 to a $400 budget, there is no basis for him to predict that share progression will be unchanged. Instead of an increase in his own tax from 20 per cent to 40 per cent, which such invariance implies, the rate may shift to 45 per cent at the higher level, in which case tax-price would increase from $15 to $16.85. For his low-income compatriots, by contrast, the tax rate may increase only from 10 per cent to 13.5 per cent, with a corresponding *reduction* in tax-price, from $5.00 to $3.37.

This numerical example suggests that, in the conditions postulated, an individual may be led, on rational grounds, to support or to oppose changes in the quantity of public goods (budgetary outlay) in large part because of the effects on the tax-price that he confronts. The model is analogous to that of the purchaser in private-goods markets who is faced with either a downsloping or an upsloping curve of supply price. In the latter, elementary price theory tells us that rational behavior considers marginal supply price, not average supply price. Hence, the prospective purchaser faced with a downsloping curve for average supply price will extend purchases beyond that level which is "optimal," while that purchaser faced with an upsloping curve for supply price will restrict purchases below that level which is "optimal."[4]

4. On some of these points, see my article, "The Theory of Monopolistic Quantity Discounts," *Review of Economic Studies*, XX (1952-53), 199-208.

This may be illustrated in Figure 3.1, in which, by the standard conventions, we assume that incremental changes are possible. Suppose that the individual finds himself at A, by his own best estimate. He, along with all others in the group, enjoys the benefits of a quantity of public goods shown by OX, for which he pays a tax-price of OT, which we assume is collected under a progressive levy on income. Assume further that the individual's marginal evaluation curve for the public good is ME. Hence, at A, the marginal value

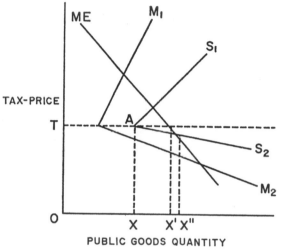

FIGURE 3.1

that he placed on the public good exceeds the tax price that he pays. If he could be insured that, in any budgetary expansion, this tax-price could remain invariant, he would support proposals for expansion up to a quantity, OX', which would then be his most preferred position. With a progressive tax, however, he can hardly predict such invariance in tax-price, even if he should predict accurately the responses of his fellows to the tax. Unless some rule dictates that increases and decreases in the budget shall be made within the restriction of constant-share progression, the individual (regardless of his own relative position on the income scale) cannot assume invariance.

Consider the case where an increase in revenue collections is accompanied by an increase in the rate of share progression. That is, at higher budgetary levels, the proportion of the cost of public goods paid by the relatively rich becomes higher than at lower budgetary levels. In this instance, the individual who is relatively rich faces a curve of average tax-price such as that shown by S_1. The curve drawn marginally to this is M_1. Clearly, rational behavior dictates here that he should vote against all proposals for expanded spending, despite the excess of marginal evaluation over average tax-price.

For an individual in the opposite position, say, a member of the relatively poor class, he may confront (at a different level) a schedule of average tax-price like S_2; the related curve of marginal tax-price is M_2. He will, of course, support all proposals for extension in spending beyond A, but, also will continue to support increased outlay beyond X," despite the fact that, beyond this level, his own marginal evaluation falls short of average tax-price.

The geometrical illustration makes clear that, unless constant-share progression is maintained, the institution of progression modifies the fourth characteristic of the tax instrument, so that 4., the amount of the tax, per unit of public good or service, to the individual, may be dependent on his own or other persons' behavior in collective choice.

As the example shows, the size of the budget, determined by the outcome of some collective-choosing process, may influence the tax-price at which the individual "purchases" the public good. Whereas under proportional income taxation, the fifth characteristic, relating to market behavior, is modified, this fourth characteristic remains descriptive. Tax-price to the individual remains invariant over differing quantities of public good under proportional rate structures. Under progression, this invariance holds only if constant-share progression is specified.

Unless some such share-proportionality is maintained, the individual is led to introduce distributional considerations indirectly into his calculus as he participates in group decisions on the size of public outlay. This effect exists, of course, over and above all of those previously discussed in connection with the difficulties in estimating tax-prices with any degree of accuracy.

The analysis demonstrates that even in some of the most familiar of tax institutions, and even within the most restrictive assumptions regarding the linkage between the tax side and the benefit side of the fiscal account, the individual who tries to participate in choosing the desired level of public goods and services cannot act upon any reasonably adequate knowledge of the alternatives. In addition, he may be led by the structure of the institutions to choose nonoptimally or inefficiently.

EXPENDITURE TAXATION

One major institution remains to be examined in the category of direct taxation, an institution that has been the subject of renewed interest in recent years. Personal taxes may be levied on consumption expenditures rather than income or wealth. The extension of the analysis to this tax is straightforward, provided that we retain the restrictive framework imposed by the first three characteristics. Under an expenditure tax the individual is able to exert greater control over the tax base than under comparable income taxation because of the greater possibility of substitution. He can vary his own tax liability within wide limits, and since all individuals in the group can act similarly, the tax-price confronted by any one person is more dependent on the behavior of others than under the other direct-tax institutions examined. The "externalities" in individual behavior tend to be increased as the tax becomes less general. The range of uncertainty as to tax-price is widened. This holds either for proportional or for progressive expenditure taxation, and the difference between these two variants is similar to that discussed with respect to income taxation.

CONCLUSIONS

Any attempt to analyze the effects of even the few most familiar institutions of general taxation on individual behavior in collective fiscal choice must include almost the whole range of orthodox incidence theory although the usage of this theory becomes quite unorthodox here. Within limits and with exceptions, the rank order of institutions arrayed for their potential in allowing individuals to choose rationally the margin of extension in public-good supply corresponds to that rank order which arrays these same institutions for efficiency in promoting rationality in the market or private-goods sector. The taxes which generate the most obvious "excess burdens," second-best considerations aside, are likely to be those which make choice behavior most difficult for the voter-taxpayer-beneficiary in the democratic models that we adopt here. The differences as well as the similarities between this and orthodox analysis should be noted. A tax generates an "excess burden" when it creates a net welfare loss over and above that which is necessary to finance a specific quantity of public goods. Orthodox theory does not examine the appropriateness or inappropriateness of this quantity. By contrast, primary emphasis here is on this latter question. Hence, insofar as the array stands in rough correspondence in the two cases, orthodox "excess burden" analysis and our own are mutually reinforcing. Insofar as "efficiency," in either public or in private choice-making, is accepted as a norm, the case for generality in taxation is strongly enhanced. This conclusion will be more fully demonstrated when the analysis is extended to indirect tax institutions.

4. *Tax Institutions and Individual Fiscal Choice: Indirect Taxation*

Recall the characteristics that describe the restrictive model of tax-price invariance:

1. the tax is newly imposed;
2. the revenues from the tax are clearly earmarked for the financing of a single public good or service;
3. the benefits from this good or service are currently enjoyed;
4. the amount of tax, per unit of the public good, to the individual, is independent of his own, or others', behavior in collective choice;
5. the amount of the tax, per unit of public good, is independent of his own, or others', behavior in market choice;
6. the amount of the individual's total tax bill depends strictly on the quantity of public good that the community chooses to supply.

As the analysis showed the fifth characteristic is violated when the individual is allowed to vary the tax base through his own behavior; the sixth condition is modified in consequence. In addition, under progressive rate structures, the fourth condition is not likely to be met.

Each of the institutions examined in Chapter 3 is normally classified in the category of "direct" taxation. The person upon whom the fiscal obligation is levied is presumed to be the person that the collectivity *intends* as the final payer of the tax. The fact that the individual may be able, within limits, to vary his own liability for the tax is not, presumably, taken into account directly in the decision concerning the distribution of the total tax load among individuals and groups. By contrast, under an "indirect" tax, the person or entity that is legally obligated to pay is not, presumably, selected with the deliberate understanding or prediction that final payment will be borne. The tax is imposed on the basis of some more or less definite predictions about the behavioral responses of such directly-obligated taxpayers, responses that are aimed at shifting or transferring the final burden onto others in the community. Final incidence of the tax is supposed, therefore, to rest with individuals who are only *indirectly* affected by the fisc; that is, with those whose net tax obligation stems from modifications in the market behavior of others in the directly assessed group. The members of the latter group serve, in a very real sense, as the set of tax collectors for the treasury. The tax liability of any individual depends *directly* on the behavior of these intermediary entities. From this it follows that, even in the absence of all behavioral response on the part of the final taxpayer, our fifth descriptive characteristic would have to be modified so that,

> 5a. the amount of tax per unit of the public good, to the individual, is directly dependent on the behavior of other members of the community in market choice, even if independent of his own behavior in market choice and also of others' indirect market responses.

We know, of course, that the latter half of this condition is not fulfilled under familiar indirect tax institutions. Nonetheless, the condition is useful as a benchmark for comparison. A specific excise tax levied on a consumption item that has zero price elasticity of demand for all individuals in the group would approximately meet 5a.

Initially, we shall concentrate on the first half of condition 5a in order to show how the additional element of interdependence that is introduced tends to increase the individual's range of uncertainty. The very indirectness of payment insures this result. The individual, as bearer of the real costs of those goods and services supplied publicly, is not assessed directly or personally. The sensation of paying funds directly to the fisc in "exchange" for the availability of public goods is absent. To reach a mental state comparable to that in which the direct taxpayer finds himself, a translation of sorts must be completed. Normally the individual will be partially conscious of the fact that conditions under which he makes market choices are modified by the tax. But to compute his own tax liability he must make a set of calculations over and above all of those required under comparable direct tax institutions. He must first distinguish between the conditions of market choice before and after the tax. Having done this, he must effect a translation of the differences into a cost or tax-price equivalent. Even if we assume that he is rationally motivated, the individual may find it almost impossible to act on the basis of any reasonably accurate evaluation of alternatives. This preliminary conclusion will become evident as we examine various tax institutions more fully.

CORPORATE INCOME TAXATION

The taxation of business income is an important means of meeting revenue needs in modern fiscal systems. If the business corporation is considered as a person, as it is in strictly legal terms, this tax belongs in the category of direct taxation, and scholars in public finance have often classified it in this way. For purposes of this analysis, however, the corporation tax cannot be treated in this fashion. Recall that individual behavior in collective fiscal choice processes is the subject of inquiry. And corporations, as such, do not participate directly. Corporations do not vote, although at a secondary level of consideration corporate interests may influence political decisions. There remains, nonetheless, a fundamental distinction between corporate behavior in the private sector and in the public sector of the economy. Corporations, as such, do "vote" with their dollars in the market alongside private individuals and families. They do not "vote" directly in public choice. For purposes of this analysis, the tax on corporate income must be classified as indirect.

As before, we want to isolate if possible the variables that enter into the decision calculus of a single voter-taxpayer-beneficiary. Again let us remain within the restrictive confines of the earlier models. Revenues from a newly imposed tax are earmarked for spending on a single public good, units of which are to be available to all members of the group. Some previously-agreed "constitutional" decision is presumed to have selected the tax on corporate income as the revenue-raising instrument. Initially, we want to avoid the problem of distributional differences among separate persons, and to concentrate on individual choice for the public good. To do so, we may assume that the individual, whose calculus we examine, is genuinely "representative," and his private economy can be described in terms of shares of ownership in corporate stock and dollars of purchases from the corporate sector.

How will such a person behave in "demanding" public goods? How will he go about making an estimate of the "price" at which such goods are made available to him?

Initially, let us assume away the whole complex of issues concerning the short-run incidence of the tax. Assume that the tax rests exclusively on the owners of shares in corporate enterprise, and that this is known. The tax does not affect corporate output. In other words, let us assume that the tax is an "ideal" one, levied on pure economic profit, which all corporations try to maximize.

If the rate of tax is predetermined, the representative shareholder can estimate, within some limits, his own share in corporate-tax liability under these highly restricted conditions. As we have shown in the discussion of the earlier models, however, the rate of tax cannot be determined independently of the decision on the quantity of public goods to be supplied. If we think of the group as voting or deciding in some other fashion on various proposals for spending on public goods, we must allow the rate of tax to be adjusted. Or, alternatively, if we think of the group as "voting" on the rate of tax to be levied, we must allow the quantity of public goods to remain dependent on the tax-rate decision. In either of these cases, the individual must make some estimate as to the size of the aggregate tax base. In this extreme model, where the tax is levied on pure economic profit, there is no direct behavioral response on the part of the corporation. However, even here, the independent variability of the tax base introduces major uncertainty into the choice problem faced by the representative individual. The situation is roughly comparable to that faced under the personal income tax when the individual has no control over the amount of income that he receives. The uncertainty is greater under the corporate tax, however, due to the greater volatility in aggregate corporate profits.

Once we modify the model to allow for some behavioral response on the part of the corporation, additional elements of uncertainty are introduced, similar to those examined under the personal income tax. Both individual and aggregate base variability are increased, and with this, uncertainty in any fiscal choice that the individual must make. And, in each instance, the individual must make the translation from corporate to personal liability. He must compute a personal liability from the predicted workings of a nonpersonal tax.

This distinguishing feature of all indirect taxes may be illustrated by an elementary comparison between the corporate and the personal income tax. Under the latter, the individual varies his own tax liability, in tax-price terms, by varying the amount of taxable income that he earns. His own ability to do so implies also that the tax-price he faces is indirectly dependent on the behavior of others who can react similiarly. In acting to reduce the tax base, each taxpayer imposes an external diseconomy on all fellow taxpayers. To an extent, this sort of personal interdependence remains under the corporate tax. Individuals may, within limits, reduce the tax-price per unit of public goods through withdrawing resources from corporate investment. And any one person's final tax obligation becomes reciprocally dependent on the activity of all other persons in making such allocative adjustments. In this respect, the two taxes differ only in the degrees of response. The additional factor that the corporate tax necessarily introduces is the "bridge" between the individual and the corporate entity. To become liable for tax, it is the corporation that must earn taxable income, not the individual. And to reduce its liability for the tax directly, the corporation must reduce taxable income. In order to estimate his own share, therefore, even apart from his own influence over aggregate investment in the corporate sector, the individual must predict how the corporation itself will behave in response to the tax. In other words, an additional decision-making entity is introduced between the individual and the fisc. A whole set of new predictions must be made concerning the decision-making processes of this in-between institution, the corporation, processes themselves involving most of the problems of group rather than individual decision making.

As in other models, the central features are clarified by posing specifically a choice situation. Suppose that the individual must decide how to vote on a public spending proposal, with revenues to be raised exclusively from a tax on corporate net income. For now, assume away net resource shifts into and out of the corporate sector. For expositional simplicity, think of the proposal as one aimed at expanding national park facilities from the proceeds of the tax, with the rate of tax, which is proportional, to be residually determined after the community decision on budget is made. Should our reference person support or oppose this proposed extension in public-goods supply? He must, obviously, make some sort of estimate as to the tax-cost that such a proposal will involve. This estimate will depend on the amount of net income that he predicts for the corporation (or set of corporations) that he owns, whether or not the corporate responses to the tax are considered. Hence he must predict the behavior of others than himself, even if the necessary interdependence among separate taxpaying units is left wholly out of account.

If his investment in corporate ownership is relatively favorable, the individual will find himself paying a relatively high tax-price per unit of public goods that are available to him. If, by contrast, his investment is relatively unsuccessful, he will find that he obtains collectively-supplied goods at "bargain tax-prices." The discrimination among individuals in actual tax-prices paid for public goods will vary directly with the rate of yield of their corporate portfolios. This relationship should yield testable hypotheses concerning individual behavior in demanding public goods and services. If such goods are characterized by positive income elasticities, which seems empirically descriptive, the individual should, *ceteris paribus,* demand a larger quantity of public goods under the corporate income tax than under the comparable personal income tax, which is, of course, levied directly on less residual components of income. Actual testing of such an hypothesis would, of course, be extremely difficult, due to the necessity for cutting through the maze of information and uncertainty differences confronted in the two institutions. A second conceptually testable hypothesis is that, given the institution of proportional taxation of corporate income, individuals whose portfolios embody relatively greater "riskiness" will tend, *ceteris paribus,* to demand a somewhat larger public-goods outlay than those whose portfolios exhibit less "riskiness." Both of the hypotheses here are derived from an analysis similar to that which was first made familiar to fiscal scholars by Domar and Musgrave,[1] in their discussion of

1. Evsey D. Domar and Richard A. Musgrave, "Proportional Income Taxation and Risk-Taking," *Quarterly Journal of Economics,* LVIII (May, 1944). Reprinted in *Readings in the Economics of Taxation,* ed. R. A. Musgrave and C. Shoup (Homewood: Richard D. Irwin, 1959), pp. 493-524.

corporate income taxation and risk-taking. In the context of this study, the proportional tax on corporate income makes the individual shareholder's "purchase" of public goods into a risky venture.

To this point we have left distributional considerations out of account. This is wholly unrealistic in regard to corporate income taxation since one of the essential features of this tax is its lack of generality. The tax is necessarily discriminatory, and this in turn implies that the position of the individual in the economic process must be considered before his reactions to fiscal choice proposals can be predicted. This, in turn, requires that we develop more specific models for corporate tax incidence. If, as was assumed above, the final incidence rests largely with stockholders, nonholders will tend to approve all extensions of spending so long as the incremental benefits are expected to be positive. Different assumptions as to final incidence, or, more importantly, as to standard attitudes about incidence, will produce different results. Beyond this, once distributional considerations are raised, models for group choice are required for any predictions about choice behavior. While these extensions are required to make the analysis complete, at the elementary and exploratory level of this study they will be left aside. The problems of fiscal choice confronted by the voter-taxpayer-beneficiary under corporate income taxation, even in the simplest of "representative" man models, are sufficiently difficult to suggest those that might arise in still more complex settings.

GENERAL SALES TAXATION

As a second major institution of indirect taxation, we shall examine *general sales taxes*. Specifically, let us look at a flat-rate, or proportional, tax levied on the value of all goods and services sold at retail in private markets. The model could, of course, be readily modified. to allow for specific exemptions or for imposition at different stages. We retain the essential features of the previous tax models discussed. We consider the tax to be newly imposed, and to finance a single good.

Similar to the tax on corporate income, some of the difficulties that any individual voter-taxpayer must face as he tries to decide rationally on the quantity of public goods that he prefers are illustrated by the disagreements, even among the experts, as to the actual incidence of this tax. If fiscal economists, who have specialized in the theory of incidence, are not agreed on just who does, in fact, "pay for" the public goods that are purchased with revenues from taxes levied on general sales, how can individual choice be made under anything other than gross uncertainty?

The individual should recognize that the tax drives a wedge between consumer-goods prices and productive-service prices. Relative to final product price levels, factor prices must fall, and, consequently, incomes earned from the sale of factors will be reduced in real purchasing power, regardless of monetary adjustments. In a perfectly-working competitive economy, the effects of the general sales tax should not differ greatly from those of a proportional tax on personal incomes or on personal consumption expenditures, depending on whether or not investment goods are included or excluded from the tax base. The prospective taxpayer·may even recognize all this in some proximate way. But it is useful to recall that the competitive model of market process is designed for explaining *general* patterns of effect. The model is not especially helpful to the individual (even he who understands it) who lives in the real-world economy, and who must decide how to vote on spending proposals, given sales-tax financing. For this choice, the tax is not similar to either the proportional income or the expenditure tax. Under either of the latter, the individual can estimate with reasonable accuracy the base upon which his tax liability will be computed. Also, since these taxes are personal, he can make his own decisions concerning adjustments to their imposition. These steps become immensely more complex under indirect tax institutions.

He will recognize that he will not, personally, be required to pay out funds to the fisc in "exchange" for public goods. Revenues are collected only from sellers. Only if the individual should serve in some functional capacity as a retailer will he be conscious of the direct fiscal transfer. The individual who does not serve in such capacity must try to estimate the differences in his market opportunities before and after the tax. As suggested, he may accept the hypothesis that factor prices will fall relative to product prices. However, this general effect of the tax will never be uniform over all markets either functionally, spatially, or temporally. Recognizing this, the individual must try, as best he can, to predict the effects of the tax on his own income shares, in real value terms. These effects will depend upon the particular supply conditions characterizing the markets for his own productive services and upon the organization of the industry utilizing these services, among many other things. What the individual must predict here are the behavioral responses of many decision-making units in the economy, other than himself. The interpersonal interdependence, the externality, that was shown to be significant even under proportional income taxation, becomes enormously complex under general sales taxation. The behavior of other persons and firms, not only in earning income, but in apportioning resources, in pricing products and services, in purchasing final output, in adjusting to price changes, is necessarily relevant to the effects of the tax on the individual. At best, predictions amount to no more than rather inaccurate "guesses." Investment in knowledge must surely stop far short of even the economist's level of prediction. The range of uncertainty that must face the individual when he makes a final fiscal decision must be extremely wide, and most persons are likely to rely on very crude rules-of-thumb, perhaps made available to them through press media and stated in very simple averages.

Despite all of the difficulties involved the individual must, nonetheless, choose (or acquiesce in the choices made for him by others). A demand or marginal evaluation schedule for the public good may be derived in a reasonably straightforward manner, since presumably the individual can make some rough estimate of the benefits he secures. On the tax or cost side, however, he may either grossly underestimate or grossly overestimate the tax-price that this institution imposes on him. No particular direction of bias seems indicated by this analysis. Relative to the model of invariant tax-price, the individual under sales taxation may choose more or less public spending. At a later stage of discussion, when the possibility of fiscal illusion is introduced, this conclusion will be re-examined.

SPECIFIC EXCISE TAXATION

The remaining important institution of indirect taxation is that of partial or discriminatory excise taxation. Many real-world systems of excise taxes, which levy charges on the sale, use, or consumption of several products or groups of products, combine elements of general sales taxation, considered above, and specific or partial excise taxation. For present purposes, it is sufficient to consider only the polar models.

We examine here the behavior of the single utility-maximizing individual as he confronts the financing of a new public good from the proceeds of a tax to be levied on one commodity only. How will he estimate the tax-price that collective supply of the public good will impose upon him? Under this model of clearly discriminatory taxation, it is more difficult to leave aside differential impacts on separate persons and groups, but we may commence the analysis by neglecting this aspect, even here. We may do so by supposing, initially, that all members of the group purchase and consume the single product that is to be taxed, say, whiskey or tobacco, and that the differential patterns of consumption are not significant enough to generate widely different patterns of response.

In such a model, as in each of the indirect tax models especially, the tax-price that the individual must pay for a unit of the public goods depends directly on the behavior of other persons in an exceedingly complex chain of economic interdependence. To estimate this tax-price, the individual must predict the reactions of those whom the legislature makes initially responsible for payment. The behavior of retailing firms must be predicted, along with the responses of resource suppliers and product demanders in the aggregate. The difficulties in making accurate predictions are evident, but it should also be noted that, precisely because of the selectivity of the tax, these difficulties are not so great as those encountered under either of the two institutions previously examined in this chapter. Textbook economics makes this point. The primary adjustments to be predicted take place via increases in the prices of the taxed commodity. Adjustments in factor prices generally, while predictable to degree, normally assume quite secondary significance. Naïve predictions made by the potential taxpayer to the effect that commodity prices will increase by the amount of the expected tax per unit will not be wildly in error if markets are reasonably competitive, if resources are not highly specialized, and if time is allowed for supply adjustments. This naïve prediction enables the potential taxpayer to make some predictions of his own about responding to the tax. The interdependence among all taxpayers with regard to the aggregate base of tax remains, but insofar as all persons are predicted to act similarly, tax-price can be estimated with some accuracy, at least as compared with alternative tax institutions.

When differential responses among individuals and groups are anticipated, the estimation of individualized tax-cost is subject to significantly greater uncertainty. Here the individual must examine his own demand for the taxed commodity relative to that of his fellows. It becomes obvious that nonconsumers, along with consumers who can themselves respond most effectively to the tax-induced price increase, will tend to secure "bargains."

The concentration of attention on individual behavior in public or collective choice as opposed to individual behavior in private or market choice should again be emphasized. Our concern is with the quantity of public goods to be supplied. In the model where partial excise taxation is the financing device, it becomes especially tempting to say that the individual's behavior in market choice is a part of his "collective" decision. This would suggest that, when he purchases a unit of the taxed commodity, say, a bottle of whiskey, he does so with the knowledge that he is buying a package that includes two components, the whiskey that is directly utilized along with the public goods that are to be financed with the proceeds of the tax. Such a tie-in model is misleading, however, since the individual will extend his purchases of the privately-consumed commodity, whiskey in this example, to the point where his marginal evaluation of this alone equals the marginal price, including tax. The fact that the public goods financed by the tax are also valued by the individual has no effect on his margin of choice for the private good. There is no way in which the individual can adjust the margin of provision of the public good through his market behavior. This choice arises only when the individual participates, not as an independently-acting purchaser-consumer, but as a voter-taxpayer-beneficiary.

SUMMARY AND CONCLUSION

In this chapter and the one preceding, some of the familiar tax institutions have been examined in an attempt to determine their relative effects on the information-uncertainty elements that must enter into any individual's efforts to estimate the costs of public goods. The institutions have not been analyzed in detail, and the many sub-models that might be introduced under each broad category have not been explored, although some of these may prove sufficiently unique to warrant special treatment. Several conclusions may, however, be drawn even from the limited analysis.

The model of tax-price invariance assumes a position all its own, as does its familiar analogue, the lump-sum tax, in the more orthodox tax theory based on the usage of Pareto efficiency criteria. The approach of this study is, of course, closely related to the welfare analysis of tax institutions, but the differences should be kept in mind. No attempt is made here to array tax institutions in terms of economic efficiency, as such. The invariant tax-price is unique for our approach, not because it exerts no influence on individual behavior in market choice, the traditional requirement for the absence of an "excess burden," but because only the absence of such influence enables the individual to choose fiscally on the basis of a well-informed comparison of alternatives.

By and large, those tax institutions that have been shown by the traditional welfare analysis to generate relatively less "excess burden" will be the same institutions that allow the individual to choose relatively more rationally as a participant in collective choice processes. There are exceptions to this rule, however, as is evidenced by the partial or discriminatory excise levy. Traditional welfare analysis suggests that this tax tends to distort the choice pattern of the consumer of private goods to a greater extent than a more general excise tax. As the above analysis has indicated, however, the individual may be able to choose a preferred quantity of public goods upon a more rational consideration of alternatives here than under a more general tax. He may be able to do so precisely because the discriminatory nature of the tax makes the effects and incidence more certain than those of the more general levy. Hence, "efficiency" in fiscal choice, which depends on the prospects for informed decisions by individual participants, may require greater distortions in market choices if the result is greater predictability. The tax on corporate income provides an even more dramatic illustration. If, in fact, this tax could be levied on pure economic profit, there are no short-run effects on market behavior of individuals or firms. The necessary conditions for Pareto optimality are not modified by the tax. However, the analysis has shown that even such a tax would introduce major elements of uncertainty in the fiscal choice problem confronted by the individual, and because of this the tax surely generates "inefficiency" in the final selection of some most preferred mix between private goods and public goods.

One significant difference between the results derived from the fiscal-choice approach and those derived from orthodox welfare analysis involves the theory of the second-best. In its various forms, this latter theory states that it is not possible to judge a single distortion as nonoptimal, on Pareto-efficiency grounds, until and unless there is some assurance that there exist no other violations of the necessary marginal conditions for optimality. Hence, even the lump-sum tax (or, in our models, tax-price invariance) cannot necessarily be predicted to generate greater over-all efficiency than other taxes of comparable magnitude. This theorem is correct, within certain limitations, when a global view of "efficiency" is taken. In the analysis of this study, by contrast, the invariant tax-price unequivocally allows for a more "efficient" fiscal choice than comparable institutions. Only under this institution can the individual participant in collective choice predict the results of group action on his own economic position with any degree of accuracy.

The discussion of tax institutions in Chapters 3 and 4 has as a central feature the interpersonal interdependence that the two-sidedness of the fiscal system necessarily introduces. On several occasions reference has been made explicitly to the "externalities" inherent in individual responses to tax imposition. This suggests that a more formal analysis could be developed within the "externality" terminology that is familiar to theoretical welfare economists.[2]

2. For a general discussion along these lines, see, my, "Externality in Tax Response," *Southern Economic Journal,* XXIII (July, 1966), 35-42.

5. *Existing Institutions and Change: The Effects of Time in Fiscal Decisions*

To this point the familiar taxes have been discussed only under certain highly restricted assumptions. Only *new* taxes designed to finance public services not currently supplied have been considered. This chapter is devoted to an examination of this single feature of taxation. How does the fact that a tax is new or old affect individual behavior in collective choice processes, and, through this behavior, ultimate group decisions? The importance of this feature has been widely recognized in both popular and scholarly discussion, at least indirectly, and is summarized in the adage: "an old tax is a good tax." To what extent and in terms of what criteria does this adage hold?

The descriptive words "old" and "new" must first be clarified. Under the rubric "new tax," as used in preceding chapters, fiscal choices were assumed to embody the imposition of some tax not previously in existence to finance public goods supply. This constraint does not require that the institution of the tax be new. An incremental addition to an existing rate of tax qualifies as a "new tax," so long as it is imposed for the financing of new services, although these, also, may represent incremental additions to existing services. The relevant requirement is that the funds for financing newly-available units of public goods and services be drawn from the financing of private goods and services. The collective decision, and the individual's participation in this decision, must reflect a diversion of resources into public goods supply.

58

This situation may be contrasted with that which is present when public goods and services are financed from revenues produced from an existing tax, an "old tax." Most orthodox fiscal analysis assumes, implicitly, that choices are made, carte blanche, presumably at the beginning of each fiscal period. Under this assumption, the group determines both the means of financing and the range and quantity of public goods and services at the outset of each period. The slate is wiped clean, so to speak, at the end of each period, and everything is commenced all over again at the start of the following period. In such a model, there is no distinction to be made between an old and a new tax.

A more realistic analysis must incorporate some recognition of the old tax-new tax distinction, and it must be based on the acceptance of fiscal institutions, as institutions. An "old tax" is one that has been approved in past periods for the financing of public goods, and one that may be, if desired, continued in existence. The initial legislative act need not, although it normally does, include more than a single fiscal period for the life of the tax. What is required, instead, is that a new diversion of resources be involved in changing the existing situation, including change to the pretax state. In other words, if the *status quo,* defined with respect to income and product flows in time, is to be maintained, the pattern of financing-spending, public and private, that exists in period t_0 will be repeated in period t_1, other things equal.

Suppose that a community in period t_0 imposes a new tax to finance a newly available collective or public good. As compared with the situation that exists in period t_{-1}, the decision to supply the public good diverts resources from private goods supply to public goods supply. Those persons who participate in the decision process, the voters-taxpayers-beneficiaries, are more or less consciously aware of the real "cost" of the newly-produced public goods, this awareness being subject to the problems of estimation that have been previously discussed under the separate taxes. Compare this consciousness, given any particular tax, with that which will be present in the situation confronting the individual member of the community at the beginning of the period t_1, when the relevant choice concerns the possible continuation of the taxing-spending process. Here a decision to supply the same amount of public goods again in t_1 and to finance this with the old or existing tax schedule does not involve a positive imposition of real costs on individuals in a temporally differential sense. As compared with the situation in t_0, existing fiscal institutions may be continued in being without any person in the group undergoing change in his economic position. In objectively measurable units, the public goods that are supplied cost the same in sacrificed private goods in the two situations. Subjectively, however, as this cost affects individual choices, and through these, group decisions, the opportunity cost of goods financed through the old tax may be substantially lower than those for the same goods financed through the levy of a new tax, given the same tax institution.

The phenomenon discussed here is not, of course, unique to fiscal choices. Any departure from a position of "dynamic equilibrium" will require a somewhat greater impulse than a continuation of the pattern of flows that have been established.[1] In the most general terms, the appropriate analogue is the physical law of inertia. It is easier to continue a flow once started than it is to start it in the first place. All that is necessary for this point to be accepted as relevant for an individual decision calculus is some acknowledgement of a temporal sequence of choices.

The analysis here concentrates on fiscal choice. As suggested, the opportunity costs that are relevant for individual choice are necessarily subjective, and these costs cannot be measured independently of choice itself. These costs exist in the mind of the individual choice-maker only at the moment of decision.[2] In any new tax situation, these opportunity costs, which serve as the ob-

1. The element of behavior here is closely related, but not fully equivalent, to that discussed by Kenneth Boulding in his homostatic theory of the firm. See Kenneth Boulding, *A Reconstruction of Economics* (New York: John Wiley and Sons, 1950), especially Chapter 2.

2. This conception of subjective opportunity costs, as distinct from objectively measurable opportunity costs, has not been properly incorporated in the standard "kit of tools" possessed by economists, despite the efforts of a group connected with the London School of Economics. For some of the more general discussion, see L. Robbins, "Remarks Upon Certain Aspects of the Theory of Costs," *Economic Journal*, 44 (March, 1934), 1-18; J. Wiseman, "Uncertainty, Costs, and Collectivist Economic Planning," *Economica*, XX (May, 1953), 118-28; G. F. Thirlby, "The Subjective Theory of Value and 'Accounting' Cost," *Economica*, XIII (February, 1946), 32-49; "The Rule," *South African Journal of Economics*, 14 (December, 1946), 253-76; "The Economist's Description of Business Behavior," *Economica*, XIX (May, 1952), 148-67; "Economists' Cost Rules and Equilibrium Theory," *Economica*, XXVII (May, 1960), 148-57.

stacle to positive choice for the individual, consist in the anticipated sacrifice of future enjoyments from resources employed in the same manner as they are *currently employed.* The psychic income that must be sacrificed in choosing to provide new public goods is visible, apparent, to the individual who chooses. He must reduce his consumption of private goods in order to secure the benefits of the additional public goods that the tax levy is expected to finance. By contrast, in an old tax, or existing tax situation, these opportunity costs, although objectively identical, appear different to the individual who chooses. Here they consist in the expected enjoyment from employing resources for private purchases that are not now being purchased. The potential employment of additional resources in private markets, and not the sacrifice of existing or current enjoyments, is the opportunity cost of public goods in the old tax case. There is, necessarily, a less evident connection between a decision to finance public goods and the costs of this choice than there is in the new-tax situation. The costs under the old tax are, to repeat, units of psychic income which are not being enjoyed currently in the same form, and which may, conceptually, come into being only if the tax is not continued.

If the analysis is correct here, there exists a threshold of response between positive choice under one institution and under the other, *ceteris paribus.* Hence, at the margin, the demand for public goods under a new tax must exceed that under the old tax if the same quantity is observed to be provided. That is to say, other things equal, the individual will tend to "vote for" a somewhat larger public expenditure under an old tax financing scheme than he will under new tax financing. In terms of the simple diagrams that were introduced in Chapter 2, this threshold phenomenon can be represented by a displacement of effective tax-price downward in the case of an old or existing tax institution.

The behavioral difference here is not, of course, unique to fiscal decision processes, and it need not arise from irrationality and illusion on the part of the participant. The behavioral difference is consistent with rationality in individual choice provided only that the costs of decision-making are incorporated in the analytical model. The making of decisions, the choosing among alternatives either in private or collective choice situations, is costly to the individual who participates. He must invest time and resources in secur-

61

ing information about the alternatives available for choice and in evaluating and analyzing this information, or else he must bear the additional costs that are involved in the greater probability of error, costs that must also be attributed to the decision process. Once these decision costs are recognized, it is clear that the repetition of a choice, over periods subsequent to the initial one in which a definite decision is made, involves considerably lower cost than the making of a decision to *change*. In the limit, the repetition or continuation of choice in later periods, *ceteris paribus,* can be evaluated at zero marginal cost; no new investment in information gathering, in evaluation, need be made unless some of the parameters of the situation should have been modified. The minimization of decision cost through time will always imply the routinization of activity, the continuation of existing rules and institutions, the repetition of past behavior, the rejection of new alternatives. Some "wedge," some threshold, will be inserted between the selection of an existing alternative and the selection of a new one.

In the traditonal approach to public finance, the adage, "an old tax is a good tax" is satisfactorily descriptive, provided that the criterion of "goodness" is the minimization of "burden" on the taxpayer. In this approach, public expenditure decisions are exogenously made, or at least made independently of tax decisions. The old tax is here less burdensome to the taxpayer than the new tax for the reasons mentioned. The adage is also useful as a rule for "government," considered to be divorced from the individuals in the jurisdiction. The old tax generates less reaction than the new tax; more funds can be raised by adherence to this rule. In this particular application, therefore, the underlying political models yield similar results. Expenditures from old tax revenues need not satisfy such rigorous standards of "efficiency" as those financed from newly-imposed taxes. This fact is, of course, widely recognized by politicians and pressure groups who support public spending programs. The primary difficulty encountered is that of securing approval of a program *initially,* in "getting over," so to speak, of the first decision to approve.[3] Appropriations in subsequent time periods are never so difficult to secure.

3. This is explicitly recognized by Walter Heller in "*CED*'s Stabilizing Budget Policy After Ten Years," *American Economic Review,* XLVII (September, 1957), 649.

Experience suggests that, almost universally, tax and public spending rates which are increased, temporarily, to meet wartime or other emergency fiscal needs remain substantially higher in postwar, post-emergency periods than before. One explanation that has been advanced for this result, by Alan Peacock and Jack Wiseman, involves the so-called "displacement effect."[4] The emergency modifies the tolerable limit of taxation that the community will accept. This explanation is closely related to, and dependent upon, some recognition of the old tax-new tax differential discussed. The two explanations can be readily translated into the same hypothesis. Wartime spending needs are such that the threshold of decision can be crossed with newly imposed taxes or with substantial increases in rate levels of existing taxes. The additional real costs, in opportunity cost terms, of the expanded spending program is accepted in the emergency setting. Once these needs disappear, however, the bias is shifted in favor of a continued high level of public activity, as opposed to a return to some pre-emergency balance between the public and the private sector. Not having to undergo the apparent sacrifice of real resources generated by new tax financing, the individual is more willing, in post-emergency periods, to approve spending on the provision of services than he should have been in the pre-emergency fiscal setting. A corollary hypothesis is, of course, that the longer the emergency, the more pronounced this effect will be; that is to say, the older the tax, the more routine the institution, the greater the likelihood that it will be continued in existence.

The institutional influence examined here may have important implications for national policy in the late 1960's and early 1970's. Concern has often been expressed about the potential reaction of the public, and its political leaders, in the event that genuine agreement on disarmament should allow for drastic reductions in military or defense expenditure by the federal government. The stabilization impact of substantial reductions in outlay, accompanied by corresponding tax reductions, might indeed be serious, given the rigidities that characterize the institutions of monetary authority. The analysis here suggests, however, the federal spending programs, considered over-all, would not be dramatically reduced, especially after the continuation of such a long period of high-level cold war spending.

4. A. T. Peacock and Jack Wiseman, *The Growth of Public Expenditure in the United Kingdom* (National Bureau of Economic Research, 1961).

Effective disarmament would immediately produce vigorous pressures to expand federal nonmilitary spending programs, and barriers to such programs in terms of additional taxes would no longer be present. The limited cuts in military outlays during the early years of the Johnson administration accompanied by the substantially increased outlays on domestic programs tend to confirm this hypothesis. The extension of the "welfare state" becomes much more predictable in the event of effective disarmament.

REVENUE ELASTICITY AND FISCAL CHOICE

A more important implication, and one that has been widely recognized, at least indirectly, in recent years, concerns the effects on public spending that follow from a tax structure which provides automatically for relatively increased revenues as aggregate income rises. Almost all real-world tax institutions of significance involve income as a base, directly or indirectly, and hence must satisfy this requirement to a degree. The effects are most dramatic, however, in those cases where the elasticity of revenue yield exceeds the income elasticity of demand for established spending programs. For example, suppose that a public spending program in operation can be maintained, over a period when national income increases, by increases in dollar outlay only one-half so large, proportionally, as the increases in income. On the other hand, suppose that the tax institution originally earmarked to finance this public service program will yield revenues, at existing rates, that increase proportionally twice as fast as national income. This combination of circumstances will bias collective fiscal decisions, relatively speaking, in favor of new spending programs. Proposals for new public outlay will be much more likely to secure favorable political response than would be the case under the requirement for new-tax financing. Hence, quite apart from income-elasticity considerations, equivalent programs for public spending will secure more taxpayer support during periods of rising national income than they will during periods of stable national income, provided only that the rate structure of taxes is such that revenues are highly income elastic. This conclusion is also evident to politicians and pressure-group leaders, as witness the fiscal experience in the United States in the 1950's and 1960's.

The fiscal-choice analysis here serves to place familiar and obvious institutional experience in a consistent theoretical setting.

Tax institutions vary significantly in income elasticity of revenue. For this reason, some distinction among the major revenue-raising categories must be made. In a period of rapidly increasing national product, that tax institution characterized by the highest elasticity will tend, other things equal, to generate the largest volume of public spending. Under this consideration, the progressive income tax, the corporate income tax, and the excise tax on specific consumption items of high income elasticity are the revenue sources to be singled out. The personal income tax, because of the progression in its rate structure, generates revenue increases in response to income changes that are more than proportional to the latter. This tax will, therefore, tend to produce more favorable public attitudes toward expanded spending programs than will most comparable fiscal institutions, other things equal, when national income grows. This conclusion cannot, however, be pushed too far, since it must be kept in mind that this tax remains direct, and, therefore, its impact is sensed to a greater degree by the taxpayer than the less direct taxes. By comparison to a proportional income tax, the progressive tax surely has the effect of making expanded spending programs more acceptable politically. The tax on corporate income must also be noted especially in this connection. Not only are its revenues highly sensitive to aggregate income changes due to the residual characteristics of corporate profits; the tax is also indirect in its effect on the individual fiscal calculus.

The institutional biases outlined here are, of course, reversible. If national income should decline, the revenue flexibility of a tax becomes an element that makes the enactment of new spending programs, or even the maintenance of existing programs, more difficult, provided only that the rules of the fiscal game require some matching of revenues with expenditures. If, in the case of a national government with money-creating powers, the balanced-budget rule is not directly observed, this reversibility may not be effective. During periods of falling national income, public spending may be maintained, or even expanded, without the imposition of newly-enacted taxes or increases in rates of existing taxes. We shall discuss the whole area of "functional finance" and its implications for individual fiscal choice in a later chapter.

MULTI-PERIOD CHOICE AND TAX CAPITALIZATION

In our initial analytical models, the tax to be levied was assumed to be a *new tax,* a restriction that we have discussed above, but, also the fiscal choice examined was limited to the *current* period of time, on both the tax and the benefit side. That is to say, we have assumed implicitly up to this point that the public goods or services provided are enjoyed only in the current period and that the tax employed to finance these services is imposed period by period, whether this be a new tax or an old one in the sense discussed above. The reason for this current-period restriction is evident: the fiscal choice situation confronted by the individual in the one-period setting is considerably less complex than that which he faces if he benefits and/or the costs should be known to extend over a sequence of time periods.

Consider now a multi-period model, while remaining within our standard reference system of the individual as voter-taxpayer-beneficiary; that is, as the ultimate chooser in the democratic political process. What modifications must be introduced in the analysis of choice behavior as a result of this change in the setting? The most obvious one arises from the necessity to translate benefits and costs that are expected to occur in future periods into present-value units. A discounting or capitalizing process becomes an essential element in the individual's decision calculus, and one that is wholly absent from single-period models. Insofar as this process itself embodies additional uncertainty, the making of decisions becomes more difficult, more costly, to the individual.

Other distortions arise that are closely related to the old tax-new tax distinction already examined. If the time pattern of both benefits and taxes is known with precision, the discounting process can be applied straightforwardly to both sides of the account, and no directional bias need be introduced. If, however, the exact dating for future taxes and for future benefits is not carried out, or if this procedure is either impossible or implausible because of the nature of the fiscal institutions involved, the capitalization may not be uniformly applied to the two sides. Suppose that a proposal is made to impose a tax on the capital value of residential real property in a community for the purpose of financing a program of vocational education. (We neglect intergroup distributional considerations here.) We want to look at the behavior of the owner of residential real property, the potential taxpayer, who is, at the same time, a potential beneficiary of the public services of the program. How will he choose the preferred rate of tax along with the desired quantity of public service? In the current-period models the problem is conceptually simple, relatively speaking. And, even in a multi-period model, if both time shapes are precisely predictable, little need be added to our previous discussion. For example, if the tax is limited to five years, which is also the designated life of the spending program, and, further, if a uniform quantity of services is to be financed each year, then the discounting process is not tedious, and it need not distort fiscal choice. Let us suppose, however, that the legislation proposed is "open ended" in time, so to speak. That is to say, both the tax and the spending program are to remain in effect indefinitely. Here the complications that are introduced into the individual's decision calculus become significant. To the degree that the tax is specialized to a particular characteristic of the individual economy, and to the degree that it is expected to remain in being over time, capitalization will occur. The owner of the property subject to tax will experience a once-and-for-all decrement in its capital value at the moment the tax becomes effective. The "burden" of the tax, over time, is concentrated in this initial period to the extent that capitalization occurs. A similar process will take place on the spending side. Prospective beneficiaries recognize that the program currently initiated will be continued. Hence, they should experience or "sense" a windfall gain at the time or the moment of effective social decision, a gain that represents some capitalized value of an expected benefits stream.

In the example here, however, it seems likely that the individual who is both taxpayer and beneficiary will tend to capitalize the tax obligation more fully than he will the off-setting benefit stream. If he does so, some distortion is introduced into the subjective evaluation of the alternatives that he confronts. The reason for this predicted difference in his treatment of the two sides of the account is found in the differential marketability of the asset taxed and the benefits enjoyed. In the example, the object of the tax is residential real property. This property is assigned to individual owners, and each parcel carries with it a current market value. The owner may dispose of a parcel, at its market value, at any time of his own choosing.

The tax acts to reduce this capital or market value to the extent that it is capitalized. On the other hand, the benefits stream, although enjoyed by the individual in common with others, and valued by him, does not provide a privately-marketable asset that allows him to secure liquid funds at his discretion. Hence, despite the fact that, in the net, the two sides may discount to the same objectively measurable present value, the individual will tend to overvalue the tax or cost side. He will consider his liquidity to be reduced by the tax, but not to be increased to an offsetting extent by the benefit stream that is anticipated. For this reason, in the example, the individual's fiscal choice tends to be biased against supporting the proposal for levying the tax and financing the program of spending on vocational education. There will be an institutional bias here against spending on long-term benefit projects. The bias or distortion here is caused by the difference in generality between the tax and the benefit side. As suggested, tax capitalization will occur to the extent that the tax is specific, and this phenomenon has been traditionally discussed in application to asset taxes. On the other hand, in the example, benefits are assumed to be generally available to all members of the group, indivisible and unassignable into separate shares. When the asymmetry runs in this direction, fiscal decisions are likely to exhibit institutional bias against spending on long-term projects yielding general benefits.

If, however, the asymmetry should be reversed, an opposing bias would appear, as a second and different example can make clear. Suppose that the tax to be imposed is a general one, say, a proportional tax on income, while the spending program involves specific and assignable benefits to owners of property, say, free water for irrigation purposes. In this model the expected benefits should be immediately capitalized into the value of the land, whereas the tax will not tend to be capitalized to any comparable extent. Accordingly, as citizen-taxpayer-farmer, the individual will be quite favorably disposed toward the initiation of long-term projects financed under such arrangements. There will be an institutional bias toward public spending under these arrangements.

The point may be further emphasized by examining specifically the situation of an individual, in each of the two examples above, who plans to leave the local community after a period of, say, three years following the period of the initial fiscal decision. In the first model,

68

he will find that the capital value of his property which he must sell has been adjusted downward for the expected tax obligation, whereas he cannot, to the same extent, "sell" the capitalized value of the expected benefits stream to a prospective buyer of his land. He could do the latter only if he could, in some fashion, sell his "membership" in the community. Recognizing that at the time of the initial decision, the individual who thinks that he might move from the community will, of course, place more weight on the tax side than the benefit side in making fiscal choices. By contrast, the individual in the second example, where benefits are more specific than the tax, will find that he can sell his property at a capital value that has been adjusted upward to incorporate the expected benefits from the irrigation water. On the other hand, a comparable adjustment in assets value downward to reflect the tax may not have taken place.

These illustrative examples should not be allowed to make the point seem more important than it is. To some extent, any local government fiscal action is specific, and, to this extent, some capitalization will occur. If the only means of entering a local community is to become an owner of real property, then both taxes and benefits will be capitalized. The implications developed are relevant, however, for the more realistic situations where nonproperty owners are allowed to participate in fiscal choices along with property holders. The analysis here obviously yields several hypotheses that can be subjected to empirical tests.

The institutional distortions that may be introduced in multi-period fiscal choice by unbalanced capitalization applies only to the initial decision concerning whether or not to approve or disapprove a taxing-spending proposal. Other important institutional influences may arise when changes in existing programs are proposed. These are fully analogous to the old tax-new tax factors previously discussed.

Suppose that the community imposes the tax on residential real property to finance the program of vocational education, our first example above, but that no cut-off date for the program is included in the authorizing legislation. Let us also suppose, at the time of the initial decision, the objectively-measured present value for the benefits stream exceeded that for the tax costs. However, let us now suppose that one or two periods have passed, and that it has become clear that the initial expectations of benefits were in error and that actual benefits are much lower than had been anticipated. Objectively considered, the program should be curtailed and the tax law repealed. However, if the tax has been effectively capitalized, by the owners of all assets subject to tax, the opportunity costs of continuing the program will "appear" to be low indeed. The "real" costs will, of course, consist in the possible windfalls that would occur in the moment of repeal. But this element of opportunity cost does not seem likely to exert such an influence on fiscal choice as it might do in some omniscient pattern of behavior. To fail to take a decision on repeal of a tax embodies an opportunity cost that, properly measured, should be no different from that embodied in the initial enactment of a tax. But the individual does not "sense" the two opportunity costs as identical, dollar for dollar, or even approximately so. The institution of tax capitalization seems, therefore, to bias fiscal decisions toward the continuation of spending projects once these are initiated, despite the fact that, during the initial consideration the bias may run in the opposing direction. This conclusion applies, of course, only to the first sort of model, in which the tax is more specific than the benefit. In the converse model, where the benefits are more specific than the tax, relatively greater capitalization of benefits takes place, and more effective opposition will arise in each period to any continuation of tax levies in existence. In this case, if spending projects turn out to be grossly inefficient, they will probably be curtailed more readily due to individual pressures on the politicians.

CONCLUSIONS

The basic hypotheses concerning individual behavior in fiscal choice situations that have been advanced in this chapter should be subjected to empirical testing insofar as this proves possible. The hypotheses are more general, however, and there are many commonly recognized versions, despite the fact that they have perhaps not been fully incorporated into the standard body of economic theory. The classical economists discussed the notion of interest as a payment for "waiting," which Nassau Senior changed to "abstinence." There is a difference, psychologically, between the meanings of these two terms, and this difference is the one emphasized in the hypotheses of this chapter. "Waiting" implies the cost of setting aside current income, current consumption, for capital formation. "Abstinence" implies this also, but, in addition, the cost of refraining from "eating up" capital already accumulated. Logically, of course, to put aside current consumption is identical with refraining from consuming invested capital, that is, from converting it into current consumption. But individuals do not behave as if "eating up" capital is identical with refraining from accumulating it in the first place. And their behavior is not necessarily irrational, for the reasons that we have examined in this chapter. The opportunity costs of holding capital are fully analogous to those of continuing a long-existing tax or one that has been substantially capitalized; these costs consist in potentially enjoyable alternatives that are not *currently* in flow to the individual. Psychologically, these costs do not serve to inhibit individual decision to the same degree as do comparable measured costs in units of *currently-enjoyed* flows of services. If uncertainty is not positively valued by the individual, this reaction is individually rational, quite apart from the costs of decision itself. Hamlet said that it is better to bear those ills we have than to fly to others that we know not of, but his statement applies also to benefits or pleasures. A decision to initiate action involves the giving up of known benefits in exchange for necessarily uncertain alternatives. A decision to continue a course of action once initiated becomes just the reverse; continuation becomes the *status quo,* and the uncertainty elements arise on the cessation of established flows through time.

6. *Earmarking Versus General-Fund Financing: Analysis and Effects**

*Although it is developed somewhat differently, the basic theoretical model presented in this chapter is contained in my paper, "The Economics of Earmarked Taxes," *Journal of Political Economy,* LXXI (October, 1963), 457-69, circulated also as No. 73, Studies of Government Finance Reprints, Brookings Institution, 1963.

INTRODUCTION

In earlier models a *single* tax institution finances a *single* public service. Decisions were assumed to be made on the preferred quantities of public services, one at a time, and the costs of each service were assumed to be measured in one tax. The next step toward generalizing the model involves the modification of this restriction. Real-world fiscal structures are seldom characterized by segmented or assigned revenue sources to such a degree, although the institution of earmarked taxes is, relatively speaking, quite important, especially at state-local levels of government.[1] Clearly, the institutional framework in this respect exerts some effects on individual behavior in fiscal choice, effects that should be subject to analysis.

The alternative to single-purpose, or dedicated, revenue sources for public services is, of course, *general-fund financing.* In the one case, that of earmarking, the individual "votes for" designated taxes to finance specific public outlay. In the other, general-fund financing, he "votes for" the same taxes to finance, not a single service, but a budgetary bundle of several services, with the precise composition

---

1. A recent survey by the Tax Foundation indicates that, in fiscal 1963, approximately 41 per cent of state tax collections were dedicated to specific functions. See *Earmarked State Taxes* (New York: Tax Foundation, 1965).

of this bundle being determined separately, presumably by some authorized budgetary authority. How will this single difference in fiscal institutions affect the individual? Which institution presents him with a more accurate basis for comparing alternatives? Will he tend to support greater over-all public outlay under earmarking or under general-fund institutions? And, if he is empirically observed to do so, what are the characteristic conditions that must be met?

Only one of these questions seems relatively easy to answer. If the individual can make separate fiscal choices for each public goods program, which a structure of earmarked taxes conceptually allows him to do, directly or indirectly, he is informed as to the alternatives that he confronts, at least to the extent that the payment institutions allow, and subject, of course, to all of the qualifications noted in previous analysis. The uncertainty that he faces is clearly less than that which is present in the comparable decision on a "bundle" of public goods or services, with the mix among the separate components in the bundle to be determined in a separate decision process or through the auspices of a delegated budget-making authority. If this mix is not announced in advance to the voter-taxpayer, he must try to predict the outcome of another decision process, in which he may or may not participate, a process that need not exist at all in the more straight-forward earmarking model where all revenue sources are specifically dedicated.

An earmarking system is closely analogous to that which normally confronts the individual chooser in private-goods markets, and, on several occasions, we have utilized the latter situation to assess the potentialities for rationality in individual behavior patterns. In private markets, the individual normally (although not universally) purchases one good at a time and separately; he makes a decision on, say, the amount of sugar per week that he plans to consume independently from his decision on the amount of gasoline or beer, although, of course, relations of complementarity and substitutability will exist. But only a fiscal system characterized by substantially complete revenue segregation would allow the individual, as a participant in political decisions, to attain a position comparable, even at a first approximation, to that which he confronts in private markets.[2]

2. The analysis here, as elsewhere in the study, retains the reference system of the individual as voter-taxpayer-beneficiary. If the reference system is changed to that of the budgetary authority empowered to determine the component mix and if this entity is considered as a "person," then earmark-

General-fund financing, is analogous to a market situation where the individual is forced to purchase a bundle of goods, with the mix among the various components determined independently of his own preferences. The specific tie-in sale is similar to general-fund financing, that is, nonearmarking. Making use of the theory of monopolistic tie-in sales in private markets, we can develop a theory of general-fund financing, and, conversely, a theory of earmarking.[3]

A MODEL OF INDIVIDUAL FISCAL CHOICE

Consider a single individual as he confronts a fiscal choice situation. Collective services are available to the community at constant cost, whether supplied singly or jointly, and this cost is distributed among individuals in such a way that each person, also, faces a fixed supply-price, or tax-price. We may think of the goods as being financed by the levy of some invariant tax-price institution of the sort described early in Chapter 3; the individual has no power to influence his own "terms of trade" with the fisc. We also assume that the services or goods in question make up a relatively small share in the total income of the community, sufficiently so to allow us to neglect income effects in the analysis of individual behavior. We seek to analyze the behavior of the individual in selecting his most preferred outlay on public goods or services, recognizing, of course, that the model provides at best only some indication of voting behavior on spending proposals that are presented to the political group for decision.

As the earlier discussion has shown, the analysis is straightforward in the case of a single public good considered independently. We can derive an individual marginal evaluation schedule or curve, a demand curve in this instance, for the good in the same way that

ing is not analogous to the market situation. The private person does not normally tie up particular sources of his own income for spending on particular items of consumption. This illustrates the dramatic difference in analysis generated by a change in the reference system from that of the budgetary authority to that of the individual as voter-taxpayer. The near-universal condemnation of earmarking in the literature of budgetary theory can only be explained in terms of this difference.

3. For recent statements of the theory of tie-in sales, see M. L. Burstein, "The Economics of Tie-In Sales," *Review of Economics and Statistics,* 42 (February, 1960), 68-73; "A Theory of Full-Line Forcing," *Northwestern University Law Review,* 55 (1960), 62-95. See also Ward S. Bowman, Jr., "Tying Arrangements and the Leverage Problem," *Yale Law Journal,* 67 (March, 1957), 19-36.

we derive such a schedule or curve for any privately-marketed good or service. The supply curve confronting the individual, the tax-price curve, is a horizontal line at the fixed tax-price, which is some predetermined individualized share in the total community cost-price for the public good. Individual or private "equilibrium" is attained at the position where marginal evaluation or demand-price equals tax-price.

We seek to compare the results from this model with those from the contrasting one in which the individual is required to choose, not his preferred outlay on a single public good or service, but instead his preferred outlay on a bundle of two or more services, with the mix of components in this bundle being determined independently. For analytical simplicity, we shall develop this general-fund model in terms of only two goods. For descriptive flavor here, suppose that we are examining the individual's choice for police-protection and fire-protection services in a municipality. The community supplies both services collectively, and we seek to determine the possible effects on individual choice behavior that may be produced by the two alternative budgetary systems. As indicated, general-fund financing introduces greater uncertainty to the extent that the individual cannot precisely know the content of the budgetary bundle. We want to leave this consideration out of account, however, and we assume that, prior to any conceptual voting process, the budgetary mix has been set and has been made known to all participants. Whether or not the individual has directly or indirectly participated in the determination of the mix is not relevant to our consideration. Given the mix as predetermined, the individual can predict with accuracy the allocation of tax dollars that are finally channeled through the budget. In this case, we try to answer the question: Will the individual vote for more or less public outlay than he would in the contrasting model where he conceptually votes on the two services independently? Will one or both of the two services in the mix be expanded by a shift from earmarking to general-fund budgeting?

The answers here depend upon the particular form that the budgetary tie-in takes. It would be possible to define this tie-in with respect to physical units of service, such as, for example, the requirement that one policeman be hired each time a fireman is hired, and *vice versa.* It seems descriptively more realistic and analytically

75

more convenient, however, if we define the tie-in with respect to a budgetary allocation between the two services. In other words, general-fund financing takes the form of a specific proportion of the total budget assigned to each of the two services. There will exist one such budgetary allocation that will insure an identity of solution as between the two fiscal institutions, "solution" being confined, of course, to the individual calculus examined. That is to say, there will always be one budgetary ratio that will cause the individual to "vote for" the same relative quantities of the two services and the same total public outlay under general-fund financing that he would "vote for" under complete earmarking. This unique solution may be called "full equilibrium" for the individual, and this solution may be used as a starting point for the more extended analysis.

GEOMETRICAL ANALYSIS

It is convenient to develop the analysis geometrically. In Figure 6.1, quantity units are measured along the horizontal axis, but these are defined in a special manner. Under the tie-in arrangement, a unit of quantity is defined as that physical combination of the two services that are available for one dollar, one hundred cents. Thus, the total number of dollars expended is directly proportional to the distance along this axis. We begin by assuming that the "full equilibrium" budgetary mix prevails, and that this is defined as the forty-sixty ratio. That is to say, forty cents out of each budgetary spending dollar are allocated to spending for fire protection services and sixty cents are allocated to spending on police protection. We can now derive demand curves D_f and D_p, respectively for fire protection and police protection services. For analytical simplicity, we use linear relationships here, but this does not modify the results. These curves are derived with respect to the physical quantity dimensions indicated by the budgetary ratio. A single physical unit of fire protection service is that quantity that is available, to the individual, at a tax-price of forty cents, and a unit of police service is that quantity that is available, to the individual, at a tax-price of sixty cents. (Note that this does not imply that the individual is able to adjust quantity privately, as in ordinary markets; the availability of a quantity to the individual at a tax-price implies only that this is the basis upon which he conceptually votes. Whether or not he

76

actually secures these results depends on whether or not a sufficient number of his fellows agrees with him.)

The vertical summation of these two demand curves, D_f and

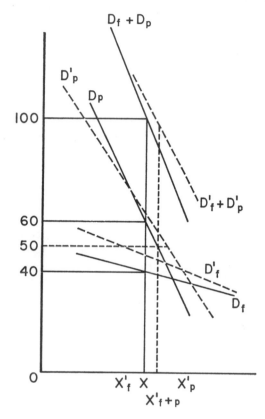

FIGURE 6.1

D_p, yield the composite demand curve labeled, $D_f + D_p$, which represents the demand for the bundle of the two services, mixed in the forty-sixty budgetary proportion. This is the bundle that the individual considers himself to be "purchasing" as he participates in collective or group choice under the general-fund scheme. By our definition of "full equilibrium," this composite demand curve cuts the composite supply curve, drawn at one dollar, along the same vertical that measures the independently-chosen quantities of fire protection and police protection. (There are elements of circularity in this geometrical construction, but these are not damaging to the analysis since its purpose is illustrative only.)

Under the conditions shown in Figure 6.1, there will be no differential effects as between earmarking and general-fund financing of the two services with the forty-sixty budgetary ratio. The individual will choose, will vote for, or otherwise use his political power to promote, the same quantity of services and the same over-all public spending under either of the two institutional forms. If separately presented, he would ideally prefer an amount, OX, of fire protection services, defined in forty-cent units, which can, of course, be readily translated into any other physical dimension. Similarly, he would ideally choose an amount, OX, of police services, defined in sixty-cent units. Or, if he is forced to choose these two services combined in budgetary bundles, defined by the forty-sixty ratio, he will choose a quantity, OX. In either instance, he will "vote for" a total budget outlay that is directly proportional to the horizontal distance, OX, on Figure 6.1.

These two distinct fiscal institutions produce different results only when budgetary ratios other than that required for "full equilibrium" confront the individual in the general-fund scheme. To examine the differences, assume now that a segregated financing system has been in effect, but that a shift to general-fund financing at a fifty-fifty budgetary ratio is contemplated, with demand conditions remaining those depicted in Figure 6.1. To determine the effects of this change, it is first necessary to translate the two demand curves, D_f and D_p, into modified dimensions, the physical quantity units now being defined as those available, to the individual, at fifty-cents. The new demand curves, drawn in the two fifty-cent dimensions, are shown as D'_f and D'_p. These are identical with D_f and D_p, except for the change in physical dimension. The effects of general-fund financing at this single nonequilibrium ratio, which now favors fire protection services differentially, can be clearly shown. As common sense should suggest, more fire protection services will be demanded in the tie-in arrangement and less police protection than would be the case under the segregated accounts. In the new quantity dimensions, OX'_f represents the "full equilibrium" or earmarking quantity for fire protection services, and, similarly, OX'_p, the corresponding quantity for police services. In other words, these are the quantities in the new dimensions that correspond to OX in the old dimensions. General-fund financing under the new, fifty-fifty, budgetary ratio will generate (as is indicated by the intersection of the new composite demand curve, $D'_f + D'_p$ and the composite supply or tax-price curve at one dollar) a preferred tie-in quantity, $OX'_{f + p}$.[4]

To this point, the conclusions are apparent. Any shift in the budgetary ratio away from that required for "full equilibrium" will insure that general-fund financing will introduce some distortion in the choice pattern of the individual. Forcing him to "purchase" two or more services in a bundle, rather than separately, will move the individual to some less preferred position on his potentially attainable utility surface. Since, under independent adjustment for each service or good, the individual could, always, if he desired, select quantities indicated by the OX' 's in the new dimensions, the fact that he does not so do suggests that the new combination is less preferred than the alternative that is available under earmarking. The distortion causes him to desire that one of the two services be expanded beyond the "full equilibrium" amount and that the other be contracted to some quantity below this. Relatively, the good or service that is expanded will be that which is favored by the budgetary ratio. The analysis remains incomplete, however, until and unless further questions are answered. Will over-all public outlay, as desired by the individual, tend to increase or to decrease, and under what conditions? What are the characteristics of those goods and services most likely to be substantially increased as a result of favorable general-fund ratios?

The construction of Figure 6.1 suggests that total public outlay need not remain the same under earmarking and under non-earmarking when the latter embodies nonequilibrium budgetary ratios, and it also suggests that the direction of change may depend upon the particular configurations of the demand functions. Examination of the model produces the following conclusions: If the ratio turns in favor of the service characterized by the more elastic demand, at the full-equilibrium quantity (as is the case in the geometrical example here), total public outlay, as this is preferred by the individual, will be expanded by the shift from earmarking to the general-fund system. Conversely, if the ratio under general-fund financing favors the service characterized by the less elastic demand, again measured at the full-equilibrium quantity, total public outlay will be contracted by the shift in fiscal institutions. These specific results hold, without qualification, only for relatively limited shifts away from "full equilibrium" positions. Relative tax-price elasticities may change as the

4. The geometrical construction in Figure 6.1 is based on a specific numerical model that is explained in the Appendix to this Chapter.

tie-in equilibrium changes. A more general conclusion is that total expenditure, as desired by the individual whose calculus we examine, will increase so long as the relative tax-price change, embodied in the budgetary ratio, is in favor of the service with the more elastic demand, with elasticity being measured at the respective tie-in equilibrium quantities of the two services. Conversely, total expenditure will fall if the ratio favors the service characterized by the lower tax-price elasticity of demand, similarly measured.

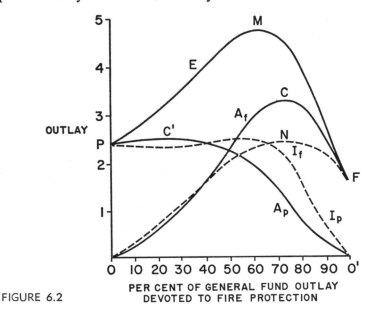

FIGURE 6.2

PER CENT OF GENERAL FUND OUTLAY
DEVOTED TO FIRE PROTECTION

Several of the relevant relationships are illustrated in Figure 6.2, which is based in the same underlying conditions as Figure 6.1. On the horizontal axis is measured the percentage of fire protection outlay in a tie-in budgetary arrangement, running from zero to one hundred. On the vertical axis is measured total outlay, on both or on each service, as this is determined by the demand pattern of the individual and the assumed cost conditions. In all cases, as before, the quantities refer only to those preferred by the single individual whose decision-process we analyze. As mentioned, Figure 6.2 is derived from the same date as Figure 6.1, which embodies linear demand functions, although a similar set of relationships could be readily derived from any postulated conditions of individual demand. The full-equilibrium ratio, defined previously as the forty-sixty one, must generate a desired or preferred total outlay under the tie-in that is equal to the sum of the preferred outlays on the two services when they are "purchased" separately, through an earmarked revenue arrangement. If a budgetary ratio with zero per cent outlay on fire protection is introduced, total outlay will be exclusively on police. Conversely, if a 100 per cent ratio prevails, all outlay is on fire protection. Hence, if income effects are neglected, the vertical distance, E, at the forty-sixty ratio, must be equal to the sum of the distances, OP and O′F.

As the ratio shifts from the forty-sixty position in favor of fire protection services, desired total outlay on both services in a tie-in bundle expands, as shown by the rising portion of the top curve in Figure 6.2 to the right of E. As this shift continues, preferred total spending increases until it attains a maximum at M, after which it falls sharply to F. As the ratio shifts from the forty-sixty position in the other direction, now differentially favoring police services, desired total outlay on the tie-in bundle falls, as shown by the top curve to the left of E. It continues to fall to point P, where no part of the budget is allotted to fire protection.

The lower four curves in Figure 6.2 break down this preferred total outlay as between the two services and as between actual and imputed components. The actual outlay on one service is readily computed by taking the indicated percentage of total outlay as shown by the ratio on the horizontal scale. The two actual outlay curves must, of course, sum to the combined outlay curve for the bundles, and the two curves must intersect at the 50 per cent position. "Imputed outlay" on a service is defined as that part of preferred total outlay on a bundle containing that service that is attributed by the individual to that service at each particular tie-in equilibrium. Imputed outlay on a service equals actual outlay only at the full-equilibrium budgetary ratio and at either extremity of Figure 6.2. For all other ratios, imputed outlay differs from actual, and the difference reflects the degree of "exploitation," negative and positive, that nonequilibrium budgetary ratios generate. Imputed outlay falls below actual outlay on the service that is favored in the budgetary mix; it exceeds actual outlay on the remaining service. This is shown in Figure 6.2. To the right of 40 per cent, imputed outlay on fire protection services, I_f, lies below the curve of actual outlay, A_f. To the left of 40 per cent, the opposite relationship holds. And, of course, the relationship for police services is the inverse of those for fire protection since the two imputed outlays must also equal total outlay on the combined bundles.[5]

Maximum total outlay is reached at M. As the ratio shifts beyond this point, desired total expenditures fall although the share of this total devoted to fire protection continues to rise. At some point, C, to the right of M, these two factors become mutually offsetting, and some maximum outlay on fire protection alone is attained. Increasing the share in a combined budget beyond this "critical ratio" will result in fewer resources being devoted to fire protection, always on the assumption that the desires of the voter-taxpayer-beneficiary whose calculus is here examined imply something about collective outcomes.

As the ratio shifts differentially to favor police services, in the model used here, total outlay falls continuously. However, because of the increasing budgetary share, the preferred quantity of police services increases to some critical ratio, C', where actual outlay on this service alone reaches a maximum.[6]

IMPLICATIONS FOR FISCAL CHOICE

The analysis demonstrates that the differential effects of earmarking and general-fund financing depend critically on the way in which general-fund budgetary arrangements allocate revenues among the several public services or goods in the bundles that are presented for choice. This suggests the question: What predictions can be made, if any, concerning the composition of a general-fund budget? To the extent that a budgetary authority is assumed able to make decisions on the mix in complete independence of the preferences of

5. The difference between actual and imputed outlay can be demonstrated on Figure 6.1 by the difference between the position of tie-in equilibrium and the corresponding points on the respective demand curves. Only at full equilibrium will this difference disappear.

6. The rising portion of the I_p curve at the left of Figure 6-2 requires some explanation. As the budgetary mix shifts in favor of police services, imputed expenditures on both services fall, as shown. However, as a smaller and smaller share of the budget is allotted to fire protection, the degree of exploitation that consumers of police services can attain reaches some maximum. Beyond this point, the "relative tax-price reduction" that the tie-in involves is progressively diminished.

The derivation of the construction is clarified in the numerical example upon which the figures are based, which is presented in the Appendix. It should be emphasized, however, that the general results do not depend on the particulars of the example or on the shapes of the curves derived therefrom.

citizens, no predictions are possible. However, if we look at a slightly different question, some interesting predictions can be made, and, in this way, the broad effects of these alternative fiscal institutions can be provisionally traced. If earmarking and general-fund financing, as institutions, are alternatives, we may predict something of the effects if we know something about the choice among these alternatives. Under what conditions is a community more likely to shift from earmarking to general-fund financing and vice versa? What responses to group pressures do such shifts reflect?

In any politically organized community, specific individuals and groups will find particular interest in promoting the performance of one or the other of the public services that are provided. Using our two-service model to be illustrative of the more general case, the predicted behavior of these separate groups can be examined. Once this is done, inferences can be drawn concerning the impact of the institutions on fiscal choice patterns. Assume that both of the services are financed initially through earmarked revenue sources; choices are made independently. It is clear from the analysis above that groups organized in support of either service would have incentives to push for a shift to general-fund financing, *if* differentially favorable budgetary ratios can be expected to result. Both groups cannot, however, simultaneously hope to secure such favorable ratios, unless one of them makes gross errors in predicting political responses. The characteristics of demand make for significant differences in the expected gain to be secured from favorable general-fund schemes. Relatively, the group that is organized in support of the more elastic-demand service stands to gain more by favorable tie-ins. Sizeable amounts of "taxpayers' surplus" can be captured from the relatively less elastic-demand service that is tied in under a budgetary bundle.[7] Not only will the favored service be allotted a larger share of each spendings dollar, but, also, total spending on

7. This conclusion is, in general, consistent with the conclusions of Burstein with respect to the tie-in sales of the monopolist. As he suggests, the monopolist, selling a product that is necessarily price elastic, will seek to tie in the sales of an inelastic-demand product. The monopolist can, of course, control the relevant ratio. Cf. Burstein, "The Economics of Tie-In-Sales," *Review of Economics and Statistics.*

The analysis of general-fund financing, developed here, is simpler than the comparable analysis of monopolistic tie-in sales. In our model, the unit cost of supplying services, either jointly or separately, is always equal to the tax-price charged to "purchasers." The government does not seek to make profits. With the monopolist, the difference between unit cost and price is a central variable that the fiscal model need not include.

both services increases. The group organized in support of this service can, therefore, afford to take some risk of unfavorable budgetary ratios in general-fund schemes. By comparison, the pressure group supporting the extension of the relatively inelastic-demand service, will not be able to secure so much advantage from comparably favorable shifts in the tie-in ratio. While a higher share of each budget dollar will be desirable, the potential "taxpayers' surplus" that is exploitable is severely limited. This group stands to gain less and probably to lose more from a change in institutions toward the amalgamation of revenues. It will, therefore, tend to opt for the continuation, or the introduction, of segregated budget accounts.

The hypothesis that emerges is that shifts toward general-fund fiscal arrangements tend to be made in response to pressures from those in support of services that will be benefited most from such arrangements. If this hypothesis is valid, and if the political response is as these groups predict, institutional changes away from earmarking produce somewhat larger public expenditures in total. This general conclusion is reinforced by the behavior of explicitly organized taxpayer groups and by that of the bureaucracy. Taxpayer associations, organized for the purpose of holding down tax rates, independently from any consideration of public-service benefits, seem likely to support the retention of earmarked revenues. By comparison, the organized bureaucracy, whose interest is diametrically opposed to those of the taxpayers, and which is interested in expanding the size of the public sector, independently of cost considerations, seems likely to support general-fund financing. This effect is over and above the specific budgetary objective of maximizing the power of the budgetary authority, which, of course, supports general-fund schemes for even more obvious reasons.

These generalizations need not, of course, apply in all cases, and empirical tests may refute the basic hypotheses that are suggested or implied by the analysis. Whether or not earmarking or general-fund financing provides, in the large, the more "efficient" fiscal institution, from the individual's own frame of reference, has not been considered. The analysis has not taken into account the costs of making political decisions, and, when these are included, general-fund financing becomes relatively more attractive, as an institution, because of the reduction in these costs that it makes possible. Considerations of this nature are put aside in this part of the study since we have assumed that the institutions are selected externally to the individual.

Numerical Appendix to Chapter 6

The geometrical construction in Figures 1 and 2 is drawn to scale from the numerical model explained here.

I. Construct two linear demand equations, one for fire protection services, one for police protection services. These equations are of the standard form:

$y = a - bx$, but the following side conditions must be satisfied.

$y_f = 40$ and $y_p = 60$, when $x_f = x_p$.

These conditions are imposed by the definition of "full equilibrium" at the 40-60 budgetary ratio.

II. Define the demand equation for fire protection services as
   (1) $y_f = 50 - .25 x_f$.

Solving this equation for x_f, when $y_f = 40$, we get, $x_f = 40$.

Now derive a demand for police protection services that satisfies the side conditions in I, as follows:

$$60 = 150 - 40b$$
$$b = 2.25,$$

giving

   (2) $y_p = 150 - 2.25x_p$.

III. Equations (1) and (2) are demand equations for the two services defined in quantity units as follows:

Fire protection—one unit is "the physical quantity available to the individual for a cost-price of forty cents."

Police protection—one unit is "the physical quantity available to the individual for a cost-price of sixty cents."

IV. From (1) and (2) construct a composite demand equation (3),
   (3) $y_c = 200 - 2.5x_c$.

This is the demand equation for the one dollar "bundle" of services, combined in the 40-60 budgetary ratio.

V. At "full equilibrium," compute *total outlay* on both fire protection services and police protection services. Compute *actual outlay* on each service, and also *imputed outlay* on each service. These results are entered in Table A-6.1, opposite the 40-60 budget-

85

ary ratio. Note that actual outlay in this solution must equal imputed outlay for each service, by definition of the full equilibrium condition.

VI. Change the budgetary ratio from that defined as "full equilibrium." Take a new ratio, 50-50.

Change the *quantity dimensions* in the two demand equations as appropriate to derive *translated* functions (1)' and (2)',

$$(1)' \quad y_f = 62.5 - .39x_f$$
$$(2)' \quad y_p = 125 - 1.56x_p.$$

VII. From (1)' and (2)', derive new composite demand equation,

$$(3)' \quad y_c = 187.5 - 1.95x_c.$$

This becomes the demand equation for the one dollar "bundle" represented by services combined at the 50-50 ratio.

VIII. Solve (3)', for x_c, when $y_c = 100$, which is the "cost-price" of the "bundle," and get,

$$x_c = 44.87.$$

IX. Now solve (1)' and (2)' for y_f and y_p, when $x_f = x_p = 44.87$. Get

$$y_f = 44.8$$
$$y_p = 55.2.$$

X. From the values derived in VIII and IX, derive *actual* and *imputed* outlay on each service and *total outlay* on both services and insert results in Table A-6.1. These values are derived as follows:

Total outlay = (44.87) (100) = 4487
Actual outlay on fire
protection services   = (44.87) (50.00) = 2243.50
Imputed outlay on fire
protection services   = (44.87) (44.80) = 2010.18
Actual outlay on police
protection services   = (44.87) (50.00) = 2243.50
Imputed outlay on police
protection services   = (44.87) (55.20) = 2476.82.

Note that total outlay must equal sum of the two actual outlay figures and also the sum of the two imputed outlay figures.

86

XI. Compute outlay figures for all remaining budgetary ratio in a similar manner and insert results as appropriate in Table A-6.1.

TABLE A-6.1

NUMERICAL VALUES AT SELECTED BUDGETARY RATIOS, WITH DEMAND EQUATIONS AS DEFINED; FIGURES ROUNDED OFF

Budgetary Ratio Fire to Police in General- Fund Budget	Total Outlay	Actual Outlay Fire Protection	Imputed Out- lay Fire Pro- tection	Actual Outlay Police	Imputed Outlay Police
00-100	2400	0	0	2400	2400
01-99	2429	24	31	2405	2398
10-90	2707	271	325	2436	2382
20-80	3079	616	711	2463	2368
30-70	3516	1055	1145	2461	2371
40-60	4000	1600	1600	2400	2400
50-50	4487	2244	2010	2243	2477
60-40	4795	2877	2299	1918	2496
70-30	4709	3296	2402	1413	2307
80-20	4000	3200	2400	800	1600
90-10	2826	2543	2169	283	657
99-01	1712	1695	1652	17	60
100-00	1600	1600	1600	0	0

7. *The Bridge Between Tax and Expenditure in the Fiscal Decision Process*

INTRODUCTION

To the individual taxes are the "prices," the "costs," of the goods and services that the government supplies for his benefit. This conception of the fiscal structure is central to this study, and our procedure has compared the individual's behavior in fiscal choice with that in market or private choice. In the market, the individual selects a preferred quantity at a given price per unit, or, alternatively, he allocates a specific outlay to the purchase of a specific good, which, at the given price, results in a determinate quantity being taken. The selection of a preferred physical quantity automatically determines total outlay, or, conversely, the selection of an amount to be spent automatically determines the physical quantity. In either case, the purchaser is assumed to make only *one* decision. It is absurd to think of his making two separate decisions, one as to the physical quantity of the good to be purchased and the other as to the total outlay to be made. Given the availability of a good or service at an invariant market price, these two decisions reduce to one and the same.

Institutionally, it is possible for the individual to make market purchases in either of these two ways. I may drive my automobile up to a gasoline pump and order five gallons, or I may, alternatively, order two dollars' worth. In the first instance, my outlay is residually determined by my decision on quantity; in the second, the quantity is determined by outlay. If I am faced with some uncertainty as to price, there need be no unique relationship between quantity and outlay at the moment of my decision. If I order five gallons of gasoline, knowing only that the price falls somewhere between thirty and fifty cents per gallon, total outlay may be anything from $1.50 to $2.50. Or, conversely, if I order $2.00 worth in this situation, I may get anything from four to six and two-thirds gallons.

From our earlier discussion, it is evident that individual fiscal choice resembles the price-uncertainty case here. In that discussion, however, we continue to assume that fiscal choice remained analogous to market choice in that only one decision is taken, with residual determination of either tax rate or total outlay (public goods quantity). Given a specific tax institution, other than that with invariant tax-price, some residual uncertainty must remain in any individual fiscal choice. The group decision may, for example, be stated in terms of a specified expenditure on public education. This will imply, in its turn, a certain rate of tax on local real property, and this rate is assumed to be residually set by the decision on spending. Or, conversely, the specifically chosen mill rate of tax for education implies a certain revenue total available for spending.

Casual observation of actual fiscal processes, at almost any governmental level, suggests that the "bridge" between the tax decision and the spending decision is not nearly so direct as these earlier models have implied. In many instances, the fiscal process appears to embody a double choice; one a choice or decision as to the size of the public spending program and the other a choice or decision on the rates of taxation. Clearly, the institutional setting that allows this apparent splitting of the fiscal decision into two parts can influence the outcome of decision.

THE NECESSARY REAL BRIDGE

In some *real* sense, there can be only one independent fiscal decision. To simplify discussion, let us again limit consideration to a single public good or service. Observed ex post, there is a specific quantity of this good or service provided. In the collective decision to supply this quantity, economic resources were committed and these were drawn from other potential employments. What these resources could have produced in alternative uses is the *real* cost of the public goods or services supplied, and this cost is directly related to the number of units. To the extent that resources are employed in the private sector, any decision to spend publicly directly implies "taxation" that is at least equal in magnitude to the money value of the spending, the measure of the value of alternative product.

The notion that the real cost of public goods or services arises from the decision to commit resources, to spend publicly, is not inconsistent with the earlier point that this decision can be made in two ways. A specific tax of X per cent can be levied with the proceeds dedicated to the provision of the public good or service. Or, Y dollars can be appropriated for spending on the good or service, with a tax sufficient to raise this amount being levied, which may be X per cent. But the logical extension of the real-cost principle suggests that taxation, in and of itself, cannot impose a real cost since there is no implication that the revenues collected are to be spent in providing public services.[1] If distributional considerations are entirely left out of account, this extension is a valid one. Within the framework of this study, the real-value approach tends to be misleading, however, because attention here is focused on the choice behavior of the individual and not on aggregative results. To the individual taxpayer, or potential taxpayer, who ultimately makes fiscal choices, the imposition of any tax implies that he will, personally, undergo some cost. He will be largely unconcerned with the macro-economic real variables of the economist. To the extent that a tax is imposed, and the funds are not spent, the only institutional means of eliminating distributional elements entirely would be that of refunding the tax revenues, in the same manner as these are received. In this case, however, no decision to tax could really be said to have been made.

Despite the necessary real bridge that must be present for the whole community between any decision to spend publicly and to impose taxes, the individual as a participant in political choice may not consider proposals to spend funds and proposals to raise taxes as directly interdependent. The degree to which he senses the underlying real interdependence will depend partially upon the institutions through which fiscal choices are made.

THE SETTING FOR INDIVIDUAL CHOICE

We have noted that the individual who participates in collective choice can never be placed in a position that is fully analogous to that which he faces in market choice. He cannot confront a one-to-one correspondence between his own choice behavior and a result or outcome. At best, in collective choice the individual can know

1. This point has been stressed effectively by Earl Rolph. See *The Theory of Fiscal Economics* (Berkeley: University of California Press, 1954).

only that, if a sufficient number of his fellows agree with him, an outcome will follow from a choice. It will be useful to specify carefully that institutional setting under which the individual's position with respect to the two-sidedness of the fiscal decision most closely resembles his position in the marketplace. If the group is faced with a decision as to the quantity of a single public good to be provided from the proceeds of a single specified tax, the individual participant should not find it impossible to construct for himself a personalized real bridge between the benefits side and the cost side of the account. In this limiting case, the residual nature of one or the other sides will be recognized. This is not, of course, to suggest that the community outcome will tend to be "efficient," even in such limiting cases. This will depend in part on the nature of the collective decision rules and upon the relative generality of taxes and of benefits among members of the community.[2]

Let us now examine the more familiar setting in which proposals are made to spend public funds *without* specifying the tax sources that are to provide these funds, and, conversely, that in which proposals are made to levy taxes *without* specifying the public-goods and services mix that is to be financed with revenues raised. How will the individual behave in this situation? Consider first his reaction to a proposal to spend on a public good that promises to yield him some measurable benefits. If he wholly divorces the spendings decision from the tax decision, he will "vote for" an expansion in outlay to the point at which his own marginal evaluation of the good or service becomes zero. Such a conceptual separation of the two sides of the account will tend to be present insofar as the individual considers both the amount and the distribution of taxes to be settled in a decision process wholly apart from the spending decision. Choice behavior of this sort is not so foreign to real-world experience as it might initially appear. There is much discussion, both in the popular press and in quasi-intellectual circles, concerning "needs" for various public services. Almost universally, these "needs" are measured or estimated independently of costs.

2. If both taxes and benefits are general throughout the community, simple majority decision rules will not distort the outcomes. However, if one side or the other should be differentially general, distortion is introduced. If benefits are specific to particular subgroups in the community, while taxes are general over the whole community, there will be a tendency to expand spending beyond "optimal" levels. The supporting analysis for this conclusion is developed in James M. Buchanan and Gordon Tullock, *The Calculus of Consent* (Ann Arbor: University of Michigan Press, 1962).

This "needs" approach to budgeting is based on precisely the model that is here discussed.[3]

At the same time that the individual "votes for," or otherwise supports, public spending programs without substantive regard for costs, the same individual, in yet another capacity, may refuse to support any new tax legislation. This half of the extreme independence model is less familiar to everyday experience, because most individuals are normally aware, at least to some vague extent, that they must accept taxes in order to secure the benefits of public goods. Nonetheless, if the individual treats the two decisions as wholly independent, one from the other, he will refuse to vote for any tax legislation.

A somewhat more realistic model is one in which some cost consciousness informs the expenditure decision, while some benefit consciousness informs the separate tax decision, but in which the two sides of the account are differently weighted. Empirical research might reveal isolated instances, but surely cases are few and far between where legislative assemblies have intentionally voted separately for a level of taxes that is more than sufficient to finance the level of spending separately chosen, debt amortization included. The direction of bias seems evident. The splitting of the fiscal decision into two parts tends to cause a "deficit" between approved spending rates and approved tax rates. Insofar as the expenditure decision fails to take into account the cost side, public services provided will tend to be extended beyond that level which fully informed consideration of alternatives would produce. Conversely, in so far as the tax decision fails to incorporate the benefit side, total revenues will fall short of the amount needed to finance that level of public services that an informed consideration of alternatives would provide. In other words, the gap between approved spending and approved taxes, in such a democratic decision model, will tend to "straddle" the unique tax-spending solution that an "efficient" fiscal decision might produce.

It is to be emphasized that the probable gap between approved spending and approved taxation that is discussed here emerges from the choices of a single individual in an institutional setting that splits fiscal choice into two parts. To this point, we have left out of account the interaction of separate individual decisions in producing a group

3. For effective criticism, see Charles J. Hitch and Roland N. McKean, *The Economics of Defense in the Nuclear Age* (Cambridge: Harvard University Press, 1960), pp. 46-49.

or community outcome. Our central concern is with the individual calculus, and the gap suggested is between the individual's preferred level of spending, as this might conceptually be expressed in a voting choice, and his preferred level of taxation, as this might be similarly expressed. Does not the existence of such a gap, regardless of the institutions of choice, reflect irrational behavior on the part of the individual? If he chooses "rationally" should he not "cut through" the possible institutional maze, regardless of complications, and recognize the underlying real interdependence between the separate decisions? To answer these questions, it is necessary to recall the provisional definition of "rational behavior" suggested earlier. To the individual chooser, rational behavior need not reflect full information for the simple reason that the securing of information is a costly process. In any specific choice situation, there is some "optimal" investment in information-gathering which seldom, if ever, will result in perfection. The institutions through which choice must be made can evidently affect this level of optimal investment as well as the degree of perfection in results.

It is useful to look at the apparent splitting of the fiscal decision in this context. Suppose that the individual faces a choice as to his preferred level of spending on a single public good or service or on some designated package of services. He is aware, within limits, of the potential benefits that these goods and services will yield to him. He chooses, of course, under conditions of high uncertainty since he cannot know the outcome of the political process, but he probably can make reasonably accurate estimates for his own personalized share in the benefits from incremental changes in the level of public-goods supply. He will sense that these services must be financed, and he may be able to make some translation into tax-cost terms. But this step will clearly require more investment in information than the comparable estimate on the benefit side. The form of the decision process in effect partially solves his information problem on one side but not on the other. The issue is presented to him in public spending terms. He must make his own translation into tax-costs.

Contrast this situation with that where the same individual confronts a choice concerning the level of taxes to be imposed, without connection to spending levels. In this case, the calculus is reversed. The institution of decision itself partially assists the individual in computing tax-costs but wholly obscures public-goods benefits. It is surely plausible to expect that most individuals will behave differently in the two cases, and, as a result, the gap suggested above will tend to emerge. In the one case the individual is reasonably well informed as to benefits, in the other case as to costs.

CLOSING THE GAP

To shift from an analysis of the individual decision calculus to that of the group requires that some consideration be given to the processing of individually expressed desires through a set of political decision rules. The effects discussed here are surely accentuated when it is recognized that each person in his spending decision will hope that the tax-costs will be shifted onto other members of the group, and *vice versa* for taxing decisions. It is useful to leave this whole question of group decision-making until a later chapter, however, even though some reference to political outcomes seems necessary. To do this, we may simply assume that the individual that we are discussing is the "median" or "representative" man in the many-person community.

In the aggregate, the potential gap between approved levels of spending and approved levels of taxation must be closed. Throughout this chapter, we are assuming that there exists an over-all restriction of budget balance. And lest the discussion here appear overly abstract, it is worth noting that conflicts of the sort mentioned here are familiar occurrences in real-world fiscal systems. Newspapers carry stories of financial "crises" faced by states and local governments; school teachers do not get paid; road contracts do not get let. How are these conflicts, actual or potential, resolved, and how can some prediction as to the manner of resolution be made? There seems to be no general direction of effect that is predictable. In the face of a potential excess of spending over tax revenues, will taxes be increased to meet the deficit, or will spending be cut? The outcome will, in each instance, be determined by the stronger set of rules, dictated in part by constitutional provisions. It is the financial conflict that brings to the surface the necessary final interdependence between spending and tax decisions and makes some resolution of the contradiction essential. This will generate a re-evaluation of both choices, and no general pattern of results can be predicted.

We know that political structures, as they operate, do incorporate institutions that tend to produce this apparent splitting of the fiscal decisions into the two parts. These same structures contain, however, other institutions that have been developed to resolve the potential conflict. Historically, legislative bodies, through which the preferences of individual citizens are most directly represented, have exercised more control over revenue or tax decisions than they have over expenditure decisions. In part this asymmetry has its origin in the development of democratic political institutions out of monarchial institutions. Representative bodies, parliaments, first achieved the power to restrict the tax-gathering privileges of the kings. Before taxes could be levied on the people, representative bodies were given the right to grant their approval. No consideration was given to the spending side of the account because public expenses were assumed to benefit primarily the royal court, at least in the early days of constitutional monarchy. Taxes were viewed as necessary charges on the people, but they were not really conceived as any part of an "exchange" process from which the people secured public benefits. It was out of this conception of the fiscal process that both the modern institutions and the modern theory of public finance developed.

The emerging of modern democratic states dramatically modified the setting for the fiscal process, but only recently has attention been paid to the necessity of revising age-old norms. As royal courts came to be replaced by executives, and monarchies by republics, taxes continued to be viewed as necessary to sustain the expenses of "government," with the burden of these taxes to be minimized to the maximum extent possible. Surprisingly little recognition has been given, even yet, to the idea that taxes must, in the final analysis, be considered as the "costs" of those public goods and services which provide benefits to the same people who pay taxes.

With the development of modern executive structures, the traditional asymmetry has remained, but, partly because of these structures, the decision conflict discussed above has been mitigated. The executive normally exercises greater control over the budget, over the expenditure plans, than it does over the revenue side of the account. Being somewhat less responsible to the desires of individual citizens than the legislature, in a compartmentalized, differentiated sense, the executive utilizes the expenditure budget as a means through which revenue projections and spending projections are reconciled. And in part it was the prevalence of just such conflicts as those discussed

95

which provided the impetus for the development of modern budgetary institutions. These generalizations are relevant largely to the American political structure, and they are somewhat less applicable to genuine parliamentary systems.

DO GOVERNMENTS ADJUST INCOME TO MEET SPENDING NEEDS?

It was concluded above that no general direction of adjustment could be predicted when the split-decision conflict arises in democratic political structures. This runs contrary to a time-honored notion in public finance. In some of the earlier works especially, the difference between the government account and the private account was emphasized in a manner that suggested one particular resolution of the conflict. "Whereas the individual or family tends to adjust its expenditures to meet its income, the government adjusts its income to meet its expenditure needs." If this "principle" has any general validity, there is a basic difference in the way in which the individual behaves in family and in public accounting structures. But does the false-analogy notion here have any claim to validity, especially in representative democracy, where, ultimately, all fiscal choices are made by the individual, directly or indirectly, and not by "government," as some entity wholly divorced from the citizens? The individual in "voting for" public outlays is "spending" in a manner that is analogous to his spending for private goods. His decision to cover this spending with tax revenues, to approve the levy of taxes on himself and others, is made in order to finance these "purchases" from the public sector. Ultimately, the income constraint applies here just as it does in private spending. What the individual does is to adjust his total spending, private and public, to his income, which itself is adjustable only within relatively narrow limits in the normal case. The traditional generalization concerning the relevance of the income constraint in restricting private spending and its irrelevance in restricting public spending is not applicable. There is no reason why tax revenues should necessarily be adjusted to meet approved patterns of public spending, as implied, rather than spending levels adjusted to meet approved levels of tax revenues. The direction of adjustment will surely depend on the particulars of each situation of conflict.

CONCLUSION

The primary sources of pressure on democratic legislatures, those for reduced taxation on the one hand and for expanded public spending on the other, arise because of the differentiation among groups in the political community. This distributional aspect of fiscal choice has been deliberately neglected here. The purpose of this chapter is to suggest that, quite apart from the intergroup or distributional conflicts that may arise, the organization of the decision-making institutions themselves may be such that the interdependent fiscal accounts are treated as embodying two apparent choices, the results of which may conflict, even in an individual calculus. It is impossible to predict with accuracy the direction of effect that this institutional influence will impose on fiscal outcomes, or to measure its over-all importance. What can be said is that this apparent splitting of decision, insofar as it is present, tends to create greater uncertainty in fiscal choice than seems necessary. In a balanced-budget context, a decision to spend publicly implies a decision to tax, and a decision to tax implies a decision to spend. Only if the actual institutions of fiscal choice are organized in such a way that this basic truism is reflected in the alternatives confronting the individual participant can these uncertainties be minimized. Much of the modern criticism of the United States Congress is directed at its failure to allow simultaneous consideration of expenditure and tax decisions. Differences of opinion may, of course, arise concerning the most appropriate means of introducing the desired symmetry in the fiscal decision process, in repairing the bridge between taxes and spending. But greater rationality in choosing the mix between public and private goods, on the part of the individual citizen as reflected through the legislative processes, depends critically on some correction of inherited error, both intellectual and institutional.

8. *"Fiscal Policy" and Fiscal Choice: The Effects of Unbalanced Budgets*

INTRODUCTION

In making a decision as to whether he should support or oppose a proposed expansion in public spending, the individual must in some manner construct the bridge between the benefits and the tax-cost. The preceding chapter examined the ways in which the institutions of choice might affect the construction of such bridge under the over-all constraint of budget-balance. This constraint, if it is known to the individual participant, facilitates comparison of benefits and costs. The next step in the analysis allows budgets to be unbalanced, and we seek to trace the effects that this single institutional change can exert on the individual's calculus in making tax decisions on the one hand and spending decisions on the other. The initial and elementary conclusion is that any comparison of costs and benefits becomes more difficult here than under a regime of over-all balance between revenues and outlay.

Unbalanced budgets are almost always possible in real-world fiscal systems. Any strict balanced-budget restriction must, at best, be considered as being imposed only an overly simplified model, preliminary to the more general model that allows for unbalance. The earlier discussion is helpful, however, in that it facilitates concentration on the effects of unbalance, as such, on individual behavior.

The apparent splitting of the fiscal process into two parts was shown to produce potential gaps between preferred spending on public goods and services and preferred levels of taxation. Until and unless these gaps are eliminated, budget deficits tend to emerge from democratic decision processes. In our previous model, the deficits remained potential because of the imposed restriction of balance. Once we drop this restriction, emergent deficits can become actual deficits. To the extent that political decision-making institutions split the fiscal choice into apparently separated tax and expenditure choices, the potential deficit predicted as a part of an individual's choice calculus will tend to be transformed through the interaction of all individuals into an aggregate result.

If deficits are allowed to arise, they must be financed. And the manner in which they are financed may itself exert important influences on the individual's ability to make a reasoned comparison of public benefits and public costs. Broadly speaking, there are only two means of financing budget deficits. One is by borrowing; that is, by issuing interest-bearing debt obligations in exchange for current command over purchasing power. The second is by printing money; that is, by issuing or creating noninterest bearing money or currency which becomes acceptable directly as purchasing power. The effects of unbalanced budgets on fiscal choice behavior must be examined under each of these two methods of financing. The second of these methods, currency creation, can only be exercised by governmental units that possess effective money-creating powers; normally, national or central governments. But national governments also assume some responsibility for the level and the movement of the aggregative economic magnitudes in the economy: income, employment, price levels. This fact further complicates the analysis here since it is evident that the *real* bridge between tax and spending decisions depends critically on the state of the aggregate economy. It will be necessary to examine how changes in the aggregate, macroeconomic changes, affect the individual's own bridge between the two sides of the fiscal account, and through this, his own behavior in making fiscal choices.

REAL DEBT AND BUDGET UNBALANCE

Even for the single individual or family, the private budget need not be balanced in each and every accounting period. "Going into debt" or borrowing either from internal or external sources almost always provides a means of resolving conflicts between income and outlay. Nevertheless, for the single family debt issue provides at best a temporary reconciliation, a breathing space, until more permanent measures for correction may be taken. The effects of the existence of borrowing, as a temporary means of covering deficits in private budgets, are probably important in some cases, but these do not warrant further consideration here.

For governmental units, the borrowing alternative to taxation as a means of financing public expenditures is almost always available, within limits. Our question is: How will the knowledge that debt can be issued to cover deficits affect the choice behavior of the individual citizen? Let us again reduce this problem to the simplest possible model. Suppose that spending is to provide only one public good or service, and that only one tax is to be utilized. The individual confronts an apparent dual decision, one on the amount of public outlay, the other on the rate of tax. However, once we allow for the possibility of debt issue, there need be no *real* bridge between an expenditure and a tax decision, even for the whole community, in the sense that resources devoted to public spending need not be withdrawn in comparable magnitude from private spending, as *payment* for the public goods and services provided.[1] If government borrowing provides the means of covering residual differences between preferred levels of spending and preferred levels of taxation, these two primary choices become *independent,* in any current-period sense, not only to the individual as he participates in collective choice, but also in real terms for the whole community. Under such conditions, a collective decision to spend does not imply a collective decision to tax currently, and a collective decision to tax does not imply a collective decision to spend currently in the same amount.

The presence of the debt alternative tends, therefore, to widen possible divergencies that may arise between the weighing of costs and of benefits in the two sides of the fiscal decision. When faced with a proposal for expanding public expenditures, the individual will tend to include a lower value for the opportunity cost of choosing favorably than he would in the balanced-budget model, other things equal. For several reasons, he will not treat the discounted value of future taxes that debt issue embodies as equivalent to non-discounted current taxes. In other words, the individual can be

1. Resources devoted to public spending must, of course, come from somewhere in the aggregate economy. If debt is issued, however, those persons who give up command of purchasing power do so in an ordinary voluntary exchange process and in no way can be said to "pay for" the benefits of the public services provided. On all this see my book, *Public Principles of Public Debt* (Homewood: Richard D. Irwin, 1958), and, for more recent discussion, see James M. Ferguson (ed.), *Public Debt and Future Generations* (Chapel Hill: The University of North Carolina Press, 1964).

predicted to "vote for" somewhat larger extensions in public outlay here than he would support in the "no-debt" model. On the other side of the budgetary process, when he is faced with a tax choice, he will not associate directly collective revenue shortfalls with curtailments in public services because of the availability of borrowing. He will be somewhat more reluctant to approve tax increases than he would be in the no-debt model. These predictions derived from models of individual behavior will tend to be transformed into collective-community outcomes.

It should be emphasized that these conclusions as to the effects of public borrowing on fiscal choice are wholly independent of the normative question as to whether or not borrowing "should" be an alternative to tax financing. The conclusions reached are both restricted and intuitively obvious; borrowing makes individuals more reluctant to levy current taxes upon themselves and others, and less reluctant to expand public spending programs.

Some vague recognition of this proclivity probably explains the origin and widespread use of constitutional debt limits that are imposed on governmental units, at all levels. In the absence of such limits, say, on a local government, the workings of democratic choice process might well produce debt issue beyond limits of "capacity," although increasing costs of credit might impose barriers to over-extension. With the imposition of limits, however, further possibilities for decision conflict arise. If a local community should approve spending of X dollars, taxation that would bring in revenues of Y dollars, but is allowed to borrow only Z dollars, when Z is less than the difference between X and Y, there emerges a conflict that must be resolved. And major inefficiencies can arise when constitutional debt limits, designed to minimize excessive debt issue, serve to inhibit what is essentially "productive" borrowing.

In one sense, local government borrowing is analogous to family or private borrowing in that it can provide only for temporary and extraordinary deficits. Without recourse to money creation, local governments must look to their own credit worthiness. There remains a fundamental difference between local government borrowing and family borrowing that should not be overlooked. In the latter, there is normally a single, responsible decision-making unit. In a democratically-organized political group, by contrast, the individual participant is aware that he is not, individually or personally, responsible for group or collective decisions. He participates in these decisions, he expresses his own preferences, and he recognizes, more or less accurately, that collective choices influence his own well-being. He will not, however, feel the same sense of what might be called "unit responsibility" that he will feel in the private family decision process. In other words, precisely because he is "individual," he will not wholly identify his own interest and responsibility with that of the political group of which he is a part. His membership in the political community allows him, so to speak, to act under a system of limited fiscal responsibility. If the democratic processes of his local government should expand debt issue to the point of default, the individual is under no personal obligation to make good on the community debt. He is in a position, for purposes of decision, much like that of a shareholder in a limited liability enterprise, but without the latter's interest in "efficiency."

NATIONAL DEBT

Any sense of fiscal identification that the individual might possibly feel as a member of a local government unit becomes less pronounced as the number of citizens in the group increases. At the national government level, there is essentially no feeling of private fiscal responsibility on the part of the individual citizen. This makes the suggested influence of public borrowing on fiscal choice more significant at the national government level, even if we remain within the individual calculus and ignore the much enhanced prospect that both tax and spending decisions at this level will involve important considerations of intergroup conflict. To demonstrate this point, examine the individual citizen's role in the 1963-64 discussion of tax reduction in the United States. What did he write his congressman, or what would he have said if he had written, and what were the underlying elements in his choice? Tax reduction was, as is usual, discussed independently of public spending. The individual was confronted with reasonably adequate measures of the additional private funds that he might secure under the proposed reduction schemes. What were the costs, to him, of favorable action on tax reduction? Clearly, he knew that these costs would not take the form of any reduction in current levels of public service provision. There were, in effect, no apparent costs that he could offset against the benefits of tax reduction promised him. He recognized that national debt (and/or currency) would be issued to finance any deficit that might have been increased as a result of the political decision process in which he participated.

Similar behavior can be predicted on the spending side of the account. If the individual citizen were asked, in mid-1963, his opinions on proposed expansions in the federal space program, he could, roughly and in some fashion, measure benefits in terms of sport, national prestige, adventure, technological fallout, etc. But what were the costs? He would not have translated the costs of the space program into increased taxes. And for a very simple reason: the individual knew that he would not have to pay such taxes. The predictable result of a democratic choice process is the generation of budget deficits when borrowing is available as an alternative to taxation unless deficit-creation is not somehow restrained by constitutional limitations.

This result is, of course, reinforced when the emergence of budget deficits is rationalized and justified on "fiscal policy" grounds. The Keynesian and neo-Keynesian arguments in support of deficits tend to accentuate and to legitimatize the proclivity toward deficit creation that democratic governments inherently possess for the reasons developed. If this tendency is so pervasive, however, the question may be asked as to why deficit-creation had not got out of hand even before the appearance of the Keynesian apologetics? The answer lies, not in the presence of genuine fiscal responsibility on the part of the individual, as citizen, or through him, on the part of his legislative representative, in the making of everyday decisions on taxes and spending. The answer lies, instead, in the fact that "constitutional" restrictions on debt issue (and/or currency creation) have been present, even at the national government level. Although it is not written down as such, the "balanced-budget rule" has been an integral part of the broader unwritten fiscal constitution of the United States. It seems probable that it is only the strength of this restriction, in part based on traditional ethical considerations, that has kept deficits within bounds of reasonable propriety in past periods. So long as the individual citizen accepts the "mythology" of budget-balance, this unwritten constitutional rule will continue to exert a limiting force on deficit creation. The effect of the Keynesian and post-Keynesian arguments is to undermine the "constitutional" status of this rule.

Once again it is necessary to state that the analysis here is not concerned with whether or not such results are or are not desirable.

Nor does the conclusion about the bias toward deficit creation carry with it any particular implication about levels of public spending and of taxation. To say that, as it operates, democratic procedure tends to generate budgetary deficits is *not* the same as saying that public spending programs are "too large." This latter implication would hold only if there should exist agreement that public debt "should" not be issued. Clearly, there is no basis for such normative agreement. Hence, all that is implied is that public spending probably tends to be larger than and taxation less than they would be in the absence of the debt (and/or currency creation) alternative.

This is a very simple conclusion that amounts to saying nothing more than that national debt, as an institutional alternative to taxation, tends to produce budget deficits. This might appear as tautological in that, in the absence of debt, deficits would not be possible, ignoring for the moment the resort to money creation. But the conclusion has more content than this version of it suggests. The introduction of the debt alternative to taxation makes the bridge between cost and benefit more difficult for the individual to construct. This is a positive conclusion and should allow derivative hypotheses to be empirically tested. The analysis does not suggest that resort to the borrowing alternative is not desirable in many situations, for reasons that can readily be developed. Nor does the analysis imply that the Keynesian destruction, or attempted destruction, of the effective "constitutional" rule of budget-balance may not have been independently desirable.

CURRENCY CREATION

The issue of public debt should never be confused with the issue of currency. Nothing has plagued modern economic policy analysis more than the persistent refusal of economists to make this distinction clearly. Public debt embodies an obligation to make interest payments in periods of time subsequent to issue. Currency involves no such obligation and, for this reason, its issue becomes a distinctly different fiscal operation. For governments that possess the authority to create money, there are two, not one, means of financing deficits that may be produced by emergent gaps between preferred spending rates and preferred tax rates. The question that is now relevant is how currency creation differs from borrowing in its influence on the fiscal choice behavior of the individual.

To answer this question it is necessary to make some assumptions about the state of the economy at the time of the operation. If resources are fully employed, or employed to the extent that increased aggregate demand will produce price-level increases without output increases, the issue of new currency is equivalent to the levy of an indirect tax on the users and the holders of cash. In this limiting case, therefore, despite the initial gap between approved public spending and approved levels of taxation, no real "deficit" in any genuine sense appears when the new-currency "tax" is employed as the residual financing device, the balancer. Insofar as the individual recognizes this and, in his choice calculus, cuts through the apparent illusion that currency issues creates, he may be more reluctant to approve new spending projects than he would be in situations where genuine public debt is the balancing device. Insofar as he is able to make the proper bridge between benefits and costs, these costs are measurable under currency creation in this model in terms of current income units. In the debt-creation case, by contrast, the comparable measure of costs must be computed in terms of present values of future income units. Insofar as future taxes are not wholly capitalized, there will be some tendency for residual borrowing to generate larger budget deficits than residual currency creation, other things equal. This conclusion depends on the assumption that the individual is able to dispel the illusion that money creation necessarily introduces. This is, of course, an important proviso, and the effects of this illusion may overwhelm those emphasized here.

CURRENCY CREATION AND UNEMPLOYMENT

The analysis must be modified when we shift out of the full-employment model. Consider now the opposite extreme; assume that there exist unemployed resources to the extent that aggregate employment and output can be expended without generating price inflation. In this situation, the financing of budget deficits by currency creation does not impose a current indirect tax on the holders and users of cash. The recognition of the possible real-world existence of this limiting case was the essential novelty of the Keynesian "revolution" in thinking about economic policy. In such a situation of deep depression, which did seem to characterize the 1930's, a decision to expand public spending does not imply an offsetting real cost to the individual, as a voter-taxpayer-beneficiary, either currently or in future periods. Professor Abba Lerner was basically correct in his early insistence that, in such situations, there is no underlying real cost of public spending, provided that it is financed by pure currency creation.[2] The *real* bridge does not exist here, in either community or individual terms, and there is no logical economic basis for the imposition of taxes. The financing of budget deficits by currency creation becomes the logical translation of economic reality into meaningful decisions as these are confronted by individuals in the group, through their legislative assemblies. In fact, the "ideal" structure in such situations is one in which only spending decisions are proposed. Failing this, the complete divorce of spending decisions from taxing decisions is desirable, and ideally rational behavior would involve the approval of expenditure expansion and tax reduction simultaneously until the growth in aggregate economic activity requires the acknowledgment of the real bridge between the two sides of the fiscal account. It was precisely to facilitate such a genuine splitting of the fiscal decision that the Keynesian and the neo-Keynesian attack on the budget-balance rule was launched. The difficulty is, of course, that "constitutional" rules may be helpful in constraining choice behavior in certain situations but may become undesirable in other situations, and vice versa. If the ultimate effects of the Keynesian attack are to undermine the budget-balance rule, fiscal choice during periods of deep depression will, without doubt, be "improved" since the institution of balance in such periods serves to distort individual choice. However, this may well be accomplished at the expense of "worsening" the results of fiscal choice during periods of high income and employment, when the rule of budget-balance does assist the ultimate choosers in making the proper bridge between the two sides of the account.

In the normal order of events, the economy will be neither in "full employment," in the sense described above, nor in "unemployment," in the contrary sense. At almost any time, an increase in aggregate demand will *both* generate some additional employment

2. For an early statement, see A. P. Lerner, *The Economics of Control* (New York: Macmillan & Co., 1944).

It is not sensible to finance deficits in such situations by the issue of interest-bearing debt. This does impose a real cost, in terms of discounted values of future taxes, a cost that is wholly unnecessary given the existence of unemployed resources to the extent assumed. The fact that the interest costs in such periods may be low does not alter the basic argument. Debt issue here can be defended only by some argument about the efficacy of rules against currency creation.

and output and some inflation in prices. The mix between the employment-output effects and the inflationary effects will, of course, vary over the phases of the so-called business cycle, but both effects will normally be present to some degree. Let us then examine the fiscal choice behavior of the individual as he might confront federal tax proposals and federal appropriations measures. Suppose that he assumes that deficits emerging from revenue-expenditure combinations will be financed solely by currency creation. How will he construct the necessary bridge between benefits and costs? He will, probably, tend to approve spending projects that require more revenue than he approves in taxes, over all phases of the cycle combined. The general bias toward deficit creation remains. But the real cost of government spending projects will vary over the different stages of economic activity, and, ideally, choice behavior should embody some recognition of this variance. It is clear, however, that this variance adds yet another element of uncertainty to the individual's decision calculus. When he writes to his Congressman approving, say, a proposed expanded program for anti-missile missiles, how much will he expect this expansion to cost him, individually and privately? Given the tax structure as it exists, and assuming that revenues were just equal to total expenditures prior to the fiscal decision under consideration, the individual knows roughly what his total tax liability is. But he now proposes to expand the rate of public spending without, at the same time, changing tax rates. How will he estimate his costs? If the program is approved, and the deficit created, price inflation and/or greater national output will result. The real costs suffered by the individual will vary greatly depending on the precise breakdown between the price and output effects of the deficit-money creation operation. If the deficit expands total output, the additional missile defense is secured at little or no cost. If, on the other hand, price inflation results, the additional defense is provided only at a real cost imposed on the individual through his holding and his usage of cash. To make any reasonably accurate translation of a spending proposal into tax-costs, the individual must predict the movement of the aggregative variables in the whole national economy. This movement, in turn, depends on the behavior of all of the economic units in the system, as well as the external variables. It is difficult to think of a situation where the interdependence involved in an individual choice calculus could be greater.

DEBT CREATION, CURRENCY CREATION, AND UNCERTAINTY

The analysis suggests that under either of the two extreme or limiting models, that of full employment or that of unemployment, currency creation as the residual financing institution should be more conducive to rational individual behavior in fiscal choice than debt issue. If employment is effectively full, currency issue becomes equivalent to a current-period tax, one that is somewhat more likely to be correctly weighted than the future-period taxes embodied in debt issue. In such situations, the deficits produced in democratic-decision processes are likely to be somewhat smaller under currency creation than under debt. On the other hand, in the Keynesian unemployment model, currency creation embodies no real cost and clearly this should produce larger deficits than debt issue, which does embody some real cost, even if not fully sensed by individual participants. The conclusion must be that in either of these two models, debt issue is a second-best residual financing device or institution.

Currency creation remains relatively more efficient as the residual financing institution for those models which allow some combination of employment-output and price effects so long as the mix between these is known with certainty. The individual will always be able, in such circumstances, to make a better comparison between benefits and costs if he knows that potential deficits are to be financed by currency creation rather than by the issue of interest-bearing debt. This conclusion must be modified, however, if uncertainty as to the mix between employment-output and price effects is present. Here second-best or relatively inefficient institutions may be supported on logical grounds, and resort to debt issue as the residual financing device may be justified. Consider a setting roughly equivalent to that faced in the United States in the early 1960's where unemployment was quite high but where controversy raged as to whether this was attributable to deficient aggregate demand or to structural factors. We may compare the two institutions for residual financing in this setting. The individual who placed most weight on the deficiency in aggregate demand would tend to assess the real costs of spending programs somewhat higher under the public debt alternative than he would under the currency creation alternative. On the other hand, the individual who placed the higher weight on structural elements in unemployment would tend to assess the real costs of spending somewhat lower under the public debt alternative than under the currency alternative. The effect of the public debt alternative is that of bringing the two assessments more closely into agreement, but providing some built-in offset to error in each. Under certain configurations of possible error, more rational choice behavior might well be produced by reliance on the debt alternative.

A REGIME OF "FUNCTIONAL FINANCE"

After the early enthusiasm for Keynesian ideas, during which policy proposals were often advanced with little regard for the structure of political decision-making institutions, a more realistic discussion of budget unbalancing, of "fiscal policy," has taken place and is continuing. How can the budget of the national government be utilized as a tool in an over-all policy for maintaining desired values for the macro-economic variables within an effectively democratic process? It came to be widely acknowledged that "functional finance," the deliberate manipulation of the budget for macro-economic policy purposes, could hardly be expected to work well when both revenues and expenditures remain within the control of representative legislative assemblies. The inherent bias toward deficit creation that we have discussed came to be recognized, along with other structural defects with fiscal policy weapons. The hope that functional finance might lead to symmetry over the whole cycle vanished. The widespread acceptance of these facts led advocates of fiscal policy to advocate modifications in the basic institutional structure. Proposals were made to shift the authority over decisions concerning both tax rates and spending rates to the executive and to remove these from direct legislative control. The executive, who is presumably under less direct fiscal pressure from the electorate, the individual citizens with whom this study is primarily concerned, was presumed able to operate more "efficiently." Tax rates and spending rates could, presumably, be moved up and down more freely so as to promote macro-economic objectives, and the inherent conflicts of democratic decision processes largely eliminated. The Commission on Money and Credit in 1961 proposed that a step be taken in this direction by granting to the President discretionary power to move first-bracket rates of the personal income tax up and down to facilitate fiscal policy action.

Let us assume that such discretionary power, additional to that now possessed, is transferred to the executive by the legislative body in some quasi-constitutional delegation. The executive would then be empowered to expand or to cut back spending projects and to reduce or to increase tax rates. The effects of such a change on individual fiscal choice, which is our center of attention, are clear if we assume that this choice is exercised primarily through the representative legislative assembly. The shifting of additional power to the executive removes effective control over ultimate fiscal decisions another step away from the individual citizen and creates for him still further uncertainty concerning the relationship between the benefits that he secures from governmental programs and the costs that he must suffer through the payment of taxes. It is obviously impossible to delegate to the executive additional "functional finance" powers without, at the same time, granting to it additional powers over the basic fiscal decision itself, that is to say, over the ultimate mix between private goods and public goods, and over the composition of the latter.

This power is already possessed by the executive to a significant degree in the current American institutional structure. It is possible for spending rates to be speeded up or slowed down, especially in the defense sector of the budget, and certain discretionary powers are also present on the tax side, notably in connection with rules for depreciation. In addition, the executive has the formal responsibility for preparing the expenditure budget, as a plan for the whole governmental fiscal operation. It would, however, be possible to shift power further to the executive, as the various proposals suggest. This change would lessen the individual's control over decisions, and to the extent that the executive remains insensitive, or less sensitive, to pressures from the electorate, the biases analyzed in this chapter and the preceding one might be reduced. In such an executive-power system of decision-making, the whole analysis developed in this study is changed in character. In such a system, where the decisions made by individual citizens are largely confined to "choosing the choosers," perhaps the traditional models of public finance theory, those which implicitly assume the presence of decision-makers divorced from the citizenry, would become more suitable.

A REGIME OF RULES

The recognition of the usefulness of the balanced-budget constraint on democratic decision-processes as well as the need to allow for budget unbalance as a weapon in macro-economic policy led to various proposals for alternative budgetary-fiscal policy rules. One of the most important of these was that for "budget balance at full employment," which was proposed in the 1940's, and widely accepted during the 1950's as the norm for policy. This rule was replaced, to an extent, by that of "budget balance at potential GNP" in the 1960's. These are defensible rules for policy, but they are rules for the sophisticated, for the expert, and they cannot be expected to inform the consciousness of the individual potential taxpayer-beneficiary, or even that of his legislative representative. Such rules as these cannot be expected to mitigate significantly the biases in democratic processes that the abandonment of the strict budget-balance rule produces.

Alternative proposals have been made for the introduction of more definite rules concerning the increase in the supply of money over time. Such a proposal could, if desired, require that new currency be issued only through the budget. In this way, budget deficits would be a permanent feature of the growing national economy, but such deficits would be held strictly within check by the monetary-growth rule. While this proposal for a monetary-growth rule, associated with Professor Milton Friedman, would be less adaptable to the day-to-day adjustments required for macro-economic objectives, somewhat more informed consideration of the benefits and costs of public programs might be possible for the individual citizen than would be the case under the more sophisticated alternatives.

CONCLUSIONS

The effects of budget unbalance on the individual's ability to make the appropriate comparisons between public-service benefits and tax-costs in a regime of effectively full employment seem clearly undesirable. The knowledge that residual gaps between preferred levels of spending and preferred levels of taxation will be financed either through public debt issue or through currency creation will surely make the individual less willing, and less interested, to construct the bridge between the two sides of the fiscal account that any fully-informed fiscal decision would require.

The strict requirement of budget balance will, however, during periods of unemployment also distort the individual choice calculus. Under the balance constraint, the individual will necessarily overestimate the real costs that public-expenditure programs involve in such circumstances. In the essentially-mixed post-Keynesian world, where elements of both the full-employment and the unemployment model are likely to be present, the relaxation of the budget-balance rule along with the absence of an agreed-on alternative makes any reasoned comparison of benefits and costs almost impossible. To the extent that governmental budgets are used to achieve what are essentially macro-economic objectives without the constraints of predictable rules, the scope for individual control over the size and composition of budgets, through ordinary democratic procedures, must be progressively reduced. How is it possible for the individual to answer the question: How much "public goods" should I "purchase"?, if, because of uncertainty concerning the relationship between the two sides of the budget account, the real "price" to the individual, of these public goods, is continuously and unpredictably changing?

9. *Individual Choice and the Indivisibility of Public Goods*

INTRODUCTION

The analytical models introduced in this book have embodied the central assumption that individual choice behavior in the fiscal process is in some sense analogous to market choice, at least to the extent that the latter may serve as an appropriate benchmark for comparative purposes. This assumption requires some defense, even at the expense of what may appear as a lengthy digression on the "pure theory of public goods." Specifically, it seems necessary to demonstrate that individual choice behavior is amenable to scientific analysis and explanation despite the acknowledged *indivisibility* of benefits from public goods and services among individuals, and, in consequence, the indivisibility of collective decisions regarding the supply and financing of such goods and services.

Does the very existence of indivisibility cause the individual to conceal his "true preferences," to behave so as to thwart the attainment of mutually beneficial results in a community or group decision process? These questions assume especial relevance due to the importance of the "free rider" argument in the modern theory of public goods. If it could be shown that, by the mere fact of common benefit sharing over large numbers of persons, the single participant in fiscal choice does not behave in a manner analogous to market choice, the methodological framework upon which this whole study rests would be quite seriously undermined. Needless to say, I shall try to show that the problems raised by the "free rider" argument do not appear in the institutional context within which individual fiscal choice is analyzed in this study. This is not to say that the argument is erroneous; it remains fundamentally valid, but it becomes relevant only in a setting for choice different from that accepted here. However, I shall note that the mere fact of collective choice exerts an influence on individual behavior not unlike that predicted to arise from free rider elements.

THE "FREE RIDER" ARGUMENT SUMMARIZED

Individuals are not likely to take actions that involve costs if they do not expect demonstrable benefits to result, these benefits being measured in terms of their own utility functions. If a person expects another person, or persons, to provide him with benefits in any case, he will not voluntarily initiate action on his own. Especially if the number of persons with whom he interacts is large, the individual is likely to consider that his own behavior in no way influences the behavior of others. In this situation, he simply reacts or adjusts to the behavior of "others" in a manner similar to his reaction to natural environment. Utility-maximizing behavior does not dictate that voluntary action toward common ends be independently or privately taken. The recognition of this fact is the basis for the "free rider" argument, one that has been discussed in connection with many of the theoretical and practical problems of group organization. As suggested, the argument has been central in the modern theory of public goods, arising out of the contributions of Samuelson and Musgrave.[1]

As this normative theory demonstrates, it is not difficult to state formally the necessary marginal conditions for Pareto optimality in a world that includes purely public or collective goods along with private goods. Difficulties arise, however, when attempts are made to translate these formal conditions into attainable results through

1. See Paul A. Samuelson, "The Pure Theory of Public Expenditures," *Review of Economics and Statistics,* XXVI (November, 1954), 387-89; "Diagrammatic Exposition of a Pure Theory of Public Expenditures," XXXVII (November, 1955), 350-55. R. A. Musgrave, *The Theory of Public Finance* (New York: McGraw-Hill, 1959), especially Chapters 4 and 6.

For works that are specifically concentrated on the "free rider" problem, see Otto A. Davis and Andrew Whinston, "Some Foundations of Public Expenditure Theory" (Mimeographed manuscript, Carnegie Institute of Technology, November, 1961), and Mancur Olson, Jr., *The Logic of Collective Action* (Cambridge: Harvard University Press, 1965).

An early and important recognition of the problem is found in Knut Wicksell, *Finanztheoretische Untersuchungen* (Jena: Gustav Fischer, 1896).

For an application to ethics, see my "Ethical Rules, Expected Values, and Large Numbers," *Ethics,* LXXVI (October, 1965), 1-13.

plausibly-workable institutions of individual choice. At this level, the private-goods world and the world of public goods are wholly different. In the former, market or exchange organization tends to produce results that meet the necessary marginal conditions, at least in some approximation and subject to explicitly definable side constraints. Individuals make their own choices, as consumers, as entrepreneurs, as sellers of productive services; these interact, one with another, in such a way that some point on the Paretian welfare surface is reached, at least conceptually. Once public goods are introduced, however, market organization "fails" in the sense that it no longer effectively channels individual or private choices in the direction of group or social optimality, as defined by the Pareto conditions. No longer are individuals, acting individually, led "as if" by an invisible hand.

The relevant question concerns whether or not the institutions within which individuals make decisions on public-goods can be so organized as to eliminate the behavior that the free-rider argument emphasizes. To accomplish this, institutions must present alternatives to the individual which embody definitive commitments on the part of others as well as himself, which make outcomes measurable in terms of his own utility dependent in some degree upon his own choice, and, finally, which reduce to some reasonable limits his own influence over the net "terms of trade." Note that these are precisely the characteristics of the institutions of market choice. The problem becomes that of arranging or organizing the institutions of the "public goods market" so as to insure that the individual behaves similarly in the two cases, or at least to the degree that the inherent differences in the nature of the choices allow.

THE WICKSELLIAN PROPOSALS

Among fiscal theorists, Knut Wicksell holds the unique position of having carried his theoretical ideas through to an examination of the political structure within which fiscal decisions must be made and implemented.[2] He proposed specific institutional reforms that would remove this element of individual behavior from its influence on fiscal outcomes. Wicksell proposed, first of all, that the bridge

2. Knut Wicksell, *Finanztheoretische Untersuchungen.* The important portions of this work are translated as "A New Principle of Just Taxation," in *Classics in the Theory of Public Finance,* ed. R. A. Musgrave and A. T. Peacock (London: Macmillan, 1958), pp. 72-118.

between tax and expenditure sides of the fiscal account be made explicit. When a specific expenditure project was presented, a whole array of possible distributions of the required tax bill were also to be presented, with each array estimated to produce revenues sufficient to cover the outlay. The expenditure project was then to be voted on in the legislature, along with each one of the tax allocations, and when one such combination secured the unanimous approval of the assembly, it was to be adopted. If no single combination received unanimous support, the expenditure project was not to be undertaken and no tax was to be levied.

Critics have been quick to look at the extreme restriction that any rule of unanimity imposes on group choice, and, generally, they have failed to see that Wicksell's scheme provides a method of circumventing the free rider problem. Under the Wicksellian set of choice institutions, the individual (or his legislative representative) is presented with a series of alternative proposals, each one of which embodies not only a definite statement of the contribution to common cost that he must, individually, bear, but, also, the allocation of the remaining total tax liability among all other members of the political group. By voting for and against such proposals, the individual is put into a position of "trading" with his fellows. Bargaining in the standard sense is not absent from this essentially bilateral trade, and the individual will be motivated to try to get the best terms possible. However, if a genuinely beneficial inframarginal project is presented for a vote, there will be some net gains to be distributed, some pure "taxpayers' surplus." Because of the bargaining opportunities, an individual or group may be motivated to vote against some proposals that will, given his own tax share, actually yield to him net benefits. He may do so if he thinks that other proposals, more favorable to him, will be presented without too much delay in subsequent rounds of voting. However, this tendency to reject alternatives which, in the absence of bargaining possibilities, would prove advantageous, is not the same as "free rider" behavior. Under the Wicksellian rules, the individual knows that, unless he approves, the proposal cannot be adopted, and he must put up with the consequences of delay, along with all others. In the free rider situation, by contrast, the individual's whole behavior is motivated by the idea that he can secure the benefits of a proposed spending project without agreeing to pay taxes.

The Wicksellian institutions of choice will not produce a unique "solution," except in the case of purely marginal adjustments. If there are bargains to be made, the final location on the multidimensional contract locus will depend strictly on the outcome of the bargaining process. Another, and related, feature of the Wicksellian rules is that, in inframarginal cases, the final location will depend on the order that proposals are presented to the assembly for votes. Since there are many tax arrangements capable of securing unanimous approval, the first one presented will be more likely to be the one selected. The order of presentation itself becomes a bargaining weapon. These features, along with the more important one involving the undue costs of delay in reaching unanimity, make Wicksell's institutional suggestions impractical, as he recognized. The point to be noted is, however, that these institutions would eliminate the "free rider" influence, as such, and that this feature of what we may call the Wicksellian "constitution" may be carried over into more practicable arrangements.

Wicksell recognized that unanimity would be difficult, if not impossible, to achieve, and he did modify this requirement to one of "relative unanimity" when he came to discuss implementation of his schemes. He did not, however, abandon his basic notion, which is surely correct, that unanimity provides the only criterion to insure that expenditure proposals are really worth making, "worth" being measured in terms of individual evaluations.

CONSTITUTIONAL RULE-MAKING

The ultimate validity of the unanimity criterion can be accepted without the implication that either full or relative unanimity should be the rule for the making of day-to-day fiscal choices. At the level of "constitutional" decision, where the alternatives are the various possible rules for making ordinary decisions for the group, it may be recognized and predicted that the costs of reaching each separate decision through a unanimity rule may be intolerably high and that some acceptance of "inefficient" results in particular instances seems warranted. The costs of reaching agreement, of higgling and bargaining, of delay, of holding out for better terms, all of these involve resource commitments and produce waste just as effectively as the making of "wrong" decisions under less perfect rules. The constitutional decision process, therefore, must weigh the advantages and disadvantages, the benefits along with the costs, of all possible rules for the making of collective fiscal choices. And,

117

conceptually, the constitutional decision process should produce some consensus on an "optimal" set of rules. Such rules may be many and varied, with particular rules applied to particular situations. Since this whole approach has been discussed in some detail in other works, it need not be elaborated here.[3]

What is of relevance to the question posed for this chapter is that, once a constitutional decision on the rule for making fiscal choices has been adopted by the community and remains in force, individual behavior of the "free rider" sort is no longer likely to occur. The adoption of *any* rule for making collective choices accomplishes in this respect precisely what Wicksell's unanimity rule does, and even more effectively. For purposes of both simplicity and realism in demonstrating this, let us suppose that the constitution dictates that fiscal choices are to be made by simple majority voting.

The individual is now asked to participate in a collective fiscal decision. Suppose that a spending proposal is under consideration, and he estimates that this will yield to him benefits that he values at $10.00. The proposal is accompanied by a tax levy which he estimates will embody a personal liability of $8.00. Will the individual be led, by "free rider" elements, to vote against this fiscal combination, even though it yields to him net benefits, or will he vote straightforwardly on the basis of net benefits? In the first place, the individual will recognize that his own vote will not necessarily be determining, and this alone may affect his behavior. We return to this consideration later, but assume that the individual will vote, one way or the other. He may recognize the possibility that other proposals alternative to the one actually confronted may arise and that some of these may involve a more favorable distribution of the tax load. Because of this, elements of bargaining strategy remain in his behavior. Suppose, for example, that the tax proposed is a proportional income tax, and that the individual has a higher than median income. He may sense that, should the particular proposal be defeated, some alternative scheme might emerge, say, a poll tax, which would produce for him $4.00 in "taxpayer's surplus" instead of the $2.00 now promised. On the basis of such considerations, he may vote against the proposal. Nevertheless, there is much less likelihood that he will do so here than in the Wicksellian unani-

3. See James M. Buchanan and Gordon Tullock, *The Calculus of Consent* (Ann Arbor: University of Michigan Press, 1962).

mity case. In the situation described here, the individual stands to gain $2.00 if a favorable vote results. Alternative tax schemes may yield him more than this, as suggested, but still other alternatives may yield him *less,* and these may eliminate or even make negative his own share in "taxpayers' surplus." For example, if he helps to defeat the proposed expenditure-tax combination, the effective alternative may be, not the poll tax, but a progressive income tax, under which he may be subjected to a net loss. It is precisely this threat of less favorable terms of trade, imposed by some majority coalition of which he is *not* a member, that will cause the individual to bargain much less strongly here than under unanimity rule. By and large, under the operation of less-than-unanimity rules for choice the individual will tend to vote in accordance with his own best estimates of benefits and costs.

A CONSTITUTIONAL APPROACH TO TAX INSTITUTIONS

This conclusion is strongly reinforced when it is recognized that the organization of separate tax-expenditure proposals is costly, and that once a proposal is defeated it is not likely to be presented again under any alternative scheme for financing. Real-world political structures as they operate allow considerably less room for strategic bargaining than even this simple majority-rule model suggests. As noted earlier, spending proposals are not normally considered simultaneously with tax proposals. A "tax structure" or "tax system" is chosen quite independently of the particular allocation of benefits in specific instances, and expenditures are voted in the knowledge that taxes will, in fact, be distributed among individuals in accordance with the tax institutions in being. This implies that the institutions of payment, of taxation, are also chosen "constitutionally," in the sense that, once chosen, they will remain in being over a whole set or sequence of possible and unpredictable spending projects.

In Part II, problems of individual choice at the level of "constitutional" alternatives will be discussed. If tax institutions are selected in some such fashion, significant departures from the satisfaction of the necessary marginal conditions for Pareto optimality in the public goods sector must be anticipated. Even for a single and purely collective good, individual marginal evaluations differ, and the meeting of these conditions would require that each and every person in the group confront possibly differing tax-prices. Samuelson and Musgrave, and others, have stressed the point that, in fiscal choice, individuals will not voluntarily "reveal their true preferences" for public goods. This is valid, however, only if individual tax-prices are directly dependent on their revealed evaluations. In other words, only if some attempt is made to "price" public goods optimally will the individual be motivated to behave strategically. If, however, tax institutions are selected constitutionally, it is clear that individual evaluations for public goods do not directly determine tax-prices. These evaluations do determine the manner in which an individual will vote on extensions or contractions in outlay that may be proposed, but they cannot directly affect the tax-price per unit at which the public good is being made available to him. Under these considerations, the individual has no incentive at all to conceal his preferences for the public good when he participates, directly or indirectly, in fiscal decisions. Even for inframarginal choices, where there may be significant "taxpayers' surplus" to be distributed among members of the group, no explicit bargaining takes place. The division of this available "taxpayers' surplus" will be predetermined in the selection of the tax institution, which takes place prior to and independently of the selection of particular spending projects. In other words, the constitutional approval of a tax institution provides a means of determining, externally and arbitrarily, the distribution of the "gains from trade" among individuals in subsequent fiscal choices.

Because of its effect on the individual decision calculus, this procedure results in greater "efficiency" in collective choice-making, as such, and these gains may be more than enough to offset the losses that must be present in the purely allocative sense. On balance, therefore, the fiscal structure which makes some separation between the "constitutional" selection of its basic institutions and the choosing of the public goods–private goods mix within the operation of these institutions may provide the most "efficient" outcomes, considered over the long run.

It is upon the basis of such a structure that we have examined various fiscal institutions in previous chapters. We have analyzed the behavior of the individual as he confronts an expenditure decision or a tax decision under the assumption that the institution of taxation has been externally determined. In other words, when we examined whether or not an individual would "vote for" or "vote against" a proposed spending project under the personal income tax, we noted that his vote, positive or negative, would not, directly, affect the final distribution of the tax load among all members of the group. This was presumed to have been settled by some "constitutional" decision that was made before the choice examined in our study of the individual calculus. Under the personal income tax, for example, the pattern of tax-prices among persons is a function of the taxable income distribution. The discrimination in tax-prices that results is in no manner related directly to the marginal evaluations for the public services voted upon by the individual, although there exists the normal relationship via the income elasticity of demand. Under such conditions, the individual has no incentive to behave as a "free rider"; rational behavior dictates that he support spending projects, the personal benefits from which he estimates will exceed tax costs. The indivisibility or the generality of these benefits exerts no influence on this choosing behavior, except insofar as this indivisibility requires collective not individual outcomes, thus preventing independent quantity adjustments.

INDIVIDUAL INTEREST IN COLLECTIVE CHOICE

The very fact that the individual must choose in the context of a *collective* decision process is, itself, important in influencing his behavior, and in a manner not unlike that discussed in connection with the so-called "free rider" motivation. This effect stems, not from the indivisibility of the benefits from public goods and services, but from the nature of the decision process when collective outcomes are settled by less-than-unanimity rules. The single person, as he participates in collective choice, will recognize that his own preferences, as expressed by his vote in the simple direct-democracy model, will not be decisive except in a certain finite number of possible configurations of preferences among other members of the political group. He will be faced with the probability that his own vote simply "does not matter." This probability becomes larger as the size of the electorate increases, given any established voting rule. This probability may lead the individual to abstain from participating in the choosing process.[4]

If participation in the collective choice process is genuinely costless, the individual should rationally participate and he should ex-

4. Anthony Downs has discussed the problem of rational abstention from voting, although not in precisely the same context as that developed here. See Downs, *An Economic Theory of Democracy* (New York: Harper, 1957), especially Chapter 14.

press his "true" preferences under the institutions that we have outlined. If, however, voting itself involves some cost, rational behavior may dictate abstention, even though net benefits may remain from favorable outcomes. This point may be illustrated by a very simple three-person model. Suppose that the individual expects benefits from a proposal amounting to one-third, if the collective decision is favorable to him, whom we call A. He does not, however, know the preferences of B and C. Assume that the cost of voting to A will be one-fourth. If a unanimous vote is required, or if he is appointed chooser for the group, he will clearly vote since net benefits exceed the costs of participation. However, what will he do if majority rule is in effect? Here he must estimate the probabilities of his being influential in determining the outcome. If both B and C are against the proposal, there is no point in A's participating in the process. Similarly, if B and C are in favor of the proposal, there is nothing to be gained from participating. Only if B and C are split on the issue can A's vote be critical. Since they can be split in two different ways, we have a total of four possible configurations of B's and C's preferences, of which A's vote will be controlling in only two. For A, the probability is one-half that he will be the critical decision-maker for the group. Applying this probability calculus, we see that A's personal "expected benefit" from voting, not from a favorable decision, is only one-sixth, less than the cost of voting, which we assumed to be one-fourth. The result is that, under such conditions, A will not participate in the "election," and the outcome will be determined by those more interested or whose costs of voting are less.

Although this example greatly exaggerates the costs of participating, it demonstrates the point to be made, and it should be noted that as the group becomes large, similar results will follow even if costs are reduced to very low levels. Note that, through his rational abstention under such conditions, the individual is not "giving false signals" or "failing to reveal his true preferences." Given the situation that he confronts, he is fully expressing his preferences by abstaining from voting.[5]

5. This point has been made with specific reference to the "free rider" problem by Davis and Whinston, "Some Foundations of Public Expenditure Theory." My own discussion of abstention is based on an extension of the Davis-Whinston argument. A related argument, in the form of a criticism of Arrow's discussion of the general impossibility theorem, has been advanced by James S. Coleman. See Coleman, "The Possibility of a Social

How will the individual make the decision whether or not to vote? In our simple example, we assumed an estimate of the net benefits (benefits minus costs) of a favorable outcome. However, as earlier chapters have shown, the securing of information about expected benefits and expected costs is itself costly, and there exists some "optimal" level of investment in the gathering of such information in each particular instance. In addition to this ignorance factor, there remain inherent uncertainties in any collective decision. That is to say, even if the individual knows that his own vote will determine the outcome, and even if he has the most complete access to information concerning expected benefits and costs, under most tax institutions that exist in the real world additional uncertainty will remain due to the freedom of all taxpayers to modify the tax base through their behavior on private market choices. In any practical situation, therefore, the individual must act on the knowledge that all three of these elements are operative. He cannot know with accuracy what his fellows are going to do with respect to modifying the aggregate tax base; he cannot invest the effort required to translate alternative collective outcomes accurately into private or personalized benefits and costs; and he cannot predict with accuracy the preferences of his fellows for and against particular proposals. Facing this set of circumstances, the individual may behave quite rationally, and yet his observed behavior may only remotely resemble rational behavior in market choices. The three difficulties compound one another. Knowing that his own vote will be determining in only a certain number of possible configurations of preferences of his fellows, the individual will be led to invest less effort in securing information about alternatives than he otherwise would do. And, conversely, knowing that he has less than perfect information, and that inherent uncertainty remains as to the effects of alternative outcomes, he will tend to abstain from voting when, if he knew the actual effects, participation might prove rational.

The recognition of these difficulties makes "theorizing" about individual behavior in fiscal choice complex, even within extremely simplified models. It is one thing, however, to acknowledge the difficulties of "theorizing"; it is another thing to refuse to make the attempt. We should try to make as much sense as is possible out of collective choice processes in democratic political organization.

Welfare Function," (mimeographed, Johns Hopkins University, November, 1964).

Whether or not suitable models can be developed, we know that, directly or indirectly, individuals do participate in fiscal choice. They make decisions; they elect representatives who make promises on fiscal matters; they occasionally vote in referenda; they support one political party or another; they join pressure groups; they write letters to their congressmen or to their newspapers; they write speeches; they write books; they talk to their neighbors. If this is acknowledged, then the influence of institutions on their behavior can scarcely be denied. Different institutions will tend to produce differing patterns of response.

The simple models are essential for the clarification of ideas, but these make both the positive results and the weaknesses of theory appear exaggerated. The three difficulties mentioned above need not serve as the major barriers to individual behavior that they seem. The uncertainties in fiscal choice are great, but these are circumscribed within limits; and there are means of reducing the costs of securing information; and individuals do have some idea as to the patterns of preferences among others.

CONCLUSIONS

This chapter has a methodological purpose, which is that of showing how the very fact of indivisibility, associated with public goods and services, does not negate all attempts to reduce collective choice making to an individual-behavior calculus. In other words, this chapter represents a defense, as it were, of the approach taken in the whole study. I have shown that the "free rider" argument, while valid in the context of independent voluntary behavior, loses its relevance when the rules or institutions for choices are laid down in advance, whether these rules be those for Wicksellian unanimity or near-unanimity, or any other, including simple majority voting. Bargaining elements remain in individual behavior, but these are largely eliminated in fiscal choice because of the fact that tax institutions are "constitutionally" selected and are not normally adjustable to specific spending proposals. Confronted with alternatives for choice under this set of circumstances, the individual has no incentive to conceal his "true" preferences for public goods. The fact of indivisibility of benefits among separate individuals does nothing to modify this conclusion.

The outcomes of collective choice must apply to all alike, and not individually, and this tends to influence individual behavior in a manner not unlike that discussed under the "free rider" argument. The individual need not participate in collective choice, and only in some positive proportion of instances will his own vote be critical or decisive. Recognizing this, he may abstain on occasions, even when net benefits are expected to result from favorable outcomes, or net costs from unfavorable outcomes. Such abstention is, itself, "behavior." But all this makes individual behavior in collective choice less amenable to analytical treatment than that in market choice.

10. *The Fiscal Illusion*

Throughout the analysis to this point, it has been assumed that individuals evaluate alternatives "correctly," to the extent dictated by utility-maximizing behavior. This is not to suggest that only observable real magnitudes are relevant. If this were the case, institutional influences on decisions would not exist. As noted, institutions can affect the investment in information, the certainty with which specific outcomes can be predicted, the motivation for individual participation, and still other elements of choice without introducing illusory aspects of behavior. This chapter supplements the previous analysis by allowing for fiscal illusions, and it examines various fiscal institutions for their effects in generating such illusions.

Differences between behavior in the face of ignorance and/or uncertainty and behavior in the presence of illusion are subtle. In either case, behavior would not be the same in the absence of the phenomena. If the chooser does not possess adequate information about alternatives and if he is uncertain, he conceptualizes the alternatives *imperfectly*. If he is affected by an illusion, he conceptualizes the alternatives *falsely*. The effects on his choice behavior may, however, be identical. Initially, it seems reasonable to suggest that probabilistic elements are more important in the first of these situations than in the second. This need not be of assistance in distinguishing results, however, for several reasons. First, an illusion itself may take the form of an expectation of greater or less certainty than "real" facts warrant. Secondly, and more importantly, the probabilistic elements that must be considered are necessarily subjective and nonobservable. And, finally, illusions may be both optimistic and pessimistic.[1]

Behavior under illusion is not necessarily irrational. The individual who behaves irrationally makes inconsistent choices; he does not behave in such a way that an external observer can make predictions, even should his utility function remain unchanged. By contrast, the individual who behaves in the presence of an illusion will act consistently; given the same choice situation on two separate occasions he will tend to make the same decision, provided that "learning from experience" does not dispel the illusion and provided that his utility function does not shift in the interim. Conceptually, the external observer can make predictions here if he knows the effects of illusion on choice behavior. This amounts to saying that "theorizing" about individual behavior under illusion is possible, whereas "theorizing" about individual behavior that is genuinely irrational is not possible.[2]

Illusion arises because of the characteristics of the alternatives

1. Behavior under illusion is most familiar to economists through the "money illusion." Individuals are presumed to choose on the basis of money values rather than real values; the reactions of labor unions in refusing money wage cuts while acquiescing in real wage cuts generated through price inflation are cited as evidence. Whether or not this actually does reflect behavior under illusion need not concern us here.

2. In one sense, behavior under illusion is "nonlogical," as distinct from "logical" or "rational" or "irrational." The term here is Pareto's, and his attribution of this characteristic to individual behavior in the fiscal process is worth citing. In a letter written to Sensini, Pareto said:

"You do well to concern yourself with the science of finance. In that field, there is everything to do. They call it a science, and it is not even an art. It is necessary to tackle the problem from two sides. One is that of pure science, that which you mention to me. The other is that of synthesis; the study of concrete phenomena, discovering whether or not there exist uniformities which can become a pure science. Don't be in a hurry. If you want, write some monographs; but for the general scientific aspects wait until your studies have well matured. The principal difficulty is that you must construct a completely new edifice.

"Emphasize that the taxpayer, who is considering to be aiming at maximizing ophelimity, gives you only one part, often very small, of the phenomena. The taxpayer does not know the many effects of taxes, or, more generally and better, of the many financial transactions; therefore his actions are not of the nature of logical action, such as occupies political economy, and for which the theory is less difficult. But they are of the nature of nonlogical action, for which the theory is much more difficult" (translation mine). G. Sensini, *Corrispondenza di Vilfredo Pareto* (Padua, 1948), cited in Mauro Fasiani, "Contributi di Pareto alla scienza delle finanze," *Giornale degli economisti* (1949), p. 156.
Note that Pareto does not rule out the application of theory to the nonlogical behavior that characterizes behavior in fiscal process.

as these are perceived by the individual; irrationality is a characteristic of the "mind." Thus, we can "explain" why an individual "sees" water in the desert mirage. The artist can create illusion deliberately out of his knowledge of ordinary sense perceptions.[3] It is evident that the institutions of social choice can create illusions, and that this aspect of such institutions is worthy of study.

THE ITALIAN SETTING FOR FISCAL ANALYSIS

It is surprising that the "fiscal illusion" has not been more thoroughly analyzed. Institutions in which the individual must participate in making fiscal choices can exert illusion-creating effects, and these may be sufficiently important to modify behavior. However, the concept remains largely outside the community of discourse that makes up modern public finance. A fundamental contribution was made by an Italian scholar, Amilcare Puviani, who published his major works at the turn of this century. These works were neglected, even by other Italians, until Mauro Fasiani reintroduced them in his widely-acclaimed treatise, first published in 1941.[4] Only during the decade of the 1950's was Puviani's contribution more widely recognized, and, in 1960, a German translation of his basic book was published.[5] The discussion of Puviani in my own essay on the Italian tradition remains, to my knowledge, the only available summary of his views in English,[6] although plans are currently underway for the completion of an English translation.[7]

The theory of public finance as it has developed in Italy is much more closely related to the structure of political institutions than has been the case with its English-language counterpart. The Italians have traditionally been explicit in their statements about the political models within which their discussion of fiscal organization

3. For an excellent account of the importance of illusion in art, and one that is interesting to the nonspecialist, see E. H. Gombrich, *Art and Illusion* (London: Phaidon Press, 1960).

4. Puviani's two basic books are: *Teoria della illusione nelle entrate pubbliche* (Perugia, 1897), and the expanded version, *Teoria della illusione finanziaria* (Palermo, 1903). The content of these works is cited and discussed at length in Mauro Fasiani, *Principii di scienza felle finanze*, Vol. I, (2nd ed.; Torino, 1951). A first edition of this work was published in 1941.

5. Amilcare Puviani, *Die Illusionen in der öffentlichen Finanzwirtschaft*. With an Introduction by Professor G. Schmölders (Berlin, 1960).

6. See my *Fiscal Theory and Political Economy* (Chapel Hill, 1960), pp. 59-64.

7. This translation is being undertaken under the supervision of Charles Goetz, University of Illinois.

takes place and for which their analysis applies. This has produced two parallel branches of fiscal theory. Some of the major figures, such as Francesco Ferrara, Antonio de Viti de Marco, and Mauro Fasiani, extended their own work to cover at least two political models, one of which is "democratic," "co-operative," "voluntaristic," or "individualistic" (these terms being used variously by separate writers) and the other of which is "tyrannical," "monopolistic," "elitist" or "monarchist."

Other scholars have worked largely in one or the other of these two broadly contrasting models, and aside from those major figures who did make the attempt to develop both models simultaneously, the various Italian works in public finance can be classified in these two sets. Puviani's approach to public finance is based on an assumption that the State is "monopolistic." In order to appreciate fully Puviani's contribution some discussion of this political model is required. The State, or the political unit, is not conceived here as an independent, supra-individual entity, in any Hegelian sense. To this extent, even the "monopolistic" model remains individualistic, as opposed to organic in basic content. The political unit is not, however, conceived to be democratic in the sense that universal participation is assumed. Instead, the State represents an agency through which one group of persons, those possessed with power, exerts its will upon persons in another group, those who are dominated. This is essentially a force theory of politics, a "ruling class" model. As such, it is akin to the Marxian conception, although it is not specifically Marxian in content. The ruling class need not possess particular economic characteristics, and economic reality need not determine the demarcation between the rulers and the ruled. The political conception is that developed more fully by both Pareto and Mosca, who observed that, as of any moment, the citizenry can be divided into two groups, the dominant and the dominated. The conception is based, fundamentally, on a denial of the possibility of effectively democratic political order.

It is relatively easy to see that, if one looks at the political process with this "vision," the theory that he constructs may be significantly different from that which he might construct should he possess the "vision" of effectively working "individualist" democracy. The hypotheses would be different, and the explanations offered for the same set of facts would sharply diverge, as is indeed demonstrated in some of the contrasts between the Western and the Marxian interpretations of current events.

Under the ruling-class conception, the fiscal structure is an institutional means through which this class, who are the decision-makers for the whole community, can exact funds from the dominated or ruled group, for providing, or financing, those goods and services that the first group wants to see provided. The ruling group may or may not be narrowly self-interested. The members of the dominated or ruled group can only react to the conditions within which they find themselves; that can never initiate action in a direct sense. This group will, predictably, resist efforts by the ruling class to impose charges upon them, and they will, understandably, be conscious of little or no "co-operation" with the rulers. The objective of the rulers becomes that of arranging or organizing the fiscal structure so that the resistance of the dominated class is effectively minimized, consistent with the securing of adequate revenues.

In this setting, the task of the fiscal theorist becomes that of explaining the behavior of the ruling class in organizing the system, in making the fundamental decisions on the public economy, and also in explaining the behavior of the dominated or exploited class in reacting to and resisting the imposition of tax charges. One means of explaining the behavior of the ruling class is that of placing one's self, conjecturally, in their position and asking: What actions should be taken if the objective is that of minimizing resistance or discontent on the part of the dominated groups? This approach is in the tradition of Machiavelli's, *Il Principe,* an approach that has been widely employed (and widely misunderstood). Puviani approached the theory of fiscal organization with the question: *If the ruling group desires to minimize taxpayer resistance for any given level of revenues collected, how will it set out to organize the fiscal system?* He made it quite explicit that he did not assume that the ruling group actually asked such a question or that it aimed directly at accomplishing this objective. Puviani argued perceptively that action on behalf of the ruling, decision-making authorities would probably be motivated largely by the short-run goal of taking the path of least resistance in each particular instance of choice. But the whole pattern of action can often be explained by a model which incorporates some *as if* objectives. All economists are familiar with such models. It is in this way that Puviani looked at the fiscal process. His answer to the question was put in the form of a general hypothesis. The ruling group attempts, to the extent that is possible, to create fiscal illusions, and these have the effect of making taxpayers think that the taxes to which they are subjected are less burdensome than they actually are. At the same time, other illusions are created that make beneficiaries consider the values of public goods and services provided them to be larger than may actually be the case. The various institutions of taxing and spending are so organized as to create this set of illusions. Puviani then proposed to examine existing fiscal structures to test his basic hypothesis. How much of the evolution of real-world fiscal institutions can be explained?

PUVIANI'S INSTITUTIONAL ARRAY

Puviani made his hypothesis too general, and in some instances he seems to stretch it almost out of recognition. Nevertheless, it is useful to look briefly at some of the institutions that he discussed and to see how he interpreted these in terms of the illusion hypothesis. Both sides of the budget were included; illusions are created through taxes and through public spending programs. The tax side is more important, however, and it will be discussed in somewhat more detail.

Fiscal illusion in the imposition of taxes.[8] Illusion in the imposition and the collection of taxes can be introduced in several specific ways, not all of which are equally important and relevant, especially in a modern setting. These several ways may be listed and discussed in turn.

1. The connection between the total amount of resources actually utilized in producing or supplying public services and any individualized share in this total may be obscured to the taxpayer. In other words, the individual shares in the opportunity cost of public spending may be hidden. Illusions of this sort can be generated in at least five separate institutions of taxation.

The first involves the use of income from the *public domain* to finance government operations. In this case, the individual taxpayers will fail to realize that, were the income not so employed, it could be returned to them in reduced levels of ordinary taxation. This institution need not be discussed in detail here. Historically, the public domain has provided a major source of public revenues, but in the last century this source has become relatively unimportant in

8. The summary presented in this section is based on two sources: Puviani, *Teoria della illusione nelle entrate pubbliche;* and Fasiani, *Principii di scienza felle finanze,* Chapter III.

nonsocialist states. In socialist states, of course, the profits from state enterprises are used to finance public services, and the illusion mentioned here by Puviani again takes its place as a factor promoting general acquiescence in the expansion of such services.

The second institution that falls within this broad grouping is more significant for our purposes. Illusion arises when the tax is actually absorbed in the payment that an individual makes for private goods and services. This situation is characteristic of *specific excise taxes,* where the tax is nominally included in the price of a private good or service. Here the individual must adjust his purchases so that the price, including the tax, stands in the same proportion to any other price as the ratio of the relative marginal utilities of the two *private* goods. No explicit recognition of the payment for a public good or service enters into the individual adjustment here. Hence, the individual is likely to be quite ignorant of the amount of tax that is paid, and he may, in some cases, be unaware of the tax altogether. The illusion is more complete, said Puviani, when a tax has been in existence for some time. Initially, when a private-goods price increases as a result of a tax, the impact may be evident to the purchaser. But as the institution remains in being for a succession of periods, the opportunity cost is not sensed by the taxpayer.

The *public debt* is the third institution that Puviani included in his first broad category. He accepted the basic Richardian proposition that the payment of a single once-and-for-all tax and the payment of a certain percentage of this sum through an annual tax in perpetuity are, in some real sense, equivalent. But, said Puviani, individual taxpayers do not act as if the two alternatives are the same. Somewhat surprisingly, he did not discuss fully the possible failure of taxpayers to discount, to capitalize, the future tax payments that public debt issue involves. He seemed to accept, at the outset, that such capitalization did take place. Even with this, however, Puviani argued that the flotation of loans, with these loans to be serviced by the payment of an annual tax, would not be resisted to the same extent as would the levy of a single once-and-for-all tax. The illusion stressed by Puviani arises because, under the public-loan scheme, the individual retains "control" over a capital value which, even though fully offset by the liability stemming from the capitalized value of future taxes, remains desirable. Because of this control over assets, the individual prefers to pay the tax in perpetuity. Such an "asset illusion" may, of course, be extended to private debt as well as public debt.[9]

A fourth, and clearly relevant, institution that Puviani included in his first category is that which involves the financing of public goods and services through *inflation,* that is, through currency creation. It seems evident that this means of financing makes it very difficult for the individual to identify his own share in the costs of the services being financed and supplied through government. Puviani stated correctly that currency inflation was similar in effect to indirect taxation under full employment.

A final means through which the ruling group, in control of the fiscal machinery, can generate an illusion that obscures the individual's share in the total costs of governmental services is the making of false promises. These take the form especially of making the individual think that various spending programs are temporary and short-lived when, in fact, these programs, once started, will be maintained in being. In this way, the taxpayer will be subjected to a considerably higher cost than he may have originally anticipated. And once a program has been commenced, it is relatively easy to present the taxpayer with the traditional "sunk costs" argument for its continuation.

2. Obscuring the real costs of public goods and services is not the only means of introducing a fiscal illusion, although it is perhaps the most important one. A second category includes those institutions of payment that are designed so as to tie the obligation to a time period or an event which the taxpayer seems likely to consider "favorable." Puviani's ingenious idea here is based on the recognition that isolated individual decisions can be influenced by temporary circumstances, and that the attitude of the individual may vary significantly with such circumstances. Common to poker games is the slogan, "big winner buys the drinks," despite the fact that, outside of the particular circumstances of the evening's play, the winner may be less able to buy the refreshments than his colleagues. "Impulse buying" is, of course, an important phenomenon in marketing behavior, but its significance for ordinary consumer choice is reduced by the repetitiveness of the marketing process. There is less impulse buying of staple commodities than there is of dollies at the county

9. I have discussed the issues here at some length in a paper, "Public Debt, Cost Theory, and the Fiscal Illusion," which is included in *Public Debt and Future Generations,* ed. James M. Ferguson (Chapel Hill: The University of North Carolina Press, 1964).

fair. The individual does not "buy" government services voluntarily and surely not on impulse. However, Puviani sensed that if
the institutions of taxation could be so arranged that individuals are
confronted with the necessity of paying taxes only during periods
when some complementary event takes place with a highly favorable
outcome, the real costs of government goods and services will seem
less onerous. Several institutions of taxation lend themselves to
partial "explanation" through this extension of the Puviani hypothesis, although there seems to be some question as to whether this
effect can be due to "illusion" in any strict sense.

Taxes on transfers, on inheritances and gifts, levied on the
donee fit well under this rubric. Assume that a rich uncle dies and
leaves an estate of a million dollars to a nephew who did not antici-
pate the inheritance. It seems clear that, on the moment of the an-
nouncement, the levy of a tax against this inheritance will not be
"felt" by the legatee in the same sense that an ordinary tax of equivalent amount would be "felt," say, five years after he had secured
the inheritance.

The same reasoning applies, however, to all taxes on transfers
of assets. Any exchange, except those made strictly at the margin,
involves net gains, presumably to both parties to the transaction.
Hence, a tax levied at the moment of completing a transaction, in
the presence of the apparent gain, tends to be less severe, in the
minds of the taxpayers, than a tax of like amount levied at another
time.

3. A third means of introducing a fiscal illusion, and one that is
closely related to the one previously discussed, is found in the charging of explicit *fees* for nominal services rendered upon the occasion
of memorable or pleasurable events. Puviani brought in marriage
license fees, hunting licenses, entertainment licenses, fees for diplomas,
etc. Slightly different, but similar reasoning led him to "explain"
such taxes as those on playing cards, pool tables, and lottery tickets.
Business licenses that are charged only on the opening of an operation can be explained on the generally optimistic attitudes of all
prospective managers.

4. The dominant class will also take advantage of shifts in public
attitudes on social issues, said Puviani, and will use these shifts as
the basis for imposing taxes. If a particular attitude is pervasive
in the community, an opportunity is provided to levy a tax that will
capitalize on such sentiment, making the burden appear less than

might otherwise be the case. Puviani seemed to overextend his provocative hypothesis here when he suggested that taxes aimed at redistributing incomes to the poor were more readily accepted when rich groups were made to fear the uprising of the poorer classes. On the other hand, there is some legitimacy in his argument that certain taxes are explicitly introduced as means of securing the acquiescence of certain groups to other social changes. For example, taxes on business profits are often introduced, and justified to business groups, as political sop to labor groups aimed at securing political support for other measures. While Puviani's comments on these aspects of tax policy are interesting, as indeed most of his work is, they do not lend themselves readily to specific results in terms of his own illusion hypothesis. He does not seem to have distinguished properly between "explaining" how certain taxes come into existence, given the political activity of several social classes, and in "explaining" individual responses to taxation. It is only in the second of these that the fiscal illusion, as such, may be observed.

5. Puviani was on somewhat more firm ground when he argued that the governing class will, in order to secure the general acceptance of a tax, threaten the body politic with the direst of consequences if, in fact, the tax levy is not approved. These "scare tactics" tend to make the alternatives to particular tax proposals appear worse than they are, and it seems evident that, to the extent that such tactics are effective, a fiscal illusion is created which can influence individual reactions. In modern fiscal settings, such tactics are probably more familiar on the expenditure side than on the tax side, and it is now more or less anticipated that the bureaucracy will threaten the representative assembly and the citizenry with disastrous consequences if specific spending programs are not implemented and continued.

6. To the extent that the total tax load on an individual can be fragmented so that he confronts numerous small levies rather than a few significant ones, illusory effects may be created. If, for example, all taxes paid by an individual are concentrated into a single levy on personal income, the individual would surely be more conscious of the sacrifice that he undergoes, presumably, in support of government services. Hence, according to Puviani, fiscal systems in monopolistic states tend to be complex and to rely relatively little on general, broad-based taxes.

135

7. A final, and important, means of creating illusion on the tax side lies in the levy of taxes under situations where the individual cannot really know who finally pays; that is, in situations where the incidence of the tax is unknown. This illusion is clearly akin to that discussed under the first category, and also to some of the discussions in previous chapters. It is clear that the uncertainty that is involved in tax institutions of uncertain incidence does exert an influence on fiscal choice, whether or not this be classified as an illusion.

Fiscal illusions in public spending. The basic Puviani analysis was also extended to the spending side of the fiscal account, although it seems somewhat less applicable here. Several of the points made with respect to the imposition of taxes can be applied in reverse to spending programs. Puviani stressed, however, the prevalence of more general practices on the spending side. One of the most important of these was the tendency of governments to conceal from public view the extent and true nature of budgetary programs. Tracing the evolution of fiscal systems historically, Puviani noted that for centuries there was no distinction made between the account of the State and the personal account of the Prince. Even when this essential separation was finally accomplished, the right of the sovereign to expend tax revenues secretly was maintained. Gradually, of course, accountability to the representative assembly was established, but, even here, the governing class tends to exaggerate the spending needs and to conceal the true state of affairs in order to secure the levy of additional taxes.

In earlier epochs, the possibilities of creating illusions in this way were greatly enhanced by the absence of systematic accounting and budgetary techniques. And even under the most modern of budgetary systems, the sheer complexity of the budget makes detailed examination impossible. At best the citizen remains poorly informed concerning the allocation of public monies. Given this necessary ignorance, governments find it relatively easy to manipulate budgetary items in such a manner as to make it appear that larger sums are devoted to the more "popular" programs.

AN EVALUATION OF PUVIANI'S CONTRIBUTION AND ITS EXTENSION TO A DEMOCRATIC SETTING

No attempt has been made to present Puviani's discussion in great detail. Many of his notions seem out of date in the 1960's.

Nevertheless, the modern critic cannot fail to be impressed by the relevance that the basic conception seems to retain. The Puviani hypothesis offers an essentially new perspective from which to look at the fiscal structure, and it can be of some assistance even as applied to a modern governmental setting.

Puviani operated on the assumption that the fiscal system was organized by a ruling class, an elite, within a larger, more inclusive, political society. In his modern extension of Puviani's ideas, Fasiani discusses the fiscal illusion in that part of his treatise called "Public Finance in the Monopolistic State." We have, in this study, deliberately adopted an opposing political framework. We have assumed that the political structure is fundamentally democratic and that fiscal decisions are made, in some ultimate sense, by all members of the political group in a sort of voting process, whether this be direct or indirect. This difference in political assumptions need not, however, imply that the Puviani analysis is without value. As Fasiani points out, all traces of an elitist model are rarely removed, even in the most "democratic" of states, and to the extent that these remain, the Puviani analysis has relevance on its own terms. I should go considerably further than Fasiani here and say that, even in a fully democratic setting, fiscal institutions, regardless of the motivation behind their original organization, can be analyzed and arrayed in terms of their tendencies to generate fiscal illusions. This essentially positive approach, which does not get involved with the "why" of institutions but which takes them as they are and then attempts to analyze their effects, is the one followed in this book. For such an approach, the political setting is not so important as it may have been made to appear in earlier chapters. Just as the Puviani analysis can be appended as supplementary to that of this study, which has presumed a democratic setting for fiscal choice, so our own study could be appended as supplementary to the Puviani analysis in a monopolistic setting. It would not be difficult to modify the discussion of earlier chapters to develop a theory of "fiscal reaction" rather than a theory of fiscal choice.

FISCAL ILLUSIONS IN MODERN SYSTEMS

Puviani looked at the whole fiscal process through a "different window" from that which has been used by English-language critics. The institutions were to be explained, in his vision, by the unconscious motiviation of the ruling class to exploit the ruled. Upon closer examination, however, we see that Puviani did little more than make explicit some of the norms for fiscal organization that were also widely accepted by the utilitarians. Interestingly enough, a theory of public finance applicable to a democratic setting was not developed at all in the English tradition. Out of neoclassical economics and utilitarian ethics there came, instead, the tax principle of "least aggregate sacrifice," as developed primarily by Edgeworth and Pigou. This principle, if it merits attention at all, must be recognized as closely akin to Puviani's fiscal illusion as a norm, for what is the purpose of creating illusion other than that of minimizing aggregate sacrifice for the taxpayer, and, through this, minimizing taxpayer resistance? Puviani was a political realist, and he made no pretense of assuming government to be both despotic and benevolent. The Edgeworth-Pigou principle, by contrast, can be applied only in a despotic setting where the despot is both wholly benevolent and all powerful. It is clearly irrelevant to a democratic setting, and since the despot need not worry explicitly about taxpayer reaction, he must be all powerful. In either conception, Puviani's or Edgeworth-Pigou, the tax side is viewed independently from the expenditure side, which of course implies a nondemocratic framework. In a democratic setting neither "least aggregate sacrifice" nor "minimization of felt burden through illusion" is appropriate as a norm for fiscal organization. Instead, the norm must be that of allowing individuals, through the structure of collective decision institutions, to "purchase" public goods and services in such a way that their choices as between these goods and services and those produced via private market process can remain as "neutral" and "nondistorted" as is possible.

If we go back to the classical economists and look at the canons of taxation laid out by Adam Smith, we find that "convenience" to the taxpayer is one norm. Taxes should be so levied as to make the payment as convenient and as commodious as is possible. This norm has been repeated in many manuals. It is not surprising that this norm of convenience should come close to that which motivates the ruling class in the Puviani conception. If we look at those institutions which have come to be accepted primarily because of the convenience criterion, these lend themselves to examination under the Puviani model.

Puviani's ruling class attempts to promote optimistic illusions; the taxpayer is made to feel that he pays "less" and receives "more" in return that he would under alternative institutional arrangements. If we drop all considerations of motivation, however, and simply examine institutions as they exist, there is no necessary presumption that the fiscal illusions present shall always be optimistic ones. Pessimistic illusion is also possible.

Withholding of income for tax payments. Since World War II, in the United States, a large proportion of the personal income tax has been collected through the withholding of tax from payments of salaries and wages to employees. The employer acts as the tax collector, and the employee does not receive directly that proportion of his salary or wage that is withheld at the source for tax purposes. This widely-hailed "reform" in the American income tax system was almost exclusively supported on the argument of increased convenience for the taxpayer. If Puviani's ghost were present, he would surely point to the withholding feature as a likely source for the generation of illusion in an almost classic sense.

Withholding would fit neatly under Puviani's first category of institutions which tend to obscure from the taxpayer his opportunity cost of supporting public services. The individual who does not have possession of income before paying it out cannot "sense" the real cost of public services in a manner comparable to that experienced in a genuine act of outpayment. In this respect, withholding affects individual behavior in much the same way as an indirect tax.

Does this imply that "convenience" to the taxpayer should not be one of the criteria for tax reform? Should the taxpayer be made to pay taxes in the most onerous manner that can be devised? The answers to these loaded questions are obviously negative. Prior to the introduction of withholding and pay-as-you-earn, the individual taxpayer was forced to pay the full amount of his annual tax liability at one time, at the springtime settling of accounts. This practice probably generated a pessimistic illusion and made the cost of government appear excessive in some appropriate relative sense. Conceptually, an "ideal" institutional arrangement might be that of allowing individuals to "pay for" governmental goods and services in a manner analogous to that which they have found most convenient for financing consumer durables. The quarterly payments of tax on declarations of income above or outside withholding probably tend, on balance, to promote "logical" response to the income tax structure. It is the absence of any conscious sense of transfer, the absence of any monthly or quarterly bill, that represents the questionable feature of withholding, and one that may tend to create a Puviani-type illusion.[10]

Progression in the rate structure of an income tax. As suggested, pessimistic illusion may be generated as well as optimistic ones, especially when no specific design-for-illusion in the Puviani sense has guided the organization of the system. It seems intuitively plausible that the institution of progression, per se, tends to create an excess feeling of tax burden on the part of the taxpayer. The effect here stems from the divergence between the average and the marginal rate of tax, and the observed tendency of persons to think in terms of marginal rates. This illusion, if present, is supported by discussions of the rate structure in the popular press and in political debates.

For some purposes, the marginal rate of tax is the relevant one for analyzing individual choices. In adjusting his behavior in the private sector, in deciding how much taxable income he will earn, the individual should act in response to the schedule of marginal rates. However, in trying to choose the quantity of public goods to be supplied, in matching the benefits of public services against the tax costs that are imposed upon him personally, the individual should think in terms of average rates, and on the schedule of these rates as the total revenue requirements vary. He may, however, be led by the progressive structure to think and act falsely *as if* public goods and services are available to him at some schedule of "negative quantity discounts," that is, at some increasing marginal price.[11]

One implication of the hypothesis here is that an individual would tend to choose a larger quantity of public services under proportional income taxation than under progression, even though his own liability under the two schemes is identical. This implication is at least subject to conceptual testing.

Social security taxes. The modern American system of old-age and survivors "insurance" seems ready made for the Puviani criticism. It is apparent to almost everyone, without detailed analysis or knowledge of the system, that the effects of promoting the insti-

10. For a discussion which reaches somewhat different conclusions, see Francesco Forte, "Osservazioni sul metodo della trattenuta alla sorgente nelle imposte sul reddito," published in *Studi in onore di Gaetano Zingali* (Milano: Giuffre, 1965), pp. 209-30.

11. If confronted with increasing marginal price over quantity, choice is distorted in the direction of causing the person to choose less than his own optimally preferred quantity. The effect is the opposite of that resulting from adjustment under quantity discounting.

tutions under the "insurance" rubric, which implies actuarial independence and integrity, tends to conceal from participants the real flows of costs and benefits. Whether or not such was the deliberate intent of the founders of the system need not concern us here. The facts are that the system, as an independent trust-fund account outside of the regular budgetary procedures of the federal government, is not actuarially sound by private financial standards, and that the plan will depend for its continued existence on the Treasury's willingness to finance currently claims made against the system. Contributors to the system finance only a relatively small share of the benefits that they receive, especially to this date (1966), and the remaining funds must be secured from current taxes collected from prospective beneficiaries. To the extent that the current contributor accepts the regular increases in his own taxes, as well as those nominally levied on his employer, under the assumption that, on balance, these are to be accumulated for support of his own retirement benefits, he will be less resistent to such increases than if he knew that such tax increases were simply required to meet current outpayments to beneficiaries. He operates under an illusion of the Puviani sort. If future claims against the system should be properly discounted, along with future taxes that are required to meet these claims, the entrant into the system would recognize that, in the net, the costs significantly exceed the benefits, both computed in present-value terms. The fact that there is no widespread resentment or resistance against entering the system supports the hypothesis that illusion is present, and is effective. Even for the employee who may recognize the actuarial bankruptcy of the present system, who is able to dispel the fiscal illusion, it may not, however, be rational to reject the scheme when he predicts that, during his own period of retirement, other prospective entrants can still be attracted by illusory claims of "insurance." The system in this manner provides a continuing means through which income transfers can be made to the aged from the currently productive elements of the population, which can be "explained" or "rationalized" to many taxpayers on the basis of contributory schemes of retirement protection. There seems little question but that, if the same fiscal transfers were proposed openly and without attempts at illusion, there would be significantly greater political resistance. This conclusion can be attained, regardless of one's own value position on the quite separate question as to whether such transfers should be decreased, kept the same, or increased.[12]

Corporate income taxation. Taxes imposed on income of corporations tend to create major uncertainty for the ultimate taxpayer, as we have previously noted, and this in itself is sufficient to allow this important modern institution to be added to Puviani's last category. The additional feature that warrants special mention lies in the tax status of the separate legal entity, the corporation. This device lends itself to an even further obscuring of the real costs of public services from the individual, who must be the final taxpayer.

Averaging in the personal income tax. Among academic specialists in public finance in the United States almost universal support has been voiced for the introduction of additional averaging features under the progressive income tax. The substantial reforms in this direction embodied in the 1964 tax legislation have been widely acclaimed. Puviani, from his wholly different approach—and unconcerned about equity—could "explain" the failure of previous attempts at such reform, and he would not have been able to predict 1964 changes by his hypothesis. If the only consideration is the minimization of taxpayer resistance, averaging would not be a reform that commands the widespread attention of Puviani's "rulers." The man who receives windfall gains, who hits it lucky, now and then, whose income fluctuates is, psychologically, more willing to pay taxes than is his neighbor who may possess the identical "permanent income." The nonaveraged progressive income tax becomes, under this explanation, one device for introducing illusion. The 1964 reforms clearly refute Puviani's illusion hypothesis in its normative sense.

Capital gains taxation. The treatment of capital gains under the income tax is closely related to the problem of averaging, and one reason for the continued favorable treatment of gains is held to be the absence of effective averaging provisions in the regular income tax. In the context of Puviani's model, taxes should clearly be im-

12. It is worth noting that the academic specialists on insurance have recently established a Committee on Social Insurance Terminology and that this committee has discussed at some length the appropriateness of using the term "insurance" to apply to Federal security programs. The argument has been, however, largely definitional, and the effects of using or not using the term seem to have been neglected. See C. Arthur Williams, Jr., "Social Insurance—Proper Terminology," *The Journal of Insurance,* XXX (March, 1963), 112-28.

posed on gains, perhaps more severely than on ordinary income. As with the 1964 averaging reforms, the favorable treatment of gains tends to refute the basic Puviani notion that the motivation behind fiscal evolution is the creation of illusion.

11. *Simple Collective Decision Models*

INTRODUCTION

In an effectively democratic political order, collective decisions emerge from a process that takes individual expressions of preference as inputs and somehow combines these to produce outcomes. Fiscal institutions affect these preferences. The influence on individual behavior is not, however, equivalent to an influence on collective outcomes. Such an extension requires a crossing of the bridge between individual participation and the final outcome of the collective choice process. It becomes necessary to translate the effects of institutions on individual behavior into effects on political results. To accomplish this, we must examine the rules that serve to combine individual "votes."

Complete discussion would require a volume. Here we can only construct very simple models that abstract from the complexities of actual political process in order to concentrate on those elements that will be of assistance in making predictions. The models used are those of direct democracy. It is assumed that fiscal decisions are made directly through voting processes in which all citizens participate. Such models are, of course, highly unrealistic in any descriptive sense. Common observation tells us that collective decisions are not made in this manner. The underlying realism of the models depends, however, not on their apparent correspondence with observed reality, but upon their assistance in developing hypotheses about political choices that can be conceptually tested. If the models allow us to do this, they are of some significance for an understanding of the fiscal process as it actually exists in its complex institutional setting. Some of the general problems involved in moving

144

from the models of the theorist to the real world are discussed in Chapter 12.

A THREE-PERSON MODEL OF EQUALS

Return to the initial models of individual demand for a single public good that were presented in Chapter 2. Recall that, in those models, elements of uncertainty, ignorance, and illusion were neglected. Initially, we stay within the same limitation here. The situation confronting the single individual is that shown in Figure 11.1. Provided only that he is not required to consider alternatives

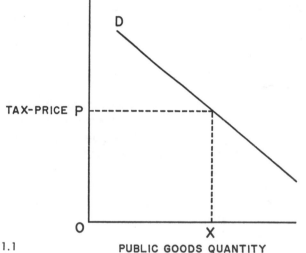

FIGURE 11.1   PUBLIC GOODS QUANTITY

on some all-or-none basis, the individual depicted will "vote for" an amount, OX, of the public good, for which he is charged a tax-price (determined externally) of OP per unit. To the individual, OX is the "optimal" quantity of the public good to be supplied. He will not be allowed, individually, to determine whether or not the community will supply more than, less than, or just this amount, since the collective decision will result from a political choosing process in which he is only one among several participants. To discuss the reaching of collective outcomes, which, once reached, must be imposed upon all members, it is necessary to examine the behavior of more than one person.

We begin with the simplest model that may be constructed. Assume that there are only three persons in the community, and

145

that these three persons are identical in all respects. (The second of these assumptions makes the model applicable for any number of persons, but it will be useful to stay within the three-person restriction for purposes of comparison with later models.) How much will this group, acting as a collective unit, decide to devote to the supply of the public good, given the structure of tax-prices as indicated?

This model is interesting, even if the results are trivially obvious, because it is the only one in which neither the *decision rule* nor the *tax institution*, as normally considered, exerts an influence on the final outcome. Provided only that the tax is a *general* one, *any* decision rule and *any* tax scheme will yield the same result, which will be that shown in Figure 11.1. This result will also satisfy the necessary marginal conditions for Pareto optimality, although this welfare implication is not our primary concern at this point.

The conclusions may be demonstrated by postulating a tax institution. Suppose that a system of equal-per-head taxes has been agreed on in some "constitutional" setting before the particular fiscal decision is to be made, with the agreement stipulating that the total tax bill shall be residually determined as a result of the voting process on the amount of the public good to be supplied. The good is available to the community at constant cost; this assumption is common to all of the models introduced in this chapter. Under such conditions, each person, were he given his own "private" choice, would desire that the collectivity supply a quantity, OX, of the good, which is, of course, equally available to all members. Each person would choose to have the collectivity expend the same total outlay. Hence, unanimity could be secured on this outcome without difficulty. Simple majority voting would in no way modify the result. Any less-than-unanimity voting rule will, in this model, produce the same outcome as the unanimity rule because the predetermined agreement on the tax institution removes any opportunity that either a single dictator or a majority coalition may have of exploiting other members of the group. Thus, *any* possible rule for making group choices will yield the same result, provided only that the tax is general and not discriminatory. Other general taxes will yield equivalent results. Since all persons are identical by assumption, a proportional or a progressive tax on income, or any other tax that is not specifically discriminatory, will impose equal tax-prices on the separate members of the group. Public spending programs are always "ideally efficient," and institutional influences on outcomes are absent.

146

A THREE-PERSON MODEL WITH UNEQUAL EVALUATIONS FOR THE
PUBLIC GOOD

As a first step toward making the model less restrictive, let us allow for only one difference among the three persons, a difference in their evaluation or their demand for the single public good. This change will enable us to isolate the effects of varying decision rules on collective outcomes independently of the effects of tax institutions. Since here we retain the assumption that the three persons are identical in all respects relevant to the levy of any general tax, any such tax will still impose the same tax-price on each person.

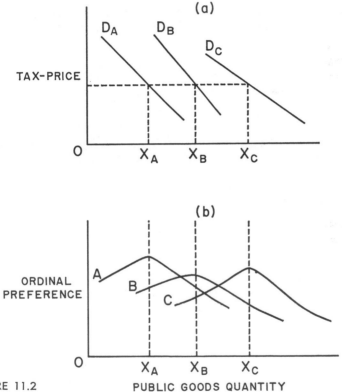

FIGURE 11.2

The three individual demand curves are shown in Figure 11.2 (a), along with the privately-preferred adjustments to the common tax-price. If he could choose independently, for the whole group, Individual A would have the collectivity provide OX_A; Individual B would have the collectivity finance, instead, OX_B units; and Individual C's most preferred quantity is OX_C. Clearly the delegation of decision-making power to a single person under these circumstances would produce different results with different "dictators." Figure 11.2(b) depicts the preferences of the three persons in a slightly different manner. Here on the ordinate we measure the ordinal preferences of the persons and a point standing higher on this scale indicates that the individual prefers this quantity (given the tax-price) to any other point standing lower on the scale. Note that, when viewed in this way, the preference schedule for each person is single-peaked, with his most preferred outcome, for the group, being that shown by his "private equilibrium" position in Figure 11.2(a). The fact that the schedules are single-peaked is important, since this characteristic insures that under a simple majority voting rule, there will be some determinate outcome. There will be no cyclical majority.[1]

If no limits are put on the number of proposals that may be put forward for a vote, the outcome represented by the single-peak for the median preference member of the group will be selected under a decision rule of simple majority. Individual A will prefer the quantity OX_B to any output that is larger. Similarly, Individual C will prefer OX_B to any smaller quantity. Hence, Individual B will become controlling in the majority decision, just as if he were delegated privately with exclusive decision-making authority for the group. The predicted outcome will be that indicated to be "most preferred" by the person whose preferences are median for the whole group. This analysis suggests that, because of the median-man construction, some analysis of collective decision-making under majority rule is possible even if we remain at the level of the individual decision calculus. If fiscal institutions are predicted to influence the preferences expressed by the median voter, they can be predicted to influence the final collective results in the same direction.

Under a voting rule of unanimity, the outcome becomes indeterminate within wide limits. In the three-man model here, unanimity may produce a result that is confined only within the limits between quantities OX_A and OX_C. If votes are taken on successive additions to output starting from small numbers, no consensus can be attained for going beyond OX_A. On the other hand, if the choos-

1. The construction and the use of single-peaked preference schedules is based on the work of Duncan Black. See Black, *The Theory of Committees and Elections* (Cambridge: Cambridge University Press, 1958).

ing process starts with some quantity larger than OX$_C$, agreement could be reached only on a reduction to this level and no more. No quantity falling between these limits could be modified by general agreement of all parties.

A THREE-PERSON MODEL WITH EQUAL EVALUATION BUT UNEQUAL TAX-PRICES

It will now be useful to isolate, to the extent that is possible, the differences that arise from changes in the fiscal institutions. To do this, we shall now assume that the separate individual demand

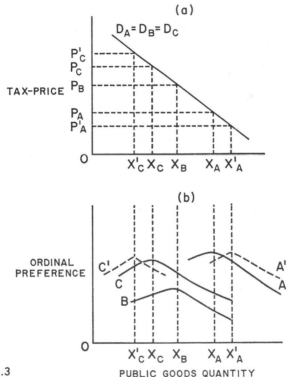

FIGURE 11.3

schedules are identical, as drawn in Figure 11.3(a). However, we shall assume that the individuals differ in some respect that may be relevant to the determination of tax-price. Let us say that they differ only in income.

Under the equal-per-head tax, the model becomes the same as that discussed two sections above in connection with Figure 11.1.

149

The same quantity would be selected under any voting rule since both demand and tax-price are identical for all participants. If, however, we introduce a tax system that relates liability for tax to income level, the individuals will confront different tax-prices. Assume that Individual A has the lowest income, B the median income, and C the highest income in the group. Proportional income taxation, let us say, will confront the three persons with a set of tax-prices shown as P_A, P_B, P_C in Figure 11.3(a). Despite the equivalence in demand, the three individuals will now prefer different quantities of the public good because of the discrimination in tax-price. In this model, as in the unequal evaluation model above, the particulars of the decision rule will affect the outcome of the political process. Under majority rule, the man with the median income tends to exert controlling influence.

Progressive income taxation does not differ from proportional taxation in terms of general results. It tends to widen the differentials between the higher and the lower tax-prices, but, under majority rule, the median-income receiver tends to remain controlling. Progression may, however, exert important effects on outcomes through shifting the preferred outcome for this median voter. To clarify this point, it is useful to introduce the notion of *symmetrical* and *nonsymmetrical* shifts in the structure of tax-prices. Assume that a proportional rate structure is in being and that progression is introduced. One means of introducing progressive rates would be that of increasing the tax-price charged to the "rich" man while reducing the tax-price charged to the "poor" man, leaving the middle or median man's tax-price unchanged. This is defined here as a symmetrical shift in rate structure, and it will not affect the outcome in this model. The median voter retains control over the majority-rule outcome, and his preferred results are not changed. However, suppose that progression is introduced by increasing the tax-price for the "rich" man, reducing the tax-price for the "poor" man *and* for the median-income man. When tax-price is modified for the median-income man, the shift is defined to be nonsymmetrical. If the shift serves to reduce this critical tax-price, the introduction of progression will have the effect of increasing the quantity of public good supplied under simple majority voting rules. The median man is confronted with a lower tax-price, and he will desire a larger quantity. Nonsymmetrical shifts need not be unidirectional; progression might be introduced by increasing the tax-price for the "rich" man *and,* also, for the median man, while reducing tax-price for the "poor" man. In this case, the effects on simple majority-rule outcomes are the reverse of those traced above. The quantity of public good supplied will tend to be reduced.

This analysis suggests that even in the highly restricted model of equal evaluation, the differential effects of progression and proportion on the supply of public goods under simple majority voting rules cannot be predicted until and unless the effects on the relative tax-price of the median voter are determined. This is an empirical fact, and useful research into the nature of real-world rate structures and changes in these structures within the context of the collective-choice models discussed here can be undertaken.

The effects of progression, as compared with proportion, under a decision rule of unanimity can be readily observed from Figure 11.3(b). The limits are extended beyond those applicable under proportion. The "solution" set of points is larger. This generalization may be more important than it initially seems. Decision making in democratic political structures may well require either more or less than the equivalent of simple majority approval. Insofar as some greater-than-majority support is, in fact, required to secure decision, the unanimity model can yield helpful predictions. The range over which a solution, under all qualified majority rules, may be found is larger under a progressive rate structure than under a proportional rate structure. The observed degree of discontent about the "proper" size of the public sector should, therefore, be greater. This seems an implication that could, in some proximate sense, be empirically tested.

A THREE-PERSON MODEL WITH UNEQUAL EVALUATION AND UNEQUAL INCOMES, BUT WITH EQUAL PREFERENCE PATTERNS

Less restrictive models are necessary if we are to develop hypotheses of extended interest. In any real-world fiscal setting the evaluations of different persons for public goods will be different and, also, persons will differ in other respects, some of which will be relevant for determining their tax liabilities. Given such a world of unequals, is there any orderly theorizing that can be carried out? Clearly if we impose no structure on the direction and extent of the variations among individuals, few predictions can be advanced. Some order may be introduced, however, if we impose restrictions on the

151

model, but restrictions that are considerably less severe than those hitherto employed.

We propose to adopt a variant on the world-of-equals model. We assume that the *preference patterns* of the separate persons are identical, but that incomes differ. That is to say, the individuals in the model would be identical in their demand behavior if their incomes should be the same, but, since their incomes are different, their demands for public goods will differ. This allows marginal evaluation or demand schedules to vary among individuals due to the influence of income effects on individual choice behavior. While still highly restricted, this model is considerably more general than those previously introduced. If income effects should be absent or relatively unimportant in influencing the choices between public and private goods, this model reduces to that which has just been discussed; in this case, the separate demand curves become identical. If, however, income effects are significant, this new model, which we may call the *equal-preference* model, allows these to be incorporated into the analysis.

In general terms, any conceivable values for the income elasticity coefficients for public goods can be analyzed with this model. We shall, however, limit the scope of the analysis by imposing the further restriction that these coefficients are positive. This means that the demand schedules of the three persons may be ordered by the levels of income over relevant quantity ranges. This is shown by Figure 11.4, where D_A, the demand schedule for the individual with the lowest income falls below D_B, which, in turn and for the same reason, falls below D_C.

The tax-price confronted by each of the three persons also varies with income under either proportional or progressive income taxation. In terms of an ordering, therefore, tax-prices correspond with marginal evaluation or demand so long as the income elasticity coefficient is positive. This suggests that there may exist some structure of ordered tax-prices that will generate a unique collective outcome for which the decision-rule is not influential. That is to say, for any given ordering of marginal evaluations for the public good, there should be some ordering of tax-prices that will guarantee what we may call "full neutrality." This result will satisfy the necessary conditions for Pareto-optimality, and, also, will not depend critically on the nature of the rules for the reaching of political choices. The condition that must be satisfied for "full neutrality" to be achieved is as follows: *The income elasticity of the tax-price schedule must be equal to, but opposite in sign, the income elasticity of demand for the public good divided by the relative price elasticity of demand for the public good.* When this condition holds, the decision-rule is unimportant, and the outcome generated under *any* rule is "optimal."

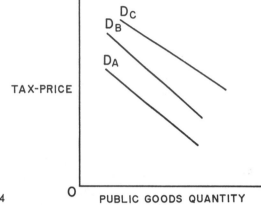

TAX-PRICE

O   PUBLIC GOODS QUANTITY

FIGURE 11.4

This principle has already been demonstrated for the case in which income elasticity of demand is zero; here the required structure of tax-prices must also have zero income elasticity. In other words, only when tax-prices are equal for all persons will the condition be met. If the income elasticity of demand for the collective good is unitary, a strictly proportional tax on income will generate neutral results *only if the price elasticity of demand for the good is also unitary.* Note that the elasticity of the tax-price schedule under proportional rates is unitary.

We are able to utilize the familiar concepts of income and price elasticity here because of our assumption that the underlying preference patterns of the separate persons are identical. This allows us to consider the shift from the choice situation of one individual to that of another at a different income level as equivalent, analytically, to a change in the income of a single person. Price elasticity of demand is normally expected to be negative; therefore, as the formula suggests, if the income elasticity of demand is positive, "full neutrality" must require that tax-price increase as income increases. Suppose, for instance, that the income of a person is increased by 10 per cent. With, say, an income elasticity of demand over this range of two, the preferred quantity of public good would increase

153

by 20 per cent. Suppose, further, that over the relevant range, price elasticity of demand is unitary. What increase in tax-price would be just sufficient to keep the individual at the same preferred quantity as before the income change? Twenty per cent is clearly the answer. Hence, if the income elasticity of the schedule of tax-prices, over this range, is also two (a progressive rate structure), a shift in his income position from the first to the second status would not influence his choices as to the most preferred quantity of public goods supply. Applying this reasoning to two persons at separate income levels rather than to one person at two separate income levels, which the equal-preference assumption allows us to do, we may say that if the tax-price schedule exhibits an elasticity of two in this case, both persons will be "satisfied" with the same public-goods quantity, which is, of course, a precondition for "full neutrality" in the sense that we have defined this latter term. If the formula is satisfied over the whole range of possible incomes, each member of the group, regardless of his income level, will "choose" the same quantity of the public good. If each person were made dictator in turn there would be no change in the amount of public good supplied as the decision-making power shifts. Given a tax system that satisfies the "full neutrality" formula, dictatorship, simple majority voting, and unanimity would guarantee the same, and Pareto-optimal, result.

What does this "full neutrality" conception suggest in regard to the actual structure of tax-prices among individuals? The relationship between income and price elasticity of demand is important in determining the rate structure that will satisfy the required condition, or, more appropriately stated for our purposes, in determining the effects of any specific rate structure that is postulated. If the income elasticity of the demand for the public good tends to be high, and positive, while the price elasticity of demand tends to be low, a progressive rate structure would be necessary to achieve the sort of neutrality noted. Or, to say the same thing somewhat differently, if these elasticity conditions prevail, a given structure of progression need not produce over-all inefficiency in the supply of public goods, and need not make the outcome so directly dependent on the political decision rule as might otherwise be the case. On the other hand, any shift downward in the income elasticity coefficient relative to that for price elasticity, tends to reduce the progressivity of the neutral tax-price schedule. And, if the income elasticity of demand should be negative, the elasticity of the tax-price schedule must also be negative to achieve neutrality. This means, of course, that persons with low incomes would in this case actually have to be charged higher tax-prices than persons with higher incomes.

Where does a "regressive" rate structure fit in this picture? By normal usage, this term characterizes systems in which the tax-price increases with income but not proportionately so. It is relatively easy to see that, for public goods possessing relatively low income elasticity coefficients, a regressive tax schedule may be necessary if neutrality is to be reached. This suggests that the whole notion of "full neutrality" be examined somewhat more carefully. Strictly speaking, the formula means only that the system is neutral with respect to the rule for making political choices. By implication, any system meeting this requirement will also be "neutral" or "efficient" in the more familiar sense that emerges from an application of the Pareto welfare criteria. Only through meeting this condition can a point on the Pareto welfare surface be attained in a Pareto-optimal manner. Note that this does not suggest that a position on the welfare surface cannot be attained nonoptimally; it may well be so attained. And, if some net redistribution is desired through the financing of the public good, the Pareto welfare surface (neglecting for now other possible violations of the necessary conditions) may be attained without satisfying the formula above, provided that the several departures from individual "optimality" are mutually canceling or offsetting. Note, however, that this nonoptimal attainment of the surface can never be inferred directly from individual choice behavior, and note, also, that in such cases, the political rule again becomes all important in determining the particular outcome that is likely to be generated. In other words, only the omniscient and benevolent despot is likely to be able to move the group to the welfare surface nonoptimally.

Our interest here is not primarily that of analyzing fiscal institutions for their effects on "efficiency" in the standard Pareto sense.[2] It is instead, that of attempting to make rudimentary predictions concerning the direction of effects on total spending for public goods that various fiscal institutions exert, via their influence on individual choice behavior. Returning to this primary emphasis,

2. For an analysis similar to that of this chapter which places somewhat more emphasis on such efficiency aspects, see my paper, "Fiscal Institutions and Efficiency in Collective Outlay," *American Economic Review*, LIV (May, 1964), 227-35; and, also, see the Appendix to this Chapter where the equal-preference model is examined in further detail.

let us remain for the time being in the equal-preference model and assume a decision rule of simple majority voting. Is it possible to make any predictions concerning the differential effects of regressive, proportional, and progressive taxation, without regard to the question as to whether or not "full neutrality" is present? Once again the critical position assumed by the median voter-taxpayer must be stressed. If any shift is symmetrical with respect to this median man, there will be no direct effect on the majority solution. The structure of tax-prices can be modified without changing the political result. So long as symmetry with respect to the position of the median man is maintained, the rate structure can be "tilted" within wide limits without affecting the quantity of public goods supplied under majority-rule institutions. If nonsymmetrical changes are made in the structure of tax-prices, the majority solution will tend to be changed and the efficiency of the system modified.

Symmetry or nonsymmetry is defined with reference to the median voter, as preferences are arrayed along some public-goods quantity scale. In the simple cases that we have to this point discussed, we have assumed that the individual evaluations are ordinally related to income, and, also, that the structure of tax-prices is ordinally related to income levels. Even within these assumptions, however, it may be possible that the median or decisive voter in a majority rule model is not the median-income recipient. To this point, we have implicitly assumed that this possibility did not exist. It should be admitted, however, that, under certain structures, the array of individuals by public-goods preferences may not correspond with their array by incomes; this should be especially noted since some of the empirical evidence to be cited suggests the presence of this pattern. In local communities that are characterized by nonprogressive tax structures, especially over the middle-upper income ranges, political coalitions may combine the upper and lower income classes in opposition to the middle-income classes. As we shall note in Chapter 13, there is considerable empirical evidence which suggests precisely this situation for American municipalities. In this case, the median voter may stand at either the lower or the upper end of the middle-income range. The analysis with respect to symmetry and nonsymmetry continues to apply, even here, although its implications with respect to actual effects of changes in rate structures cannot be so readily advanced. The situation can arise only when the "progressivity" in evaluation among persons exceeds the "progressivity" in tax-price structure.

THE RELEVANCE OF THE EQUAL-PREFERENCE MODEL

The equal-preference model is highly restrictive. Individual demands for public goods, as for private goods, differ for reasons other than differences in incomes. If this is admitted, however, are there any restrictions that can be placed on a model of behavior that will still allow conceptual predictions to be made? Here it is, I think, necessary to rise to the partial defense of the equal-preference model. When properly considered, the model is less restrictive than it at first appears. Individual tastes differ, one from the other; this may be, and must be, acknowledged. But is there a pattern to such differences or must they be assumed random? If we examine particular goods, private or public, a widely scattered pattern of demand would surely be observed. Some people just do not like garlic; others do. Similarly, for foreign aid. If, on the other hand, we examine the whole package of private goods, or the whole package of public goods, would such wide differences in tastes be observed? Differences would remain, but these may be relatively narrow, except as related to income levels. The final and critical test is provided when income effects are examined. If, for the consumption of the whole package of public goods relative to private goods, the differences in incomes among persons tends to overwhelm or to swamp the differences in tastes, the model that has been introduced here retains considerable relevance for our purposes.

If individual differences in the demand for public goods, on the average, are not related to individual differences in income or wealth, the levy of taxes on the basis of these characteristics makes little economic sense and surely leads to serious distortions in the allocation of resources. Implicit in the development of the familiar institutions of general taxation, which have used personal incomes or assets as the bases for computing individual tax liabilities, has been the assumption that all members of the group, generally, share in the common benefits of public services, and that these benefits may be, in some way, related to income-asset positions. This is not to suggest that modern tax institutions have evolved out of a "benefit principle" of taxation, as such. But even the so-called "ability-to-pay" principle carries with it some implied "willingness-to-pay" which, in turn, implies that general charges should be related to

157

income-asset levels presumably because individual demands are so ordered.

The appropriateness of any general tax principle, or the possible efficiency of any general tax institution, depends on the effective limitation of the collective sector. The services financed through tax funds must be appropriately "chargeable to the whole community," which is to say, they must provide general, nondiscriminatory benefits. If this "principle" is not followed, and the public sector is used to provide services that are designed to benefit specific subgroups in the community, the model of equal-preference is clearly inapplicable, as are general tax institutions. It would, for example, clearly be inappropriate to apply an equal-preference model when discussing the financing of irrigation projects by the United States government. And, more importantly, it is also inappropriate, on the basis of efficiency considerations, to utilize general tax institutions for the financing of such special benefit services.

IGNORANCE, UNCERTAINTY, AND ILLUSION

In this chapter individual participants have been assumed to act on the basis of complete information concerning alternatives. As earlier chapters have shown, such an assumption is untenable, and individuals must make voting choices under conditions of ignorance, uncertainty, and illusion, with these factors varying significantly from one institution to another. The effects are to make the outcomes of any political decision process less predictable for the simple reason that individual choices are less predictable.

The process of reaching agreement may actually be somewhat less costly than it would be under conditions of more information. An individual faced with genuine uncertainty as to alternative prospects may tend to agree more readily with his fellows than he would under certainty where his own interest is more sharply identified. This appears to be a positive advantage, and it suggests that fiscal institutions which embody considerable uncertainty and which create illusion possess attributes of "efficiency" that are often overlooked. This is no doubt correct, but the efficiency involved in reducing the costs of reaching agreement, under any decision rule, will tend to be offset by the greater costs, or inefficiency, in an allocative sense. Despite the fact that the individual does not know with certainty the effects of alternative outcomes, there continues to exist some "optimal" outcome, for him, if he could know what this is. And departures from this "optimal" outcome, viewed ex post, reflect allocative inefficiency. Thus, institutions that generate uncertainty in the mind of individual choosers tend, at the same time, to reduce the costs of reaching political agreement and to increase the costs of the "mistakes" made in some allocative sense. These two elements would have to be compared in each particular instance to determine the over-all effects of the separate institutions.

CONCLUSIONS

The problems that arise in the construction and use of political decision models are evident from the discussion. Despite these, the critical position assumed by the median taxpayer-voter in most of the models of majority voting allows an important step to be taken toward converting the analysis of individual choice behavior into one that retains relevance for group choice. If we can, in some fashion, locate the median voter, we are then able to predict the direction of effect that the various institutions will exert on fiscal choice through an analysis of the decision calculus of this individual. This device enables us to utilize much of the theory of individual choice behavior developed in previous chapters while crossing the bridge to collective choice.

The relevance of the whole analysis depends on the appropriateness of the simple majority-voting models as reflections of real-world political process in democratic governments. Obviously decisions on taxes and public spending are not made in glorified town meetings, even at the local government level. The critical question is whether or not the simplified town meeting can serve as a model with which we can analyze the much more complex process through which fiscal decisions get made. There is no way in which this question can be answered other than through the testing of hypotheses that emerge from the model against observed experience. The fact that, in some superficially descriptive sense, decisions do not seem to be made in this manner, tells us relatively little about the predictive power of the models.

Appendix to Chapter 11

PARETO EFFICIENCY UNDER EQUAL-PREFERENCE MODELS

In this Appendix the relationship between schedules of tax-prices and variations in individual marginal evaluations over income changes will be examined more carefully. The derivation of the formula for full neutrality presented in the text of Chapter 11 will be clarified, and some of the efficiency implications of familiar taxing institutions will be suggested. The analysis is restricted to the equal-preference model, and the framework assumptions made in the discussion of the main text continue to hold here.

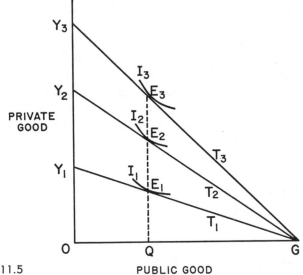

FIGURE 11.5   PUBLIC GOOD

Assume that there exists a proportional tax on income and that this is the only means used to finance a single public good. What characteristics of individual preference patterns (and, by assumption, these are the same for all individuals) would have to be present in order for full neutrality to be guaranteed? The problem is illustrated in Figure 11.5. On the ordinate are measured private goods, on the abscissa, public goods. A system of proportional income taxation is represented by the fan-like array of "budget lines" intersecting on the abscissa at G. For an individual with private goods (income) of Y_1, the "budget line" that he confronts is T_1, and the slope of this line is the tax-price that he faces in any decision as to the amount of the public good to be supplied. Similarly, the individual at income Y_2 faces the "budget line" T_2, etc.

By definition of a purely collective good, all members of the group must consume or have available the same quantity of the public good. Assume this quantity to be shown as Q in Figure 11.5. The question becomes: What characteristics of the preference map must be present to insure that Q units of public good, financed by the schedule of tax-prices indicated, satisfies the conditions required for full neutrality? The answer is now evident from the construction. The indifference curves must be tangent to the successive budget lines along the vertical drawn from Q. As an individual is moved from E_1 to E_2 to E_3, both income and tax-price increase. The increase in income tends, normally, to make him prefer a larger quantity of the public good; the increase in tax-price tends to make him prefer a smaller quantity. The necessity that the *same* Q satisfy the individual at the different income levels (or different individuals at different income levels in this model) requires that the income effect on his demand for the public good be precisely and fully offset by the price effect.

If proportional income taxation is to meet this condition, the income elasticity coefficient must be the same as the price elasticity coefficient, with reversed sign, since we know that the income elasticity of the tax-price schedule under a proportional rate structure is equal to one.

A progressive tax is illustrated in Figure 11.6. Note that, as drawn, the tax-price to the individual remains constant over the variations in the quantity of public goods; the "budget lines" remain linear. This assumption is not essential to the analysis, but is used here for convenience only.* The elasticity of the tax-price schedule under progression is greater than unity; the budget lines increase in slope more than proportionately with income increases. In this configuration, if the price effect is to be completely offset by the income effect, the income elasticity of demand must exceed the price elasticity in absolute value, the ratio being just equal to the elasticity of the tax-price schedule. This is the formula presented in the text of Chapter 11, and it retains general validity.

The analysis may be extended by constructing schedules of tax-

* For a discussion of nonlinear "budget lines" of this nature, see R. A. Musgrave, *The Theory of Public Finance* (New York: McGraw-Hill, 1959), p. 122. Note that Musgrave's figure is similar to the constructions introduced here, but that he uses this for a somewhat different purpose.

price and of marginal evaluation. In Figure 11.7, income (or private goods) is now measured along the abscissa and tax-price along the ordinate. For any specific quantity of public good, say Q, which we assume is supplied to the community at constant cost, there will be a schedule of tax-prices that will confront the individual as he moves along the income scale. Thus, under proportional taxation at, say, 10 per cent, the individual will pay a total tax-price of $100 if his income is $1000, and a total tax-price of $1000 if his income is $10,000. These totals can be translated readily into tax-prices per unit, once we know the cost per unit of the public good and the number of individuals in the community along with their appropriate income levels. If some greater Q must be supplied, the 10 per cent will have to be increased, imposing thereby a higher tax-price per unit on all members of the group.

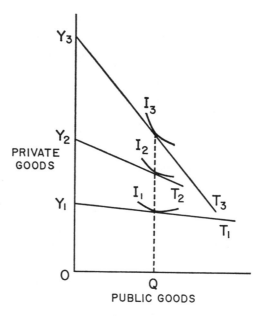

FIGURE 11.6

In Figure 11.7, the line labeled R is drawn to represent a schedule of tax-prices under proportional taxation, for a given quantity of public good. If the full neutrality position depicted in Figure 11.5 is to hold, the line, R, must also represent the schedule of marginal evaluation. This schedule or curve is derived by plotting the slopes of the successive indifference curves along the vertical

162

from Q in Figure 11.5 against income. If a progressive tax structure is to accomplish full neutrality, as in Figure 11.6, the line of marginal evaluation must lie along, and correspond with, a line of tax-price such as R' in Figure 11.7. A regressive system is depicted as R''.

The analysis remains limited, however, unless departures from full neutrality are introduced, and the construction of Figure 11.7

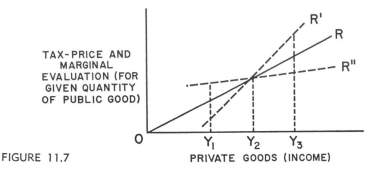

FIGURE 11.7

TAX-PRICE AND MARGINAL EVALUATION (FOR GIVEN QUANTITY OF PUBLIC GOOD)

PRIVATE GOODS (INCOME)

facilitates this extension. Assume that the marginal evaluation schedule lies along R, and that a system of proportional taxation would accomplish full neutrality. Let us examine what will happen when a decision is made to shift to a system of progressive taxation. As we have noted in connection with earlier models, it is necessary to distinguish between *symmetrical* and *nonsymmetrical* changes in the tax-price schedule with respect to the position of the median voter-taxpayer. If the change from proportion to progression is accomplished with the tax-price confronted by this median voter remaining unchanged, the total revenue collected from the group remains unchanged, and the "political equilibrium" that prevails under simple majority voting is not modified. The same quantity of the public good, Q, is supplied. The outcome remains Pareto-optimal despite the fact that the shift is not, in itself, Pareto-optimal. If we neglect the other necessary conditions (e.g., effects on the supply of effort) we can say that such a symmetrical shift from proportional to progressive taxation amounts to a movement from one point on the Pareto welfare surface to a different point, the differences being exclusively distributional. The shift is equivalent, in effect, to a set of income transfers between the rich and the poor. Therefore, if the tax-price schedule is shifted from R to R' in Figure 11.7, the supply of public goods will remain unchanged, and the excess of tax-price over marginal evaluation for the "rich" is just equal to the excess of marginal evaluation over tax-price for the "poor." There is no way that the "rich" man can overcompensate the "poor" man, or vice versa. The point may be illustrated by supposing a three-man group, one each at income levels Y_1, Y_2, and Y_3, in Figure 11.7.

A symmetrical shift to a regressive structure of tax-prices is analytically similar in all respects to a move to progression. One such shift is shown by R'' in Figure 11.7. The "poor" man is exploited under this structure, but he cannot bribe the "rich" man to change, and the position of the median man remains unaffected.

Symmetry need not characterize a change from one tax-price schedule to another. Let us now assume that for the given quantity of the public good, Q, the tax-price schedule in existence is that shown by R in Figure 11.7, and, as before, assume that this schedule guarantees full neutrality. That is to say, given cost and distributional conditions, the marginal evaluation schedule is also shown by R, for this Q. Now suppose that a change to a progressive rate structure is made, but that the change is nonsymmetrical with respect to the tax-price confronted by the median voter. In this case, the quantity, Q, will no longer remain the "equilibrium" quantity, as determined by simple majority voting.

Non-symmetrical shifts can, of course, be weighted in either of the two directions. The tax-price faced by the median voter may be increased or decreased. If it is increased, the equilibrium quantity of the public good will be reduced; if it is decreased, the equilibrium quantity will be expanded. Other things equal, therefore, a change from a system of proportional taxation to one of progression may decrease, leave unchanged, or increase the quantity of public goods that will tend to be supplied in response to the desires of majorities. The direction of effect here will depend on whether or not, relative to the marginal evaluation schedule, the rate change is symmetrical or nonsymmetrical and, if the latter, the direction of the weighting. These results can be shown readily in a table, as illustrated in Table 11.1, where a five-person group is considered. Incomes are shown in Column 2. A proportional rate structure of 10 per cent yields a total revenue of $750, and, for simplicity, assume that the public good is available to the community at a cost of one dollar, allowing a quantity of 750 units to be initially supplied. Assume further that at the tax-price of $0.20, the median man, C, is in "private" equilibrium, as indicated by his demand schedule, shown in Table 11.1

(b). Column 5 of the Table represents a symmetrical progressive structure. Columns 6 and 7, by contrast, represent nonsymmetrical progressive structures relative to the proportional structure in being at the outset. In the first, Column 6, note that the tax-price to C is reduced, and C will, therefore, desire 900 units of the public good instead of the 750 previously provided. Similarly, in the rate structure shown in Column 7, C will demand only 500 units of the public good because the tax-price that he confronts will have increased. In neither of these situations is 750 an equilibrium quantity.

TABLE 11.1 (a)

Indi- vidual	Income	Marginal Evaluation	Total Tax 10 per cent	Symmetrical Progression	Nonsymmetrical Progression	
					Right	Left
(1)	(2)	(3)	(4)	(5)	(6)	(7)
A	$1000	$100/750	$100	$ 0	$ 25	$ 0
B	1000	100/750	100	0	25	0
C	1500	150/750	150	150	100	200
D	2000	200/750	200	300	300	275
E	2000	200/750	200	300	300	275
			750(750)	750(750)	750(900)	750(500)

(b) Demand Schedule of Individual C for Public Good

Tax-Price	Quantity
200/750	500
150/750	750
100/750	900

These results can be depicted geometrically in Figure 11.8. Assume that the marginal evaluation schedule exhibits unitary income elasticity, as before, and that it is shown by R. In a new political equilibrium reached under majority voting, the position of the median voter, with income Y_2, will be more favorable than under proportional taxation if the non-symmetrical shift is weighted to the right. In the construction, if the new tax schedule is that shown by R', the median voter pays less than the average amount of tax; his tax-price is lower than under proportion, and the equilibrium quantity of the public good is increased. The result is nonoptimal in the Pareto sense. The "rich" man can now afford to bribe the "poor" man into modifying his vote, were such bribery possible, something which he could not do under symmetrical progression. He can do so because the excess tax that he now pays is greater than the excess benefit, at the margin, that the "poor" man receives. Thus, in shifting from proportion to progression nonsymmetrically, the supply of public goods has been shifted, and a position off the welfare surface is the result.

If progression is introduced nonsymmetrically, but is weighted to the left, the opposite results hold. The median man now faces a higher tax-price than under proportion, and he will exercise his influence on majority outcome through demanding fewer public goods. The situation, after the new equilibrium is established, is shown by the configuration, R", in Figure 11.8.

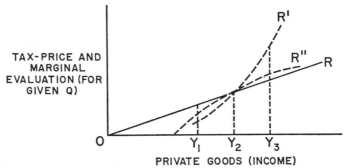

FIGURE 11.8

The same analysis that has been applied to the introduction of a progressive rate structure could be applied to the introduction of a regressive structure. This extension will not be carried out here. The analysis can, of course, be applied to any conceivable configuration of tax-price and marginal evaluation schedules.

To what extent is the analysis useful in helping to answer real, rather than hypothetical, questions? Although, once again, heroic assumptions are required, plausible predictions can be made. It seems that the income elasticity of demand for public goods is positive and probably not greatly different from unity in value. For purposes of analysis, we can also assume that the price elasticity is unitary. In this case, strict satisfaction of the conditions for full neutrality requires a system of proportional taxation. If the effective structure of tax-prices is also roughly proportional, when all tax institutions are considered jointly, we can conclude, with some degree of accuracy, that majority voting rules probably generate roughly an "optimal" outlay on public goods, provided these goods include only those that are genuinely collective in the general sense. If, on the other hand, the effective structure of tax-prices is observed to be sharply progressive, and, also, if the median voter is observed to receive less than the average income, and to pay less than the average amount of tax, the situation becomes comparable to that noted with curve R′ in Figure 11.8. The result is probably nonoptimal because, relatively, the quantity of public goods is in excess of that which is "efficient" in the Pareto sense. By contrast, if the effective structure of tax-prices, under the same assumed conditions of income and price elasticities, should be regressive, the situation is nonoptimal due to an undersupply of public goods. Empirical research into several aspects of these relationships can, of course, establish better grounds for making over-all judgments.

The elasticity assumptions can, of course, be questioned, along with parts of the model, and changes in these will lead to different general predictions. Recall, also, that the whole analysis has been based on the equal-preference model. This need not be so restrictive as it appears, however, when real-world predictions are attempted. The empirical data that may be secured on the marginal evaluation of public goods will be drawn from cross-section statistical surveys. At best, some composite preference map, typical of or approximating that for the "average" or representative taxpayer-voter, may be derived. To this sort of data, the equal-preference model can be appended without difficulty.

Observation of political experience can yield helpful suggestions as to the direction of divergence between schedules of tax-price and of marginal evaluation. If there seems to be no observable relationship between income levels and the reactions of individual citizens to proposed extensions in public spending programs, there may be little divergence here, and full neutrality may be closely approximated. If, on the other hand, the "poor" are observed, generally, to approve extensions in spending, while the "rich," generally, oppose them, the direction of "tilt" between marginal evaluation and the tax-price schedule is suggested, or vice versa in the opposing case. One extremely interesting case, which is suggested to be relevant by some of the empirical work that will be reported in Chapter 13, involves the "poor" and the "rich" combining forces to approve extensions in public spending programs over the opposition of the "middle" income groups. This can be "explained" by the models developed here in plausible fashion. If the elasticity of the marginal evaluation schedule is unitary, as shown in Figure 11.9 by R, and the tax-price schedule takes the form of the curve shown by R' in the same figure, this political result will follow. Note that this seems a possible shape for the tax-price schedule in municipalities

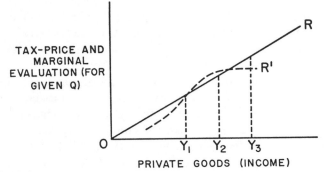

FIGURE 11.9

where the lowest income groups largely escape tax, and where the bulk of the revenues are collected from general property taxes. Note that, in the configuration of Figure 11.9, the man with income Y_1, not Y_2, is the median voter, since preferences for the public good are not arrayed in the same ordering as incomes. Other "explanations" for such results are also possible, of course, but the fact that the tools developed here can be extended to cover such results is perhaps indicative of their power on the one hand and their limitations on the other.

12. *From Theory to the Real World*

INTRODUCTION

The scientist, whatever his subject, works with models. He simplifies, he abstracts, he deliberately leaves out of account elements that serve to complicate his analysis. To an extent his very success is determined by the elegance of his refinements. In the process, however, care must be taken lest the vital explanatory factors be discarded, lest the model become so abstract, so general, that it ceases to have the basic discrimination that is required if it is to retain relevance for real-world application.

The social scientist, who seeks to explain social institutions and human behavior under such institutions, faces problems of particular difficulty. The unit subject of his analysis is the individual person, an active decision-making being, not an automaton. To the extent that man can choose, and does choose, the scientist cannot predict or explain his behavior accurately. Add to this complication the almost open set of possible influences on behavior, and attempts to make predictions with even modest success become formidable enterprises.

The economist, among social scientists, occupies a favored place, although surely his is precarious enough. Man's behavior in the market place, as a buyer or seller of goods and services, is somewhat more predictable and hence somewhat more amenable to scientific analysis than is his behavior in many other capacities. To the extent that individuals behave "economically," economic theory is an exact science, and conceptually refutable hypotheses may be developed. Imposing operational content on the science is a more complicated task, since there is no way of knowing to what degree individuals do behave "economically," even in their most restricted

169

market activities. Nevertheless, as experience has shown, the economic motivation has proved sufficiently dominant in many cases to allow hypotheses to be tested against actual observations of behavior.

INDIVIDUAL BEHAVIOR IN POLITICS

Man behaves, man chooses, in many other capacities than that of simple buyer and seller in the market place. Man behaves politically. He votes when given the opportunity, or chooses to abstain from voting. He joins pressure groups. He makes campaign contributions. He runs for office. He writes letters. Can this behavior be subjected to scientific analysis?

It is perhaps not surprising that "political science" is not on all fours with "economic science" in explanatory potential, and that the implications of "voter sovereignty" have not been worked out in theoretical models comparable in sophistication with those of the economists which incorporate "consumer sovereignty." When we refer, in everyday language, to *economic* behavior we have a common reference point. And to say that an individual behaves *economically* we really mean that, when confronted with a relevant choice, he chooses "more" over "less" in terms that are measurable by some outside observer, say, income wealth, or another objectively measurable variable. By contrast, what would it mean to say that an individual behaves "politically"? There are many answers or interpretations, and it becomes difficult to construct analytical models for precisely this reason. So many elements influence or may influence behavior in political choice that abstraction seems impossible, and the would-be scientist feels himself lost in a complex world of description, empiricism, and history. No genuine theory exists, and prediction, or even elementary understanding, seems beyond his capabilities.[1]

We know, however, that some analysis about political behavior can be helpful in our understanding of social institutions. The scientist who does not initially despair may go part of the way toward

1. In such situations, the need for "theorizing" becomes all the more important.

"We are putting the cart before the horse when we think that a science of politics must be different from other sciences because political behavior is random and haphazard. It is not because political behavior is random and haphazard that we do not have much objective knowledge about it. It is because we do not have much objective knowledge about it that it seems random and haphazard" Charles Frankel, *The Case for Modern Man* (New York: Harper & Bros., 1956), p. 132.

explanation, even if he recognizes that he must stop short of the rather unenviable position attained by the economist. Man's behavior in politics can be explained and predicted, within limits, even if these are more restrictive than those found to be necessary with respect to the explanation of behavior in the market place.

As a preliminary stage, it is useful to stretch the economist's model to political choice and to see how much of an explanation is forthcoming. It is obvious that there is some explanatory value here since man behaves to some extent economically even when he steps outside the market and enters the polling booth. He continues to confront alternatives that may be reduced to economically measurable criteria, and his behavior in choosing among these alternatives can be tested against the simple propositions of elementary economics. Casual empiricism alone suggests that the validity of an economic model of individual behavior in politics extends over wide areas of real-world choice. It is the California congressman who pushes for federal outlay on irrigation; it is the urban congressman who supports urban renewal programs; it was the Boeing-area senator who grumbled about the TFX; it was on the slogan that he could get more defense plants for Massachusetts that Teddy Kennedy was elected.

THE ECONOMICS OF POLITICS

As a larger share of the resources of the total economy come to be allocated through public or collective decisions, the relevance of this extension of economic analysis to political choice-making is increased. In one sense the fiscal mechanism,· the institutions of government finance, are the economic elements of the whole political process. Man chooses politically; the results of his decisions may be translated in several different dimensions, but one of the most important is surely that which is measured in the dollars and cents of tax costs on the one side and the dollars and cents of conceptually measurable benefit values on the other. The political decision, no less than any other, can be discussed sensibly in cost and benefit language, and benefits and costs can be measured to some reasonable degree of accuracy. Public finance, as a branch of scholarship, as a science, on the borderline between economics proper and political science is the *economics of politics*.

The institutions of government finance are economic as well as political ones, and their impact on the individual citizen and his

171

behavior in response to this impact can be described and analyzed economically. This has, of course, long been acknowledged; public finance has been a subdiscipline of economics. As noted, however, the impact of fiscal institutions has been almost exclusively examined with reference to the individual's response in the market place, the peculiar domain of the economist's competence. The individual's response and reaction in the political choice process has been largely neglected. This explains why the preceding chapters seem to be devoted to topics foreign to the professional research of the field.

WHAT IS INDIVIDUAL BEHAVIOR IN POLITICS?

Does it follow that because fiscal institutions affect individual behavior in market choice they necessarily must affect such behavior in political choice? If, for example, it is meaningful to examine the effects of the progressive income tax on the work-leisure choices of the individual, is it necessarily also meaningful to examine the effects of this same institution on the individual's choice concerning the public sector—private sector mix? The second of these introduces *individual behavior in political choice* explicitly, and even to look at this we require a setting for analysis, a model, that is not needed in the first, or orthodox, approach. It is essential to specify just what this behavior is. What do we mean by the terms? What is individual behavior in politics?

We have sidestepped this issue in earlier chapters by employing oversimplified models of political process. If we are to justify the relevance of such models, we must relate them to the real world in which the individual lives, responds, and ultimately chooses. To this point, in analyzing fiscal institutions we have assumed that the individual citizen participates more or less directly in voting choices on public spending programs and that final decisions are reached on the basis of very simple decision rules such as majority voting. The analysis was designed to enable a few broad and general predictions to be made about the way in which the fiscal institutions might influence an individual's vote or potential vote on alternative spending programs.

To the realist, who looks at the world of politics as it exists, the whole analysis may appear as wasted effort, as the dreamspun stuff of an armchair romanticist, who talks about direct democracy and whose models imply continuous referenda on all choices by a well informed electorate. If the analysis is to retain validity for either scientific explanation or, ultimately, for the development of norms for improvements in the fiscal structure, it must be defended against such charges.

We begin from the simple fact that political decisions do get made. Somehow, someway, somebody decides how much money shall be spent publicly, how this shall be distributed among various items of outlay, and what tax institutions shall be employed to collect it. The task of the scientist is to explain such decisions and to construct if possible analytical models that will enable predictions about the shapes of such decisions under varying circumstances.

WHO CHOOSES FOR THE COLLECTIVITY?

Before explanation and analysis can begin, the decision unit must be identified. Who makes political decisions? Who chooses *for* the group? What does "democracy" mean in terms of individual citizen participation? How much control over decisions or outcomes do individual citizens possess? How much "should" they exert? How much control is required for a political order to be classified as "effectively democratic"? These questions have not been sufficiently discussed and even less have they been appropriately answered. But answer them we must if sense is to be made out of the fiscal decision process, regardless of who exercises final control.

Implicitly analysts have often assumed that political decisions are taken by some central decision-making entity that is effectively divorced from individual citizens. This model has been in the background of much of the scientific discussion of economic policy and especially of fiscal reform. Along with the origin of the subject, this model grew out of the political reality of centuries past, when despots did exercise choice for the collectivity of persons over whom they reigned. In a certain respect, it is intellectually notorious that the same political model should have held its dominance throughout the epochs of revolution and change to presumably democratic structures. (Indeed it would be an irony of history if such models come again to have relevance when political structures again become effectively despotic.) Despite the warnings of Knut Wicksell and a few others, economists and political scientists alike have carried on their work *as if* the despot still reigns supreme, *as if* a single decision-making entity makes political choices for the whole collectivity, *as if* these choices are not really influenced by citizens.

Critical observation should prompt either one of two separate responses here. Observing political reality as it exists, the scientist may, as Pareto did, say that all of the discussion about democratic process is fictional, that in any social order there exists a central minority that "rules," which makes political decisions for the larger group of which it is only a part. Alongside this ruling class, there also exists a larger group of persons which is ruled, dominated by the ruling group, and which possesses power over political decisions only to the extent that reaction and response to imposed conditions generates feedback effects to the calculus of the decision makers. If such a ruling class model does emerge from a critical study of political reality, the consistent application of such a model should clear away much of the confusion about democratic process. It would then allow the analyst to get along with his work of developing models of behavior, in this case limited to that of the ruling class, which he could presumably identify. Only the reaction mechanism of the dominated classes need be subjected to analysis.

Alternatively, the appraisal of political reality in modern Western collectivities might reveal processes that Pareto did not see, processes through which the citizens of the collective group effectively participate in the formation of group decisions. In this model, choices made *for* the people are also made *by* the people. There are no first-class citizens; there are no readily identifiable members of the political group who are, somehow, destined to be the philosopher-kings, who are especially selected to make decisions for the larger group of which they form a part. There is no ruling class ruling over the ruled. And, in some ultimate sense, each citizen possesses roughly equal power to influence the outcomes of the political process, in general and in detail.

The hardheaded realist will probably conclude that there is something to be said for both models here; in any time and place, in any given political order, there are surely elements of a ruling-class that are operative. But, also, there are surely elements of democratic process, of citizen control, in almost any political order. Different orders can be arrayed and discussed in terms of their correspondence with each of the two contrasting models. And any particular order can be analyzed to an extent under either of the two models. Consistency in analysis requires, however, that the models be treated as separate, and alternative, explanatory devices. If the analyst chooses to work within the confines of the democratic model, he must commence at the level of the individual citizen-voter, and he is obligated to explain how the choices of this citizen-voter are translated into collective decisions.

THE FOUNDATIONS OF A THEORY OF DEMOCRATIC FISCAL CHOICE

We have emphasized that this study is limited to the individualist-democratic model of political order. The analysis of fiscal institutions must, therefore, begin with the choices made by the individual participant in collective fiscal decisions. It is important once again to stress that the foundations of a theory of individual fiscal choice in this respect do not exist. Any work here must commence with such foundations and build gradually toward what will hopefully become a comprehensive structure. The methodology of this book embodies as its central proposition the hypothesis that *individuals make fiscal choices*. They do determine the size of the public sector, along with the distribution of the costs and benefits. This being the case, it follows that their choices may be influenced by the institutions through which the fiscal process takes form. People will tend to respond differently under different institutions, and it is this set of responses that this book explores.

We know that individuals do not make their decisions under nearly so simple conditions as the various models of direct democracy might suggest. The effects of individual choices on the collective outcomes finally produced seem to be exercised in a much more indirect and roundabout fashion, and, for these reasons, the whole process seems much less amenable to analysis than the simple models suggest. These represent attempts to abstract from the indirectness and to look at human behavior in an idealized structure. As such, the method employed is not different from that used in any theory. Because the approach is a novel one, however, it is useful to try to relate these models to the behavior of individuals as they seem actually to behave in confrontation of the institutions of the real fiscal world.

Consider now the position of a single person who is not a political office holder. He earns an income in the privately organized economy. He owns assets of various types under property laws applying in his political jurisdiction. He spends his income, or a portion of it, on various goods and services that are available for private purchase in organized markets. He also pays taxes to one or more governmental units, and these taxes may be imposed on him in one or more specific ways; that is, through one or more fiscal institutions. He

175

receives benefits from public or collective services made available to him and his fellow citizens by one or more governmental units, and these benefits may be more or less specific, and these may be received from one or many public spending programs.

This reference individual is not faced with a day-to-day recurring decision as to his "fiscal purchases." Indeed, for most purposes, he probably considers the whole tax-expenditure process to be wholly outside his own network of choice; that is, as something that he cannot, privately or individualistically, modify. Saying this, however, is not equivalent to saying that the individual in an effective democratic structure will act in the same way that he would act should the fiscal institutions be imposed upon him by a ruling despot or ruling class. Potentially, the individual knows that he may, along with a sufficient number of his fellows, change the collective results embodied in the levels of taxes and expenditures, and, if required, the institutions through which these results are attained. The distinguishing difference between the attitude of the individual in effectively democratic and effectively nondemocratic structures lies in power of potential choice that he possesses. In the former, the individual remains, at all times, a potential participant, whether or not he actually participates.

The elected office holder, either in an executive or a legislative position, also recognizes the potential choice that resides finally in the citizens. And in his representative function, he selects specific fiscal outcomes that he predicts will "satisfy" a sufficient number of citizens. To the extent that he does so correctly, he can retain his own position. To the extent that he fails to do so, he will be replaced by another who more closely reflects citizen attitudes and choices. The political leader may, of course, modify citizen "wants" by persuasion, just as the seller of products in ordinary markets does. But, as in the latter case, the power to modify permanently the choice patterns of individuals seems to be narrowly circumscribed.

Indirectly, therefore, political decisions are made by individual citizens. If this is accepted as the basis for analysis, then we are quite justified in examining the impact of the various fiscal institutions on these decisions, and we are authorized to do so in terms of the most simple analytical models that are possible. If, when all is said and done, we accept the fact that individual members of the political community must themselves determine the rate of increase

176

in public relative to private spending over time, then we are surely justified in trying to predict how their attitudes toward this decision may be influenced by, say, the institution of the public debt, even if, in any descriptive real-world context, legislative bodies seem to make final budgetary choices.

THE CONSTRUCTION OF HYPOTHESES

Ultimately, the models of political choice-making depend for their validity on the predictions that they enable us to make, upon the explanations of political results that they provide. To what extent can refutable hypotheses be formulated, and to what extent can empirical testing of these hypotheses be performed?

Two separate steps are involved here, and these must be carefully distinguished because, as we shall show, the second step is considerably more difficult than the first. It is possible that conceptually refutable hypotheses can be developed which will add to our explanation of political process without the corresponding empirical testing, which simply may not be possible in many circumstances.

This point may be demonstrated with reference to a single example. Consider the predicted effects of fiscal earmarking, the analysis that was contained in Chapter 6. There it was suggested that total spending tends to be greater under general-fund financing than under earmarking when budgetary ratios favor public services that are characterized by relatively elastic demand. This is obviously an hypothesis that is conceptually refutable. However, the actual testing of this hypothesis empirically may prove to be extremely difficult, if not wholly impossible. In the first place, the predicted response occurs only when all of the conditions postulated in the particular model hold. In the model, we assumed a constant per-unit tax price, that is reasonably certain to the chooser. Previous analysis revealed, however, that the ordinary institutions of taxation necessarily embody considerable uncertainty as to the level of tax-prices. At the outset of an attempt to test the earmarking hypothesis, therefore, we are thrown into predicting the behavior of the individual under uncertainty. This alone makes corroboration more difficult and narrows the range of significant results.

Secondly, even if we leave this difficulty aside, the predictive hypothesis holds for only the one individual whose calculus is analyzed in the one-man model. More accurately, the hypothesis concerns only the direction of the individual's vote in public choice processes.

177

But even in the most simple of the direct democracy models, there is no one-to-one correspondence between individual choice and collective results, unless, of course, all individuals are identical. Collective results emerge from the whole set of individual choices, as these are combined by a set of decision rules. These rules are extremely intricate in the complex world of modern democratic process. We are, in essence, forced to fall back on the notion that the model of individual behavior is somehow "representative," in the Marshallian sense, so that its conclusions are relevant for the group as a whole. Beyond all this, the particular hypothesis depends on the demand elasticities for the various public services having been independently measured and made known to the observer. And, since these elasticities vary with tax-prices, the structure of discrimination in tax-prices among separate individuals can modify the outcomes dramatically.

The difficulties of testing the hypotheses, considered in their totality, are indeed immense; this much must be acknowledged. Their immensity should never be minimized, but neither should it be overstressed. Many of the same problems are encountered in any economic research. Most of the refutable hypotheses of positive economics hold only under the familiar "other things equal" assumptions, and other things are seldom equal. Nevertheless, within limits certain of the fundamental propositions of economic theory can be empirically tested.

The task confronting the tester of hypotheses in "positive politics" is considerably more difficult than that facing the positive economist for one simple reason so far not mentioned. Economic theory develops hypotheses about individual behavior in markets where, presumably, each individual acts on his own. The hypotheses may, therefore, be tested with reference to numerous individual experiments. With behavior in political process, the results are far more scanty for the reason that outcomes must apply simultaneously to *all* individuals in a political group. Private or individualized "decisions" or "preferences" are not directly observable in political outcomes, although here, as some of the research reported in the following chapter suggests, some indication of these can be secured by various interview and questionnaire methods.

For the reasons noted, empirical testing of the basic hypotheses is rarely possible in any pure sense. Despite this, in some perhaps rough and ready manner, we can apply the theory of fiscal institutions in "explaining" certain facts from the real world. Once again, refer to the earmarking hypothesis discussed in Chapter 6. Before the development of the analytical model, Julius Margolis had presented the evidence for the interesting relationship between outlay for public education and the form of the political institutions under which this service is financed. He observed that communities which finance public schools from general funds tend to spend more on this service than communities which finance schools through independent school districts.[2]

It is reasonable to claim that the hypothesis developed in Chapter 6 "explains" these observed results, even if we possess no independent measure for the relative elasticity of demand for educational services at prevailing tax structures in American local communities. It seems reasonable to assume that, relative to other general public services at the local level, the elasticity coefficient for education tends to be high. If such plausible generalization can be accepted, then certain facts of the real world can be interpreted as corroborating hypotheses.

In the analysis of earmarking, several secondary or subsidiary hypotheses were advanced. By and large, it was suggested that organized taxpayer groups, as such, should be more favorable to earmarking devices than remaining groups in the community. Similarly, it was suggested that public officials, the bureaucracy, should tend to favor general-fund financing and to oppose earmarking schemes. These are clearly hypotheses that are empirically testable, and which would, if corroborated, tend to support the central hypothesis of the model. Such subsidiary hypotheses should be tested, even if, in some cases, the effort might seem to represent "proving that water runs down hill." Indeed, several of the hypotheses developed in preceding chapters from complex analytical models may be tested rather directly by appeal to ordinary common sense.

For example, Chapter 5 was devoted to an analysis of the principle that "an old tax is a good tax," and the specific hypothesis that emerged was that spending programs would be accepted more readily if financing is available from existing sources than if such financing requires the levy of "new" taxes. This hypothesis seems demonstrably to be valid, and its corroboration requires no special-

2. See Julius Margolis, "Metropolitan Finance Problems: Territories, Functions, and Growth," in *Public Finances: Needs, Sources, and Utilization* (National Bureau of Economic Research, 1961), especially pages 261-66.

ized research. A mere reading of the daily newspaper reports on congressional deliberations is sufficient here. Other hypotheses might be checked similarly against the facts of everyday political experience.

This should not be taken to imply that sophisticated empirical testing conducted in accordance with the strictest rules of procedure is not to be encouraged. The point is rather that where such testing is not possible, the analyst need not despair. Social science can always be made more tractable by a generous dosage of good judgment and common sense.

13. *Some Preliminary Research Results*

INTRODUCTION

Little is known about individual actions and attitudes in collective, and specifically fiscal, choice. Scholars have simply not been interested in the behavior of individuals as political decision-makers. Once a democratic model for the political order is accepted, however, the gaps in our knowledge become apparent, and the need for many man-years of research is evident. Once we acknowledge that individuals as voters, or potential voters, in a broadly democratic political order ultimately determine the size of the public economy along with its composition, we are obligated to try to find out as much as we can about their choices.

Very little research has been done; what has been done is widely scattered; much of this remains incomplete, and the questions asked have been the wrong ones. Despite all this it may be helpful to report provisionally on what has been accomplished; this will in itself point up the need for further effort rather than indicate definitive conclusions.

INFORMATION AND IGNORANCE: THE MARKET ANALOGUE

Several preliminary steps must be taken before systematic attempts can be made to formulate testable hypotheses. In this respect, the earmarking analysis used as our reference example in the preceding chapter is not characteristic. Elemental gaps in our knowledge must be filled in before anything like a sophisticated set of hypotheses about fiscal behavior can be developed.

The first thing that we need to know is the amount or degree of information possessed by individual citizens when they make actual or potential fiscal choices. How much do individuals know about the fiscal institutions under which they live? Earlier we have utilized individual behavior in ordinary market choice as a sort of benchmark with which comparisons of behavior in nonmarket choice can be made. It will be useful to follow the same procedure with respect to the information content of choice situations. Traditionally, economists have assumed that choosers in the market possess substantially full information about the alternatives that they confront. Only within the last decade has the whole set of problems summarized in the term, "theory of information," come to be examined thoroughly.[1]

It is widely recognized that even for day-to-day market choices the individual may not be in command of anything approaching complete knowledge about the alternatives that he faces. There are several reasons for this ignorance. First of all, given the fact that securing information is costly, the optimal degree of investment in search may produce results that fall far short of genuine omniscience. Secondly, choices may be such that uncertainty cannot be eliminated even under maximum investment in information gathering. Thirdly, the individual may operate under an illusion that he is more informed than he actually is; he may be ignorant but not aware that he is. It becomes difficult, if not wholly impossible, for the external observer of individual choice behavior to make distinctions between these several situations. In any one of them, the rationally motivated behavior of the individual may produce results that are not desired or intended.

When we look at the individual's behavior in fiscal-collective choice, all of the problems of information emerge with renewed force. We know that the average person possesses far less information about the costs and benefits of public goods and services than he does about the costs and benefits of private or market goods and services. But just how ignorant is the average voter-taxpayer-beneficiary about the fiscal alternatives that he confronts? How much does he really know about the impact upon him exerted by the various fiscal institutions, existing or potential? How much is he obligated to pay in taxes? What are the costs of the public services that he enjoys? How much value does he place on the benefits from

1. See, for example, the important paper by George Stigler, "The Economics of Information," *Journal of Political Economy*, LXIX (June, 1961), 213-25.

these services? Does he make any effective translation of benefits into tax-costs?

To raise such questions as these suggests the paucity of research that has been aimed at answering them empirically. Consider the most direct question of the group: How aware is the individual of the amount of taxes that he pays? How much do public services cost him, computed in dollars of tax liability? Even this elemental question must be factored down into several subsidiary ones before is can be partially answered. The degree of information possessed by the individual will vary with the tax institutions under which he pays. Earlier chapters have demonstrated that the tax awareness should be greater under direct than under indirect taxes. A logical starting point for research might be, therefore, the individual's estimation of personal tax liability under the most widely employed and most important direct tax, that on personal incomes.

ESTIMATED LIABILITY UNDER THE FEDERAL INCOME TAX

Enrick Studies. This was the purpose of the studies carried out by Norbert Enrick of the University of Virginia in 1961, 1962, and 1963. This research involved interviews and questionnaires circulated in the Charlottesville-Waynesboro, Virginia, area in 1961 and 1962, followed up by nationally-circulated questionnaires in 1963. In each case, samples were drawn by accepted randomizing procedures.

Enrick asked two simple questions of each person. First, the individual was asked to *guess* the total amount of federal income tax that he had paid in the preceding year. Secondly, he was asked to look at his personal records and to find out how much he *actually* paid for that same year. Questioning was conducted in the last half of the calendar years so as to examine tax awareness at some time other than the springtime settling period.

The results of Enrick's study were not surprising. Even under the individual income tax, people are not well informed concerning their own personal liabilities. Only slightly more than one-half of the respondents (55 per cent) were able to estimate their own tax liability within plus or minus limits of 10 per cent. More than one-fourth of the respondents erred in estimating their liability by more than 20 per cent. Over-all, there was some slight tendency for the respondents in Enrick's sample to underestimate their tax liabilities, although this finding was not a dominant one. The samples were drawn from all income levels, but there was no demonstrable relationship between the percentage error of tax estimation and the level of income of the respondent. This provisional finding was, itself, of some importance since it tends to refute the hypothesis that withholding, as an institution, makes people less conscious of the taxes that they pay. Corroboration of this hypothesis would have required that high-income receivers (who have a smaller share of total tax liability withheld) demonstrate more accurate estimates.[2]

Estimated Liability Under Withholding: The Wagstaff Study. To some extent at least, the personal income tax was converted into an "unconscious" tax for many taxpayers through the inauguration of withholding provisions in 1943. It seems plausible to suggest that this institution, in and of itself, affects the tax awareness of the individual, despite the fact that this suggestion was not corroborated by Enrick's limited survey.

To ascertain more specifically liability awareness under withholding was the purpose of a second University of Virginia study completed by J. V. Wagstaff in 1963, some months prior to the tax legislation of 1964. Wagstaff surveyed more than a thousand taxpayers whose income was subject to withholding. He asked each of them to estimate both his gross income per pay period, before any deductions, and the amount of tax withheld from this income per pay period. This information on taxpayers' estimates was then compared directly with payroll and withholding records made available to Wagstaff by employing firms.

As in the comparable Enrick study, Wagstaff found that individuals are not well informed as to their income-tax liabilities. In this case, some 52 per cent of the respondents were able to estimate tax liability within an error range of plus or minus 10 per cent, thus confirming the general validity of Enrick's similar result. Some 30 per cent erred in their estimates by more than 20 per cent, plus or minus. As with the Enrick study, there was no dominant tendency for either overestimation or underestimation by the group taken as a whole, although here, in contrast with Enrick's results, there was a slight indication of overestimation. Wagstaff produced more interesting results when he broke his respondents down by income groups. He found that, as a subgroup, respondents with incomes

2. The results of Norbert L. Enrick's studies are reported in Enrick, "A Pilot Study of Income Tax Consciousness," *National Tax Journal*, XVI (June, 1963), 169-73, and in "A Further Study of Income Tax Consciousness" *National Tax Journal*, XVII (September, 1964), 319-21.

lower than the median for his whole sample tended to overestimate the amount of taxes paid. By contrast, the above-median income subgroup tended to underestimate the amount of tax. Both of these findings were significant statistically.

An additional feature of Wagstaff's study that is highly interesting concerns the relationship between attitudes toward tax fairness or equity and tax consciousness. As a preliminary question, Wagstaff asked all respondents whether or not they considered the personal income tax to be "fair." He then isolated those respondents who held the tax "fair" from those who claimed it to be "unfair." He found that there was a surprisingly accurate estimation of tax liability among individuals in the group who considered the income tax to be "fair." By contrast, individuals who responded that the tax was "unfair" tended to have a significantly wide margin of error between estimated and actual tax liabilities.[3]

Since the Enrick and Wagstaff studies are not comparable in any direct sense, no definitive conclusions as to the differential influence of the institution of withholding on tax awareness seem warranted. Since the errors in estimation were somewhat greater in Wagstaff's survey, some corroboration of the "unconscious tax" hypothesis is suggested. But additional comparative data on tax awareness of persons not subjected to withholding is required before any conclusions here can be definitely established. Wagstaff's data need to be compared with closely comparable data for persons whose income is not subject to withholding; in this way, a reasonably clear testing of the "unconscious tax" hypothesis would be possible.

Schmölders' survey. One of the most persistent workers in the whole area of fiscal consciousness for many years has been Professor Günter Schmölders of the University of Cologne, Germany. Schmölders' primary concern is simply that of learning more about how individual citizens think about the fisc, and he has explicitly called for a new branch of public finance, which he calls "fiscal psychology."[4] His research, for the most part, has been directed toward ascertaining taxpayer attitudes. We shall refer to this at

3. Wagstaff's study was completed in the form of an unpublished dissertation at the University of Virginia (as was Enrick's initial study). See J. V. Wagstaff, "Tax Consciousness Under Withholding," on file at the Alderman Library, University of Virginia. The results are summarized in J. V. Wagstaff, "Income Tax Consciousness Under Withholding," *Southern Economic Journal,* XXXII (July, 1965), 73-80.

4. G. Schmölders, "Fiscal Psychology: A New Branch of Public Finance," *National Tax Journal,* XII (December, 1959), 340-45.

several points later in this chapter, but at this point one of Schmölders' surveys may be mentioned in connection with estimation of liability under personal income taxes.

Schmölders asked his respondents what percentage of their gross income they thought they paid in income tax, and then he compared these results with external estimates for the appropriate percentages actually paid. These external estimates were based on general rates assigned on the grounds of occupational category and income class. As in all of the studies of this type, Schmölders found that taxpayers were not well informed. In addition, his results indicated that individuals, on the average, tended to overestimate their liabilities under the tax.[5]

Awareness of high-income taxpayers of marginal rates. A recent Michigan study attempted to ascertain whether or not high-income taxpayers were aware of the marginal rates of personal income tax. The major finding was that almost one-third of the respondents (27 to 31 per cent), all with annual incomes in excess of $10,000, were unaware of the marginal rate of tax which they paid.[6]

On the basis of the limited studies that have been completed, the only conclusion that seems possible concerns the limited extent to which individuals are informed, even about their own liabilities under the personal income tax, surely the one tax in the structure upon which we should expect a relatively high degree of accuracy.

TAX AWARENESS UNDER INDIRECT TAXATION

We know that individuals are likely to be less informed about the costs that indirect taxes impose on them than they are about the costs of direct taxes. Our knowledge concerning the magnitude of their ignorance and the direction of their errors in estimation is even more limited than that relevant to direct taxation. Schmölders

5. Schmölders' survey was conducted in 1958, and it involved interviews with 1986 persons, selected on a quota sampling basis. The particular question reported here is only one of a large set asked of respondents. For a report on the project, see Günter Schmölders, *Das Irrationale in der öffentlichen Finanzwirtschaft* (Hamburg: Rowohlt, 1960), with special reference to the part mentioned on pages 84-86. The methods and procedures of the survey, along with more extensive results are reported in, *Steuern und Staatsausgaben in der öffentlichen Meinung der Bundesrepublik* (Kohn: Westdeutscher Verlag, 1960).

6. These results are reported in: Bruce L. Gensemer, Jane A. Lean, and William B. Neenan, "Awareness of Marginal Income Tax Rates Among High-Income Taxpayers," *National Tax Journal*, XVIII (September, 1965), 258-67.

found that, in many cases, taxpayers are not able to distinguish between commodities and services that are subjected to specific excise taxes and those that are not. For the most part, individuals are aware that taxes are important components in the final prices of the standard sumptuary goods, such as liquor or tobacco. However, for remaining nontaxed "luxury" goods included in the questionnaire from one-third to one-half of the respondents believed that a tax existed when it did not.[7] The ignorance as to rates of tax was even more serious. For the cigarette tax, only 14 per cent of the respondents were accurate within a 10 per cent rate range. Approximately equal numbers of respondents estimated the tax to be higher and lower than it actually was. With the tax on sugar, an even smaller per cent made accurate estimates as to rate, and, this rate being considerably lower, there was a general tendency toward overestimation.

Schmölders also asked the question: How much additional income do you think you would get if all excise taxes should be removed? Including the turnover tax, the appropriately computed answer was estimated at some 10 per cent of family income on the average. His findings were that lower income families tended consistently to overestimate the weight of the taxes, while upper income families tended to underestimate them. This finding is consistent with that of Wagstaff, reported earlier, with respect to the personal income tax.

In 1954, Robert Ferber attempted to determine the awareness of American consumers of the excise-tax reductions introduced earlier in that year. He found that not more than 30 per cent of the respondents were aware of the tax reductions in any case, and, for some goods, this figure was as low as 16 per cent. Consistent with Schmölders' results, Ferber found that a significant share of respondents could not distinguish taxed and nontaxed products.[8]

It is clear that much more research is required before we can really know much at all about individual information on burdens of indirect taxes. For specific excises, where the real incidence is reasonably predictable, such information is surely limited severely. For the more important indirect sources of revenue, such as general sales taxes, turnover taxes, value-added taxes, and corporation in-

7. These results are reported in Günter Schmölders, "Unmerkliche Steuern," *Finanzarchiv*, Band 20 (1959), 23-34.
8. Robert Ferber, "How Aware Are Consumers of Excise Tax Changes?" *National Tax Journal*, VII (December, 1954), 355-58.

come taxes, where the incidence is in dispute even among experts, the ignorance of the taxpayer-voter must be great indeed.

GENERAL TAX AWARENESS

In an extensive British survey, completed in 1965, individuals were asked to estimate total amounts of taxes paid (direct and indirect) and these estimates were compared with reasonably computed totals. Somewhat in contrast to Schmölders' results, there seemed to have been general underestimation. Those who overestimated tax liabilities seem have been relatively concentrated in lower-income groups in the sample, independently confirming one of Wagstaff's results. Respondents were also asked to estimate the proportion of income paid in taxes for the country as a whole. Here the results indicate reasonably accurate estimates if only averages are employed, with low-income groups again exhibiting higher tax awareness. Dispersion about the averages suggests, however, that respondents were not at all well-informed as to average levels of tax.[9]

TAX ESTIMATION AND TAX AWARENESS

Individuals make fiscal choices not on the basis of how accurately they estimate tax costs, but rather on their consciousness or awareness of these costs along with their predictions as to magnitudes. The ignorance of the individual concerning his tax liability does not measure "consciousness" at all accurately. The more informed the taxpayer is, the more "tax conscious" he is likely to be. Hence, ignorance becomes, in some rough sense, a measure of "unconsciousness." To the extent than an individual is genuinely unaware of the existence of a tax, he will tend to be more acquiescent to its imposition, even if, when it is brought to his attention he tends to overestimate its impact.

For our purposes, fiscal institutions should be classified, if possible, in terms of their net impact on individual choice behavior. Tax institutions can affect behavior in two ways: first, the institution can affect the transmission to the individual of an awareness of public-services costs. Different institutions will generate different results in this respect. Secondly, once the individual is fully aware that the tax exists (as he must be when confronted with a question-

9. *Choice in Welfare, 1965.* Institute of Economic Affairs (London: October, 1965), pp. 30-33.

naire asking for his estimates of liability), the form of the tax may affect the degree as well as the direction of error in estimation. These two separate effects of taxes should be distinguished.

The studies to which reference has been made are largely directed to the second of these effects. Enrick's, Wagstaff's, and some of Schmölders' work are aimed at finding out how accurately the individual can estimate his tax liability and what is the direction of his errors. Much less work has been done on finding out whether or not the individual is even aware that a tax exists. Here Wagstaff's finding that employees subject to withholding tend systematically to underestimate their gross incomes suggests that the institution of withholding, as such, reduces income tax awareness. This can be valid despite the accompanying finding that, when questioned concerning the amount of income tax withheld, there was some tendency toward overestimation, especially among lower income groups. If, from such data, we should try to make some predictions as to the net impact of withholding on fiscal choice behavior, some comparison of the relative strengths of these offsetting effects might be required.

Similar conclusions follow for Schmölders' rudimentary findings on indirect taxes. As suggested, individuals are not even conscious that such taxes exist in many instances, and, on the other hand, many think that taxes exist which do not. However, when taxes that do exist are brought to their attention, certain groups tend to overestimate the extent of their own liability.

BENEFIT ESTIMATION AND AWARENESS

Information on the individual's estimation or awareness of his tax liabilities is meager; but, by comparison, it is plentiful. Almost no empirical work has been directed at determining the individual's estimation or awareness of the value of the benefits that he secures from the availability of publicly-provided goods and services.

Logically, we can think of classifying public goods and services in two categories similar to the direct tax-indirect tax classification on the other side of the fiscal account. But if we try to apply such a classification on the spending side, problems immediately arise. What is a *direct* public good or service? On the tax side, directness implies that the levy is upon the person who is expected to bear the final incidence. Defined in this manner, there is no necessary connection between *directness* and *generality* in taxation; a direct tax could be highly selective or discriminatory. However, the standard institutions of direct taxation also tend to be those of *general* taxation, while those of indirect taxation tend necessarily to embody discriminatory features. This leads to the commonly accepted link between indirectness and nongenerality. When we consider the public expenditure or benefit side, however, the situation is almost reversed. A *direct* public service, one that involves the most direct linkage between the individual recipient and the fisc, must, almost by definition, be discriminatory or selective. On the other hand, the most *indirect* public good or service, those that are the most remote from the individual's private economic situation, tend to be the most *general*. Unless this asymmetry between the two sides of the account is kept in mind, confusion is likely to arise when discussing direct and indirect benefits from public goods.

Direct benefits are those which come closest to providing individuals with money payments, freely convertible into goods and services as desired. It follows that we should expect persons to be more aware of these benefits than those from public goods that yield value only in quite specific and nonindividualized forms. For example, the benefits that the individual secures from national defense spending are surely indirect; he cannot convert Polaris submarine patrols into anything which he can privately enjoy, even to the extent of placing a roughly comparable value upon them. Hence, we should predict that he will be less conscious of such benefits than he will be of those which he secures under various social welfare programs.

Empirical testing of benefit awareness under the several types of public programs would be helpful, but the relevance of such data for the purposes of this study should not be overemphasized. The individual's awareness is, for our purposes, relevant only to the extent that his choice behavior may be modified predictably. On the tax side, it is reasonable to assume that, other things equal, the institution that reduces tax consciuosness or tax awareness tends to modify individual choice in the direction of greater public outlay. It is difficult, however, for reasons to be discussed, to apply symmetrical predictions on the spending side. Can it be maintained that, other things equal, the public spending program that generates the lowest "awareness" on the part of the individual beneficiaries tends to bias individual choice in the direction of lower tax rates? The difficulty here lies in the fact that the provision of public service benefits is the *raison d'être* of the whole fiscal structure. Analysis is meaningful which suggests that differing tax institutions, all of which draw generalized purchasing power from the individual, may exert differing effects on his choice of public goods, generically defined. One cannot, however, simply reverse this statement and say that analysis of the effects of differing budgetary compositions on levels of taxation is equally meaningful. The point is that differing budgetary compositions represent differing fiscal "purchases," so to speak. Again an analogy with markets will be helpful. One can say that the *manner of paying* for goods, oranges or apples, may affect the quantity purchased. One cannot say, in reverse, that whether or not oranges or apples are purchased affects total outlay. Of course it will. But wholly different choices are involved in this case, and comparison becomes essentially irrelevant.

It follows that the *institutions of providing public goods and services* are relevant to our purposes only to the extent that choices are comparable; that is, only to the extent that the *same* public goods mix is selected under the varying institutions. While it may be presumed that an individual beneficiary is less aware of a remote and indirect public good, such as defense, than he is of a direct welfare payment, his choice, at the margin of adjustment, need not be affected. This is because, in any sort of "political equilibrium," the various budgetary items will tend to be extended so as to yield roughly equi-marginal benefits. At this point, the representative taxpayer-beneficiary should value marginal extensions of the various public services in some roughly comparable manner. This "equilibrium" may or may not be "optimal" in some other sense, but this does not concern us here. Our task is simply that of determining what effects, if any, structural institutions of the fiscal system exert on the final adjustment. How can the institutions through which public goods and services are made available to the individuals affect their choice calculus in the collective decision-making process?

On the benefit side, the question then reduces to: Are there institutional differences that may affect the *directness* or the *indirectness* and hence the awareness of the individual beneficiary for *comparable* public services? If the issue is posed in this way, the relatively limited range for institutional variability on the spending side can be more readily appreciated. National defense may be financed through any number of different tax institutions; but how many spending institutions can be utilized to provide the citizen with national defense? How can institutional variations here affect the individual's awareness of benefits? For genuinely general public goods, such as defense, there are few structural changes that can be possible. For public goods and services that are somewhat less remote from the individual, there are some institutional variations possible, and, with these, research hypotheses can be formulated and tested.

Consider collective outlay on elementary education. What variations are there in the institutions through which this might be provided, and how might these variations affect the willingness of citizens to bear the necessary tax costs? Suppose that a local community proposes two alternative schemes: In the first, all collective outlay takes the standard form of direct operation of a free public school system. In the second scheme, all families with school-age children will be provided with tuition grants or vouchers that they may use in paying for privately provided but qualified educational services. These are two distinct institutional arrangements for providing comparable services. In each case, assume that the same tax institution is to be employed, say, local property taxation. Will the community choose to finance precisely the same outlay under each scheme? It seems evident that there may be differences in individual choice behavior under the two schemes. For those families that are direct beneficiaries, the voucher plan tends to make the outlay more direct perhaps, and these families would probably choose to spend more collectively under this than under the alternative institution. For those citizens who are taxpayers, but who are not direct beneficiaries, the results might be reversed; the voucher plan might well make the benefits seem more remote, because concentrated directly on specific beneficiaries. To my knowledge, no research has been directed specifically at finding empirical answers to such questions. Such research would be difficult because observed institutional variations here are much more narrow than comparable variations on the tax side.[10]

The elementary education example is discussed here because it does suggest that institutional hypotheses may be developed and

10. An analysis of predicted outcomes under various institutional schemes for financing and operating educational systems is contained in W. Craig Stubblebine, "Institutional Elements in the Financing of Education," in *Education and the Southern Economy*, Supplement to *Southern Economic Journal*, XXXII (July, 1965), 15-34. Stubblebine does not, however, claim to examine empirical evidence to test his hypotheses.

tested for those goods and services that are comparable, such as public outlay for medical care, for housing, for social services generally. Different institutions for providing roughly comparable benefits can have different effects here, and where such differences in institutions are observed to exist, empirical research that asks the right questions can yield highly valuable results.

Choice in Welfare: The Institute of Economic Affairs Surveys. British surveys conducted in 1963 and 1965 indirectly provide some evidence of benefit awareness of individuals under several existing welfare programs.[11] The emphasis of these surveys was upon securing information on individual preferences for alternative institutional arrangements, as such, and not upon examining the possibly differing results under such alternatives, which is the information directly relevant for our purposes. However, certain by-product results of this survey suggest levels of benefit evaluation at least in rough opportunity-cost terms.

In the 1963 survey, public attitudes on the provision of medical care, education, and pensions were ascertained. With respect to medical care, respondents tended to underestimate seriously costs of providing standard quantity units, for example, a week's hospitalization. The lack of cost awareness was even more emphatically shown in the fact that some 36 per cent of the respondents thought that NHS contributions were sufficient to finance fully the National Health Service when, in actuality, such contributions provide less than one-fifth of the total revenues. Similar, although less startling, results were found with respect to public attitudes on the costs and benefits of public education. Some 18 per cent of the respondents explicitly considered it unnecessary to pay for education "either directly or through rates or taxes." By contrast with their answers in medical services, however, the respondents tended to overestimate the costs of public educational services that were provided, and also the costs of providing educational services privately. With respect to the public pensions schemes in Great Britain, some 35 per cent of the respondents genuinely considered the operation one of "insurance," with the pensioner having accumulated sufficient reserves to meet the full costs of benefit payments. In fact, both the employer and

11. *Choice in Welfare.* Institute of Economic Affairs (London, July, 1963). The results of this survey are discussed in Ralph Harris and Arthur Seldon, "Welfare and Choice," *The New Society* (No. 43), 25 July 1963, pp. 14-16. Also, *Choice in Welfare, 1965.*

the employee contributions account for only some 10 per cent of total revenues for the program.

The 1965 survey attempted to determine respondents' awareness of the total value of social benefits received from all government welfare programs. Here, as in the estimate of taxes, there was general underestimation, and the range of estimation was wide. No attempt was made in 1965, as there was in 1963, to secure benefit estimates for particular programs.

For purposes of this study, the most interesting result of both British surveys is the revealed failure of individuals to make any effective translation of public-service benefits into tax costs.

THE RELEVANCE OF THE "ECONOMIC-INDIVIDUALISTIC" MODEL

A second broad area for empirical research involves tests of the possible explanatory range of the central "economic" hypothesis of our individual collective-choice models. Quite independently of the information content problem, to what extent do individuals choose among collective alternatives on the basis of criteria that may be externally measured? Even if an individual should be accurately informed as to both his own tax liabilities and the value of the public service benefits that he receives, both in total and in per unit terms, will he choose in such a manner that an economist can make some rough predictions? Unless this question can be answered affirmatively, little progress can be made toward developing a "scientific" theory of individual behavior in fiscal choice.

As suggested in Chapter 12, casual everyday observation of politics tends to corroborate the central hypothesis here in numerous ways. Elections are contested, and campaigns are waged, at least in part, on issues that can be reduced to direct and measurable economic content. Behavior of the electorate is surely influenced, to a degree, by predictions as to measurable gains and losses. It remains useful, nonetheless, to extend research well beyond this range of casual observation, and to test the validity of the central hypothesis more specifically if possible. And the construction of applicable and relevant subsidiary hypotheses is not nearly so easy here as the behavior of politicians make it appear. The analyst must be able, independently, to identify the effects of the fiscal variables examined upon the circumstances of the individual participant before he can develop any testable propositions concerning individual response. Such identification is often difficult. Specific conclusions must be made concerning the incidence of both taxes and public benefits, and the real or actual incidence must be distinguished from the apparent. To the individual chooser, it is the apparent incidence of taxes and benefits that affect his choice.

Schmölders' work has already been mentioned several times. He has not been concerned with testing hypotheses in the direct sense, but some of his subsidiary findings can be adduced at the outset to provide corroboration of the "economic" motivation in the fiscal preferences of individuals. In a survey of individual attitudes on the desirability of public or governmental support for private industry, he found that those persons from the industries most likely to secure grants were the most likely to respond favorably. Similarly, he found that governmental employees made up the group most likely to say that public services were worth more than the tax costs of providing them.[12] These particular results are, of course, presented along with many others concerning general public attitudes toward the fisc, and it should be emphasized here that Schmölders does not consider directly the testing of the economic motivation hypothesis.

Michigan Studies. The problem of identifying individual interest can be resolved with ease only for some of the cruder tests. Individual utility maximization cannot always be related directly to income, wealth, or economic position. Unless, however, some such direct relationship is assumed, specific testing of the utility maximization hypothesis becomes difficult. By and large, individual utility may be related to income level for purposes of examining individual responses to tax alternatives. If high-income receivers are found to express a relative preference for sales taxes over income taxes, whereas low-income receivers are found to express the opposing preference, some support for the explanatory value of the economic model is provided. This result was forthcoming from the study of tax preferences conducted in Michigan in 1959 by Elizabeth David.[13] She also found, not unexpectedly, that property owners tended to be less favorably inclined than were renters toward the use of the property tax as a revenue raising device. Generally speaking, David's survey corroborates the hypothesis that the economic positions of

12. Günter Schmölders, *Das Irrationale in der öffentlichen Finanzwirtschaft.*
13. See Elizabeth Jane Likert David, "Public Preferences and the Tax Structure: An Examination of Factors Related to State and Local Tax Preferences" (University of Michigan Microfilm, 1961).

individual citizens is an important determinant of their attitudes on fiscal alternatives.

In a survey conducted by the Survey Research Center of the University of Michigan in 1960 and 1961, and reported by Eva Mueller,[14] the role played by economic self-interest in determining respondent attitudes was shown to be a significant, although not necessarily a dominating, explanatory factor. Public programs aimed at providing benefits to low-income groups (aid to the poor, the unemployed, hospital and medical care, public works) tended to be viewed more favorably by the lower-income members of the sample. Aid to small business and highway outlays tended to be more heavily favored by the higher-income groups. All groups, regardless of income level, seemed to favor expenditures on education and on aid to the aged. This finding, along with certain other features of the survey, suggested that economic self-interest in any narrow sense, fails as a self-contained, all inclusive explanatory hypothesis.

One of the more interesting findings of the Survey Research Center project was the attitude expressed by higher-income individuals with respect to relative expansions in public spending programs of all sorts. On the basis of a crude and unsophisticated version of the self-interest hypothesis, higher-income groups should be predicted to be less favorably inclined toward additional public goods and services than the lower-income groups. However, the data collected here suggested that, on the average, the two groups that view expansions in spending programs most favorably are those at the two extreme ends of the income scale. This result was, for example, quite clear with respect to educational spending.

Does this sort of evidence contradict or refute the utility-maximization hypothesis more generally considered? No refutation seems indicated when it is recognized that the higher-income individual may place a higher evaluation on the "spillover" effects of public spending than persons in lower-income groups, and, also, that the pattern of tax incidence may not be so progressive as the relevant ratio of income and price elasticities of the public services provided. In other words, the degree of what has been called "Samuelsonian publicness" in any particular public service may increase substantially as income levels increase. This would allow a so-

14. See Eva Mueller, "Public Attitudes Toward Fiscal Programs," *Quarterly Journal of Economics,* LXXVII (May, 1963), 210-35.

phisticated form of the hypothesis to remain valid in "explaining" the survey data.

Wilson-Banfield Studies. Attitudes toward fiscal alternatives as expressed by respondents to interviews or questionnaires can be extremely helpful in filling out the many gaps in our knowledge. It is commonplace, however, that such expressed attitudes do not necessarily enable us to predict behavior accurately. When confronted with genuine choice, individuals may not respond in the way that expressed attitudes might indicate. Somewhat more conclusive tests of the central behavioral hypothesis may, therefore, be carried out if actual choice behavior can be observed. Such tests are, of course, difficult to conduct since individuals do not normally choose directly among fiscal alternatives. Nevertheless some testing is possible where data on voting referenda can be secured, and where numerous observations can be found.

Municipal referenda on spending programs can provide the basis for such tests, and experiments utilizing these data have been completed by James Q. Wilson and Edward Banfield of Harvard University.[15] Their work is noteworthy in that it sets out explicitly to test an hypothesis: voters act as if they are trying to maximize their net family incomes. This hypothesis leads to the prediction that the lowest income groups would vote in favor of most public spending programs that are proposed by municipal governments. The upper-income groups should be expected to oppose most proposals for spending, whereas middle-income groups should be expected to be highly selective.

Results tend to confirm the behavioral hypothesis for low-income groups. However, upper-income groups also tend to vote heavily in favor of many spending programs that provide them with little direct benefits. Opposition to municipal spending programs tends to be concentrated in the middle-income ranges.

These findings corroborate the attitudinal surveys reported by Mueller. To an extent at least, the crude income-maximization hypothesis seems contradicted by the data. Wilson and Banfield "explain" the behavior of the upper-income groups by the importance

15. See James Q. Wilson and Edward C. Banfield, "Voting Behavior on Municipal Public Expenditures," in *The Public Economy of Urban Communities,* ed. J. Margolis (Resources for the Future, 1965), pp. 74-91. Essentially the same results are reported in James Q. Wilson and Edward C. Banfield, "Public-Regardingness as a Value Premise in Voting Behavior," *American Political Science Review,* LVIII (December, 1964), 876-87.

of "altruistic" motives, or by "public-regardingness." A more sophisticated version of the utility-maximization hypothesis would, also, "explain" the same data. In one sense, the presence of "altruism" as a motive is the same thing as including "redistribution" as a "good" in the individual's utility function. This construction suggests both the strength and the weakness of the economic model. Properly stretched, the model can be helpful in "explaining" almost any observed behavior. But precisely to the extent it does, it becomes useless as a predictive hypothesis.[16]

The Gillespie Study. The Wilson-Banfield and the Mueller findings become less damaging, even to the crude form of the income-maximization hypothesis, when these are examined in juxtaposition with the research results of W. Irwin Gillespie.[17] His work represents an attempt to measure, empirically, the net incidence of the over-all fiscal structure, federal and state-local, including the expenditure or benefit side as well as the tax side. In his standard model, which incorporates perhaps the most acceptable set of assumptions as to benefit and tax incidence, Gillespie found that, on balance, federal tax-spending patterns favor low-income receivers as expected, treat a fairly wide range of middle-income receivers neutrally, and impose net burdens on high-income receivers. For state-local systems, by comparison, he found that low-income receivers are again favored. But the two remaining income groups are treated differently than they are under the federal system. Here the middle-income receivers are subjected to net fiscal burdens while the high-income receivers are treated neutrally.

This pattern for state-local fiscal incidence strongly implies that opposition to extensions in public spending programs at these levels would be concentrated among middle-income receivers even if a crude income-maximization hypothesis is accepted. In this respect the Wilson-Banfield results, which are exclusively drawn from state-local data, tend to corroborate rather than to refute the hypothesis with respect to the behavior of both the low-income and the middle-income groups. And, since high-income groups are subjected, on balance, to neither net burdens nor net benefits at the state-local

16. It is plausible to suggest that the Wilson-Banfield results, along with the Mueller attitudes, can be illustrated by the configuration presented in Figure 11.9 in the Appendix to Chapter 11.

17. W. Irwin Gillespie, "The Effect of Public Expenditures on the Distribution of Income" in *Essays in Fiscal Federalism*, ed. R. A. Musgrave (Washington: Brookings Institution, 1965), pp. 122-86.

level, their behavior in supporting spending programs provides considerably weaker refutation of the hypothesis than might have been supposed independently of the Gillespie findings.

Gillespie results should be helpful to future researchers in framing hypotheses to be selected and tested. It would seem appropriate to examine voting data in legislative assemblies at the state-local and at the federal level separately to determine whether or not opposition to spending programs by high-income groups tends to be more prevalent at the federal level.

The Davis Studies. If voter choices in referenda on spending or taxing programs are not directly available, the central hypothesis of economic model may be tested by reference to comparative data from various fiscal jurisdictions characterized by differing economic circumstances. This is the approach that was taken by Otto A. Davis of Carnegie Tech in his research on local public expenditures. The first study concentrated on public school outlay in the Pittsburgh area.[18] Implicit in this approach is the assumption that elected public officials, in this case members of local school boards, act in accordance with the preferences of individual citizens. With this assumption, the results emerging from the deliberations and decisions of representative assemblies can be taken to reflect accurately the preferences of citizens and these results can be used directly to test hypotheses about the choice behavior of individuals.

Davis looked first at the problem of explaining the per pupil outlay on public schools in the various districts of his area. There are, of course, the orthodox or standard explanatory variables here which can be expected to account for a major share of the inter-district variations in spending. These are the familiar variables for per capita incomes, population density, property values, level of education. Davis' main emphasis was on the question as to whether or not additional variables designed to reflect the economic-individualistic model of choice behavior could add to the total explanation of variability. Specifically, he sought to predict the directions of influence exerted on the outcomes by several additional variables of this sort.

Some of these variables were: (1) value of industrial property, (2) per cent of voters owing property, (3) per cent of total popula-

18. See Otto A. Davis, "Empirical Evidence of Political Influences Upon the Expenditure Policies of Public Schools," in *The Public Economy of Urban Communities*, ed. J. Margolis (Resources for the Future, 1965), pp. 92-111.

199

tion in schools, (4) per cent of school children in public schools. He predicted independently that the first variable, value for industrial property, should positively affect public school outlay since this provides a source of revenue not wholly borne by local residents of the districts. Secondly, he predicted that the larger the per cent of property owners in the jurisdiction, the lower the outlay since most local revenues are raised through the tax on real property. He further predicted that there would be a negative relationship between public school outlay per pupil and the per cent population in school and the per cent of children in public schools.

The second study, undertaken jointly with James L. Barr,[19] attempted to determine whether or not the economic positions of the median voters in Pennsylvania counties, defined in terms of property holdings, provide some of the explanation of variations in local spending levels. Specifically, the study examined the hypothesis that the ratio between the median's voter's property holdings and the assessed valuation of all property in the local jurisdiction was inversely related to per capita spending levels. Statistical results indicated that the directions of effects were those predicted, and that the hypothesis was of explanatory value. Other variables must, of course, be added for any satisfactorily "complete" explanation of intercounty expenditure variance.

Davis' results, in both studies, while admittedly inconclusive, do not contradict his central hypotheses. Significant corroboration should not, of course, have been expected. The data upon which the empiricist must draw remain crude indeed, and many elements influence the final outcomes of collective decision processes.

Much more research, perhaps especially of the sort undertaken by Wilson-Banfield and by Davis and Barr, is required before the genuine predictive power of the utility-maximizing model of individual choice behavior in politics can be determined. No one would, I presume, claim for this model or hypothesis exclusive domain in a fully-developed theory of fiscal-collective choice. The limited studies that have been completed support the view that the model can provide important explanatory assistance, but that errors can be easily made if this alone is relied on for positive prediction.

The Influence of Fiscal Institutions. The several areas of research that are useful for our purposes are all closely related. Studies

19. James L. Barr and Otto A. Davis, "A Political and Economic Theory of the Expenditures of Local Governments," (Mimeographed: Carnegie Institute of Technology, 1965).

designed to fill in the gaps in our knowledge about individual fiscal consciousness or studies designed to test broadly the applicability of utility-maximizing models of individual behavior are, in one sense, antecedent to the research that is more directly related to the theoretical analysis of preceding chapters. Here the emphasis was on making predictions about the effects of fiscal institutions on individual choice behavior, and through this, on collective outcomes. The most direct research is that which aims at testing these predictions themselves, not their underlying presuppositions.

As in the case of testing the validity of the economic model generally, casual observation and introspection should not be overlooked merely because these are unexciting research tools. To an extent, these are the most useful tests that can be employed; they are cheap to conduct and they are probably more convincing than more complicated methods. One of the institutional predictions made in Chapter 5 concerned the effects of an old or an existing tax institution. The hypothesis here is so widely known and accepted that it would warrant the effort of only the most pedestrian of doctoral candidates to check it out and corroborate it. The general prediction concerning the relative impact of direct and indirect taxation on individual behavior is almost equally evident from ordinary experience. This is perhaps best exemplified in the persistence of the corporation income tax in the federal revenue structure despite its opposition by almost all those who discuss "tax principles." Note that when, in 1963, proposals were made to reduce both the corporate income tax rate and personal income tax rates, the 1964 legislation, as finally approved, resulted in a larger-than-proposed cut in personal rates but a smaller-than-proposed cut in the corporate tax rate. There could hardly be stronger corroboration of the hypothesis that the corporation tax, because it is not directly sensed by the individual voters, tends to generate a greater degree of acquiescience than the more direct personal income tax.

One of the most important institutional elements of the political decision structure with respect to its effects on individual behavior in making fiscal choices is the apparent separation of decisions on taxes and on public spending programs, decisions that must, in some underlying real sense, remain interdependent. The discussion of this problem in Chapter 7 suggested that the predictable results of a budgetary process that allows fragmentation of decision are ex ante deficits between approved tax revenues and approved spending, deficits which must under some balanced-budget rule be adjusted ex post. As the analysis suggested, this tendency toward ex ante deficits can be predicted, independently of any predictions as to whether, in the final adjustment, total public outlay will be less than, equal to, or greater than that which might be produced under alternative decision processes where the two sides of the fiscal account are simultaneously considered.

The Fragmentation of Choice: Survey Research Center Results. The general prediction is amenable to testing in several ways. One indirect test is provided in the Survey Research Center's attitudinal study reported by Mueller, and mentioned previously. Respondents were asked whether or not more, the same, or less public spending should be undertaken under each of several program categories. No mention was made of the means through which the additional necessary funds for financing the programs might be secured. The results, reproduced from Table II in Mueller's paper, are shown in the second column of Table 13.1. The same set of questions were then asked with the additional proviso "even if taxes must be raised."

TABLE 13.1

Program	Per Cent Respondents Who Think More Should Be Spent	Per Cent Respondents Who Think More Should Be Spent, Even If More Taxes Required
Help for older people	70	34
Help for needy	60	26
Education	60	41
Slum clearance	55	n.a.
Hospital and medical care	54	25
Public works	48	n.a.
Defense	47	30
Small business	37	n.a.
Highways	36	13
Unemployment benefits	29	10
Parks, recreation	27	7
Space	26	14
Agriculture	20	6
Foreign aid	7	2

Source: Table II, p. 215, in Eva Mueller, "Public Attitudes Toward Fiscal Programs."

The change in response is striking; the per cent indicating that more should be spent under the tax-bridge situation is shown in the right-hand column of Table 13.1.

Although the limited value of such attitudinal surveys for genuine choice behavior should always be stressed, these results seem to suggest, quite clearly, that individuals do not, in general, translate meaningfully between the two sides of the fiscal account. Insofar as the decision process allows them to think in terms of approving spending programs independently of tax costs, a deficit will tend to be produced. Note that, on the basis of the responses shown in Table 13.1, a majority of respondents would favor additional spending on the first five programs, but that no single program could have secured majority approval if the accompanying tax increases should be required. Note, also, that the ordering of preferences for the various programs is changed in the two situations.

In the 1963 British survey previously cited, respondents were asked whether or not programs should be extended, but only under the tax-bridge situation. Here a majority of respondents (51 per cent) indicated a preference for expanded outlay on education, while 41 and 43 per cent respectively favored expansions in outlay on public health and public pensions.[20] Somewhat interestingly, these percentages were reduced to 41 (education), 32 (health), and 34 (pensions) in the 1965 survey.[21]

Reid's Study of Veterans' Bonus Legislation. More definitive tests of the hypothesis that separation of tax and expenditure decisions exerts important influences on behavior can be made by an examination of democratic choice itself. Given a multiplicity of governmental units, comparative analysis becomes possible, provided only that the institutional arrangements under study differ significantly among separate units.

An excellent opportunity to test the hypothesis was provided by the actions of the separate states in enacting legislation granting cash bonuses to veterans of World War II and the Korean War. This was one of the objectives of a University of Virginia study completed by John J. Reid in 1961.[22] Twenty-one states enacted

20. *Choice in Welfare, 1963,* Table XII.
21. *Choice in Welfare, 1965,* Tables XXI, XXIV, XXVII.
22. See John Joseph Reid, "The Veterans' Bonuses: An Analysis of a Collective Decision" (Unpublished Ph.D. dissertation, Alderman Library, University of Virginia, 1961).

bonus legislation after World War II and twenty states after the Korean War, these being essentially the same groups. In twenty-six states, bonuses were proposed but were not finally enacted. Since the exogenous factors that might influence such a spendings decision would seem roughly comparable in all states, this divergence in results should enable some predictions to be made as to the effects of institutional differences if such are found to have existed.

Bonus legislation was presented for public referenda in twenty-seven states, a feature that allowed a direct examination of individual choice behavior in the voting booth. In fifteen of these twenty-seven states, the question presented to the electorate was framed in such a way as to impress upon the voter the necessary accompanying tax costs of the bonus. In some cases, approval was tied explicitly to the approval of a corresponding tax levy; in other cases, voters were merely asked to indicate their preferences for the tax increases that would be necessary. In the remaining twelve states, the question as to the bonus was presented without reference to tax costs.

The results that Reid observed tend strongly to corroborate the hypothesis that spending programs secure approval more readily when the tax-bridge is not present. In each of the twelve states where the bonuses were proposed without note of tax costs, the referendum was favorable. Of the remaining fifteen states, bonus proposals were rejected in six, or 40 per cent, of the total.

Although not directly testable, Reid also found that the action on bonuses in state legislatures (in states where no referendum was required) tended to be influenced significantly by the degree to which the necessary tax costs were tied into the positive approval of the bonuses.

Birdsall's Finding. Similar corroboration of the hypothesis can be found in William C. Birdsall's study.[23] He noted that, in November, 1955, a referendum proposal was submitted to the electorate in New York state calling for the authorization of a $750 million bond issue for highway development. The state's legislature had, prior to the referendum, enacted a fuels tax increase that was scheduled to go into effect *only* upon favorable adoption of the referendum proposal. The proposal was then defeated, 54 per cent to 46 per cent. Only one year later, in November, 1956, a similar proposal calling for the authorization of a $500 million bond issue

23. See William C. Birdsall, "Public Finance Allocation Decisions and the Preferences of Citizens: Some Theoretical and Empirical Considerations" (Unpublished Ph.D. dissertation, Johns Hopkins University Library, 1963).

for the same purposes was passed, with a 66 per cent yes vote. The second proposal differed from the first only in that, in 1956, the referendum decision was in no way tied to an increase in the fuels tax.

Birdsall's finding in this one instance cannot, of course, be taken for more than one isolated corroboroation of the hypothesis. However, when this is added to the Survey Research Center material on fiscal attitudes and to Reid's study of veterans' bonuses, the corroboration of the hypothesis becomes more impressive. These various strands of evidence, coupled with the introspective plausibility of the hypothesis, provide perhaps ample grounds for making firm predictions concerning the direction of effects exerted by the fragmentation of the budgetary process.

POLITICAL INSTITUTIONS AND FISCAL INSTITUTIONS

It is not easy to draw a sharp distinction between institutions labeled as "fiscal" and those that might be called "legal," "political," or "constitutional." Such institutions as earmarking, annual budgeting, the separation of revenue and expenditure decisions, etc. are "political" at the same time they are strictly "fiscal." But there exist, beyond these, institutions or rules that are essentially political without being limited to fiscal choices. I refer here to the rules for reaching collective decisions. There are numerous ways of attaining outcomes in democratic politics, and constitutions exist which specify such variations.

Once it is recognized that political or collective decision processes are not means of arriving at "truth judgments," at "right" answers, but are, instead, simply the processes through which individual choices as to alternative outcomes are combined for producing collective results, it becomes obvious that different rules can generate differences in outcomes. In another work, the theoretical background for an analysis of varying rules for political choice has been presented.[24] As with the specifically fiscal institutions already discussed, however, little empirical research has been directed at determining the influence of the several possible rules.

One area where empirical research seems possible is in the approval of school bond issues by the electorate of the various school districts in the United States. Here we have a multiplicity of

24. See James M. Buchanan and Gordon Tullock, *The Calculus of Consent.*

units making roughly the same decision and we should be able to compare results. And, because of differing state constitutional and legislative provisions as to the rules under which local school districts make decisions, some influence of these rules on final outcomes should be noted. In a University of Virginia study, begun in 1963, John Robert Cooper tried to predict the influence exerted by a few of the basic rules for decision on such bond issues. In many jurisdictions, simple majority approval in a referendum is required. In many others, a qualified majority of those voting is required, with the percentage "yes" vote varying over a rather wide range. In still other jurisdictions, the majority, simple or qualified, must be computed on the basis of all registered voters. Still other districts operate under a property-ownership qualification for voting in bond elections.

Cooper arrayed the differing requirements in terms of apparent restrictiveness as follows: Simple majority, majority with a property qualification, special majority greater than 51 per cent, special majority with property qualification, and, finally, a majority of all eligible voters. He then hypothesized that the proportion of bond issues approved would tend to fall as one moves down this array. The data, which were limited to issues presented for referendum votes in 1961, only partially support the general hypothesis. More bond issues tend to be approved in jurisdictions where only a simple majority is required than in those where a qualified majority is required. As with some of the other findings reported in this chapter, this result seems almost intuitively obvious to anyone who adopts a broadly general democratic decision-making model and who imputes any rationality to voter participation. It is useful, nonetheless, to have corroborating evidence from the real world. Cooper's results, in this respect, are in full agreement with previously completed and more limited surveys.[25]

Predictions contained in the hypothesis concerning the effects of property qualification were not supported by the data. Accepting some version of the crude income-maximization hypothesis, and recognizing that taxes on real property must provide funds for servicing and amortizing debt, the limitation of suffrage to property owners in bond referenda would be predicted to reduce the pro-

25. See John Robert Cooper, "Institutional Factors Affecting the Outcomes of School-Bond Referenda." Upon final completion, anticipated for 1966, this study will be presented as a Ph.D. dissertation at the University of Virginia.

portion of approvals. Cooper's study fails to support this prediction. Broadly speaking, the percentage of bond issues approved remains approximately the same with and without the property qualification, other aspects of the referenda remaining the same. In part this seemingly paradoxical result is explained by the fact that, in the sample drawn, those jurisdictions subjected to property qualifications tend also to be those where average income levels are relatively higher. If the Wilson-Banfield findings, mentioned earlier, are applied here, this tendency toward a high percentage approval even with the property qualification becomes understandable.

THE SEVERAL STATES

Hypotheses concerning the eff_cts of fiscal-political institutions on choice behavior can be tested only in those situations where different institutions can be observed to operate under circumstances that are, in other respects, broadly similar. A multiplicity of jurisdictions becomes a necessary condition for research. For this reason, most of the research reported in this chapter, and indeed most of the research that seems possible, relies on the availability of data from the separate state-local fiscal systems. Data on choice behavior under the institutions of the federal or central government are available, but these can reveal little or nothing about the effects of different institutions of fiscal choice simply because no controls, no contrasting institutions, exist with which results might be compared. This fact severely limits empirical research on fiscal process.

Researchers should, nevertheless, consider themselves to be fortunate that data on state-local systems are readily available in substantially complete form, especially for those years when censuses of government are completed. With these data researchers should be able, with the aid of sophisticated techniques, to isolate the effects of some of the most important institutional variables.

One approach suggested is that of trying to "explain" the variations in state-local expenditures over the several states. Here the standard and familiar explanatory variables: income, population, property values, urbanization, have been shown to explain a substantial proportion of the interstate variation. To test the relevance of the institutional approach, the researcher needs to add to these familiar variables those which represent the apparently important fiscal-political institutions and try to predict the directions of influence.

A preliminary research study along these lines has been partially completed by Jack Forbes of the University of Virginia. In an attempt to isolate the influence of political-institutional variables on fiscal choice, Forbes chose as his basic dependent variable *per capita state-local expenditure as a percentage of income.* He then tried to explain the variance in this value among the separate states. Note that the task here is not that of explaining the variance in levels of spending among the states, the problem that has been often examined. Forbes sought to explain what might be called the variance in the propensity to spend publicly out of income in the several states. To a large extent, the major explanatory variable for differential spending levels, that of per capita income, is eliminated here. The level of per capita income remains as an explanatory variable for Forbes' purposes only to the extent that the income elasticities of demand for public goods diverge from unitary.

What influence on this propensity to spend publicly from income is exerted by the several possible political-institutional variables? Initially, in his study, Forbes examined the prospects of isolating the effects of some thirty separate variables. Despite the availability of *Census of Governments* data, however, particular variables reflecting institutional differentials are not readily converted into statistically usable forms. As a result of his refinements, and recognizing data limitations, Forbes finally settled on the following list of independent variables for inclusion in his multiple regression.

X_1—number of governments per capita.

X_2—degree of state-local reliance on revenue from the federal government.

X_3—degree of local government reliance on revenue from the state.

X_4—degree of local expenditure autonomy.

X_5—degree of local tax autonomy.

X_6—degree of reliance on indirect taxation in the state-local system.

The predicted signs for the several coefficients in the regression equation were as follows. It was predicted that the influence of X_1, X_4, and X_5 on the dependent variable, per capita state-local spending as a per cent of per capita personal income, would be negative. That is to say, a larger number of government units, a higher degree of local tax and expenditure autonomy, would, other things

208

equal, reduce the propensity to spend publicly from income dollars. These predictions as to the negative influence were based on the notion that, to the extent that governmental-fiscal decisions are "brought closer to the people," more rational collective choices would be made, and that the direction of this influence would be toward reduced spending. A contrary prediction as to signs could have been made here if the important consideration was estimated to have been the economics of scale in public spending programs. It was predicted that the signs of the coefficients for X_2, X_3, and X_6 would be positive. The prediction for X_2 and X_3 requires little explanation; surely state-local spending would be expected to increase with increased reliance on external revenue sources, at either level. The positive sign predicted for X_6 stems from the notion that indirect taxation tends to generate a fiscal illusion and serves thereby to conceal from the taxpayer-voter the real weight of tax, and hence causes him to support a somewhat higher level of public spending.

The predictions as to signs were not supported in the case of X_1, the number of governmental units per capita. The predictions for X_2 and X_3 were supported by the data. Predictions for X_4, local spending autonomy, were supported, but not those of X_5, local tax autonomy. In the case of X_6, the degree of reliance on indirect taxation, the prediction was not supported by the data. The results suggest that state-local spending from income dollars tends to increase with the level of direct taxation, rather than decrease as the hypothesis predicted.

Using only the institutional variables listed above, and using 1957 data, Forbes was able to "explain" some 41 per cent of the variation in the dependent variable, per capita state-local spending as a per cent of per capita incomes. To these he added three additional and more familiar, independent variables, those for per capita personal incomes, for degree of urbanization, and for population density. With these added, the explanatory potential of the regression increased to 45 per cent. Independently considered, the three noninstitutional variables "explain" 30 per cent of the variation, indicating of course some auto-correlation among the institutional and noninstitutional variables.

The Forbes' study remains incomplete and its detailed results will not be presented in this summary treatment. The study is important for present purposes, however, in that it suggests both the relatively unexplored territory for useful statistical investigation of the influences of many institutional variables on the results of fiscal choice and the fact that such investigations will encounter serious data collection, methodological problems. The data are not such that the influences of the specific institutions can be readily isolated and examined. But the attempts can be made. And the refutation of each hypothesis adds something to the stock of our understanding.

CONCLUSIONS

The research reported in this chapter varies widely, both in rigor and in relevance for this study. The results should be considered primarily as suggestions for further work by the competent technicians that increasingly come to take their places in the ranks of professional scholars. The model of fiscal choice behavior that this book elaborates, that of democratic decision-making where individual preferences do count, has never been widely adopted by specialists. For this reason, the data that are available have rarely been examined in terms of the various hypotheses that emerge from the model. Few of these hypotheses have been formulated, and still fewer have been put to even rudimentary tests. The work reported on here is not that which characterizes a single-purpose, methodologically-fixed, workshop. Much additional development must take place before this stage is attained. There must be additional effort devoted to deriving relevant, and potential testable, propositions. Research at the empirical level will continue to be limited by the availability of suitable data. Those which do exist are largely fortuitous, since collection has never proceeded with the appropriate questions in mind. The main conclusion seems obvious and elementary. The range and scope for potentially productive research embodying both the development of imaginative hypotheses and the testing of these seems almost unlimited.

PART II

THE CHOICE AMONG
FISCAL INSTITUTIONS

The economist does not know, and should not know, and should not be concerned as to whether his theories, his models, his instruments or research, serve or should serve a few, many, one, or none at all. If they are not correct, others will expose the errors, modify them, perfect them.

Luigi Einaudi, in his Inaugural Lecture for the academic year 1949-50 at Torino. Cited by Aldo Scotto in "Luigi Einaudi," *Economia Internazionale,* XV (February, 1962), 35.

14. *The Levels of Fiscal Choice*

INTRODUCTION

In Part II an attempt will be made to examine the individual's choice among fiscal institutions, as institutions. This level or stage of individual choice behavior, which may be called "constitutional," differs from that discussed in Part I as well as from that which has concerned traditional public finance theorists. The three separate levels or stages of individual fiscal choice should be explicitly distinguished.

Individual choice behavior in traditional public finance theory— individual responses in market choice to imposed fiscal patterns. In the orthodox approach, the individual does not make either public-goods choices, as considered in Part I, or institutional choices, to be considered in Part II. Or, to state the same thing somewhat differently, these choices are not normally investigated. The fiscal and the institutional choices for the collectivity of individuals are assumed to be made externally to the individual's own potential choice system. He is presumed able to choose only in his private market behavior as he reacts to the various tax-expenditure mixes under institutional structures that are externally imposed upon him. The behavior of the individual, as choice-maker, remains the center of analysis, but it is the individual's private choice among market alternatives, as the latter are modified by the imposed fiscal structure. A typical problem posed in traditional public finance theory is: Given the institution of the personal income tax for raising government revenues, and given the level of rates that are imposed, how will the individual's choice in allocating his time between work and leisure be made, and how will this choice be influenced by a change in the level of tax rates or by a switch to an alternative institution?

Individual choice behavior under given fiscal institutions—individual responses in fiscal-collective choice under imposed fiscal institutions. In the discussion of Part I, we moved one stage or level beyond the traditional emphasis on market-choice reactions of individuals. In a democratic political order, individuals also *choose* the amount of public goods and services that the community will purchase and supply to its citizens. The individual, along with his fellows, makes public-goods choices as well as private-goods choices. The institutions through which these choices are organized may influence his behavior. An attempt was made to analyze this choice behavior and to predict the direction of effect exerted by a few of the commonly observed institutions of modern fiscal systems in democratic countries. For purposes of this analysis, the institutions themselves were assumed to have been selected externally to the individual's own choices. A typical problem under the approach of Part I is: Given that revenues are to be raised through a progressive tax on personal incomes, how will this fiscal institution influence the individual's choice in allocating resources between public goods and private goods?

Individual choice behavior in selecting among fiscal institutions. Under a democratic political order, individuals do more than choose in the market place and participate in collective choice under given institutions. Ultimately, at some "constitutional" stage of decision, they must also select or choose the structural framework for choice itself; they must choose the institutions under which both day-to-day market choices and ordinary political choices are implemented. It is extremely important that the separate levels or stages of individual choice be considered separately. We may, as in traditional public finance or as in Part I, examine the effects that the institution of the personal income tax exerts on an individual's behavior in either the market place or the voting booth. But at some "earlier" stage of decision, we may also examine his behavior in selecting the particular institution of the income tax over other revenue-raising alternatives. At this level of analysis, we try to compare the personal income tax with other institutions, say, the corporation income tax. For the approach of Part II, a typical problem is: How will the reference individual choose among the several possible alternative tax institutions through which he will exercise ordinary fiscal choices as to the amount of resources devoted to public goods and services?

214

THE INTERDEPENDENCE OF CHOICE

There are three levels of fiscal choice. The individual asks himself: first, how will I choose to pay for the collective goods and services that are to be provided; secondly, how much will I choose for the collectivity to provide; and, thirdly, once some group choice is made, how will I react to the changed market conditions that confront me? While it is essential that these three levels of choice be separated analytically, it should also be clear that the three are inherently interdependent. As in most situations of choice, "idealized" behavior requires, or seems to require, simultaneous adjustment of all the choice variables. Specifically, the individual's choice of a tax institution will depend on his choice for a public goods quantity and mix and upon his choice of a private market reaction to collective fiscal outcomes. Any satisfactory theory of normative behavior on the part of the individual must work out the process through which these three sets of choices are simultaneously made.[1]

THE COST OF DECISION MAKING

Such idealization ignores, however, one element of the decision process that can be of major importance. This is the costs of making decisions themselves. In a world where individual decisions can be made in complete isolation one from the other, this cost element may be neglected for most purposes. But in a setting where individuals must, somehow, participate in attaining some sort of consensus on collective outcomes that must, once settled, apply to all, these costs may become large indeed. Once this is recognized, even idealized individual choice need not require simultaneous determination of all values for the choice variables. In this context, it may become rational for the individual to consider his choice among rules or institutions independently from his own particular choices to be exercised within the operation of these institutions or rules. In other words, it may become rational for the individual to discuss his choice among alternative institutions under which subsequent choices will be made independently from these later choices or his predicted reactions to them.

1. The most complete attempt to work out such a model is contained in Charles J. Goetz, "Tax Preferences in a Collective Decision-Making Context" (Unpublished Ph.D. dissertation, Alderman Library, University of Virginia of Virginia, 1964). Portions of this work are contained in Charles J. Goetz, "A Variable-Tax Model of Intersectoral Allocation," *Public Finance*, XIX (February, 1964), 29-43.

This separation of the "constitutional" decision from what may be called the "operational" decision of the individual is important, and it is essential to the logic of Part II. It may be illustrated with reference to fiscal institutions and fiscal choice, the particular emphasis here, although it is more generally applicable. Consider the decision or choice calculus of a single reference person in a political community. He tries, we shall assume, to articulate his preferences with respect to the share of economic resources to be devoted to public rather than to private uses. He must decide on the institution of payment for public goods, the tax structure. He must decide on the quantity and mix of public goods to be supplied under this structure, the size and composition of the budget. And, finally, he must decide how he will react to the modified conditions of choice that he will confront in the market place as a result of the fiscal setting.

These decisions are interdependent, as noted, but when he recognizes the costs of negotiating agreements with his fellows on the institutions of payment for each and every budget, the individual may prefer, on efficiency grounds, to separate the institutional decision from the standard budgetary decision. In other words, he may agree that the group should decide, "constitutionally," on the institutions under which fiscal (budgetary or public-goods) choices shall be made, quite independently of these choices themselves. He may say, to himself and others: "I simply do not know what public goods and services I shall want and in what quantities over a whole range of future budgetary choices, but can we not discuss the institutions under which we shall pay for *whatever* public goods and services we decide to supply to ourselves, and in *whatever* quantities we decide to supply them? In specific terms, can we not decide, constitutionally as it were, whether or not we shall raise public revenues through an income tax or through a sales tax?"

Such a treatment of the institutional structure in some independent "constitutional" process will reduce the costs of arriving at ordinary budgetary decisions on the quantity of public goods and services to be supplied. The imposition of such institutional constraints amounts to setting the rules of the "fiscal choice game," whereas without such constraints the game is really without rules at all. This conclusion holds regardless of the ultimate rules for reaching collective decisions, these also being assumed to have been determined constitutionally. Whether political decisions are reached on the basis of Wicksellian unanimity, simple majority voting, or anyone of the many other variants and combinations that are possible, the independent selection of fiscal institutions reduces decision-making costs. It does so because it removes from the direct budgetary calculus a whole set of bargaining counters that would otherwise be brought into play.

It should be emphasized that the incorporation of decision-making costs in the model does not necessarily imply that rational behavior requires a separation of the institutional and operational levels of choice. There seems no way of demonstrating, a priori, that either this procedure or that of simultaneous choice of all relevant variables is relatively more "efficient" in any particular circumstances. Under certain conditions, it is surely rational for the individual, and for all individuals, to choose the fiscal institutions for the supply of public goods along with this supply itself. Under certain other conditions, efficient behavior surely suggests the opposite. If this latter set of conditions are accepted as possible, then we are justified in Part II in examining the calculus through which the individual selects a fiscal institution independently of the particular characteristics of the public-goods choices that may be confronted.

INSTITUTIONS AS RULES

How will a member of a political community go about making a personal choice among alternative fiscal institutions? The precise setting of the problem is important, and this can perhaps best be described in terms of an explicit model.

Assume the existence of a political community in which all day-to-day decisions on the supply of public goods are to be made by simple majority voting in some town-meeting fashion. Each individual knows, in advance, that any and all proposals for fiscal action will be decided in this manner. Any citizen may present to the group motions concerning the level of public outlay on particular items, or on the levels of tax rates producing revenues for those items. Further, we assume that a given individual has no way of predicting just what proposals are likely to be presented to the group for choices, and even if he should be able to make some rough predictions in this respect, he has no way of predicting just where his own preferences would fall with regard to specific motions. In other words, the individual cannot predict whether, say next year or ten years hence, a motion will be made to spend X dollars draining the boondocks. And, even if such a motion is to be made, the individual cannot now tell whether or not he would join in support or in opposition since he knows neither his own tastes in future periods nor his own economic position.

Suppose, now, that a "constitutional" session of the group is convened, and the group is asked to decide, collectively, on an institution of taxation. That is to say, some such institution is to be selected which will, if and when approved, be used to finance *whatever* expenditures that may be proposed and approved in future periods. To return to the example, the individual's future behavior with respect to support or opposition to draining the boondocks would depend, in part, on the way such spending is to be financed. Now, however, he is asked to choose a way of financing all possible spending proposals that may be approved, independently of any knowledge of the pattern of approved motions that may emerge over time. The institution so chosen is to be imposed as a constraint, as a rule, under which particularized choices as to the content and the magnitude of public spending shall be made in a whole, indefinitely determinate, series of fiscal and accounting periods.[2]

The selection of a fiscal institution becomes closely analogous to the choosing of rules for an ordinary game. The player does not know, at the time when he must agree with fellow players on the rules under which the game shall be played, what particular set of rules will be privately most beneficial to him in subsequent rounds of play. He cannot know this with accuracy since he cannot predict what alternatives he will face, and he cannot know the constraints under which he must operate. The inherent uncertainty in choice among rules makes consensus among separate players much more likely to be attained than might otherwise be expected. If a potential player in an ordinary card game, at the time of agreeing on the rules for play, should be able to predict the cards that he will hold in each successive round of play, he will, of course, be quite definite as to his preferred set of rules, and he will fight very hard for the adoption of this set by the whole group. However, to the extent that other prospective players are equally omniscient, agreement on a single set of rules can never be attained.

2. The problem as posed here with reference to the choice among fiscal institutions is methodologically equivalent to the problem of choosing constitutionally among alternative rules or institutions for reaching collective decisions. Cf. James M. Buchanan and Gordon Tullock, *The Calculus of Consent.*

On the other hand, if no prospective player can predict his own position in the various rounds of play anticipated, consensus on rules moves within the realm of possibility. In this situation, each prospective player will be motivated to select a set of rules that will seem "efficient" or "fair" in the private or individualized sense that, whatever may be his own position, he will stand a "fair" chance of winning. The central element of conflict among prospective players that arises once individual positions are identifiable is eliminated to the extent that such identification becomes impossible.

For our purposes, the game setting becomes that of choosing among fiscal institutions. How should the individual prefer to be taxed over a whole indeterminate sequence of periods in which spendings decisions will be made by the group if he knows neither what proposals will be presented and adopted nor what his own particular preferences regarding proposals will be?

FROM PRIVATE INTEREST TO "PUBLIC" INTEREST

Throughout this book, and in earlier works, analysis has been grounded on the choice calculus of the single individual, as a choosing unit, and he has been assumed to act so as to maximize his own utility. This is not, of course, the appropriate place to discuss the general methodological implications of this approach, but one point should be made in passing. Political scientists, and others, often refer to "the public interest" as something that exists independently of the separate personal or private interests of the individual members of a community. The approach taken here does not recognize the existence of such a "public interest," and individuals are presumed to act simply as utility-maximizers, although utility functions need not be narrowly defined.

The approach to fiscal institutions taken in Part II allows some reconciliation of the purely individualistic and the public-interest conception of political order. If the choosing individual is placed in the position of selecting among institutions, among alternative rules of the game, and if he cannot predict with any degree of accuracy his own particular position on subsequent rounds of play, his own private interest will dictate, as suggested above, that he indicate a preference for a set of rules that seems "efficient." That is to say, his own utility-maximizing behavior will, in this setting, lead him to choose rules that will be efficient for the group, taken as a whole. And consensus among all members on a common set

219

of rules becomes conceptually or potentially possible. The analysis suggests, therefore, that if individuals are appropriately placed in positions where they are required to choose "constitutionally," they can be led, by their own self-interest, to act as if they are furthering the general or public interest in some properly meaningful sense. In this setting, no conflict arises between private utility-maximizing behavior and political obligation.

This conclusion has important normative implications, some of which will be discussed more fully in a later chapter. It suggests that where possible social choices should be made under conditions where individuals find themselves in such "constitutional" situations. The utility function of the individual chooser provides different signals for behavior in such situations from those that it provides when individual positions are more readily identifiable. No explicit incorporation of interpersonal considerations need be introduced; the utility function need not be changed so as to include arguments for either the utilities or the activities of other persons. However, because the reference individual may, in any subsequent "round of play" assume any one of many specific positions, his own utility-maximizing behavior will lead him to select institutions that are *generally* efficient. And, since all members of the group may be in roughly similar situations, agreement on a *generally* efficient set of rules becomes possible.

THE QUESTION OF RELEVANCE

Are fiscal institutions actually chosen under conditions that remotely resemble those postulated here? Are institutional choices made separately from day-to-day choices? Exhaustive research into the political process is not required to establish the general conclusion that the models of decision do have considerable relevance for real-world events. Nothing more than everyday observation is required to reveal that fiscal institutions are debated, discussed, and finally selected quite independently of public-goods choices. For example, the political discussion on tax reform in the United States in 1963 and 1964 was carried on largely without any consideration of the choices of spending programs that might be consequent to the reform. In part this partitioning of the fiscal decision process may well be due to fundamentally irrational or inefficient elements, and a greater allowance for the real interdependence among fiscal variables at all levels might well be highly desirable. The effects of one aspect of this partitioning have been discussed in Part I. The independent consideration of the institutional choice tends to impose constraints on ordinary budgetary choice, and, because of this, to generate inefficiency of the standard sort. If, for example, a proposal is made for a particular spending program to be financed under an existing, and presumably nonadjustable, tax structure, the required support may not be generated, despite the fact that, should some alternative tax distribution be introduced, support would be readily forthcoming.

The considerations advanced in this chapter suggest, however, that such admitted inefficiencies that stem from the independence of institutional and operational choices may be offset, at least in certain cases, by the greater efficiencies of decision-making under the fully partitioned system. A priori, it seems impossible to say that the whole fiscal choice process should not, ideally, involve a distinct conceptual separation between the institutional set of decisions and the ordinary or day-to-day operational set. The facts are that we observe such separation in almost all political jurisdictions.

A REHABILITATION OF TRADITIONAL NEOCLASSICAL PUBLIC FINANCE?

The classical and neoclassical theory of public finance, especially as this has been developed by English-language scholars, has been criticized for its emphasis on the tax side of the fiscal account and for its relative neglect of the expenditure side. Analysis in this tradition proceeded as if taxes are exogenously imposed and as if revenues were drained out of the economy upon collection. Einaudi's term, "imposta grandine," which, literally translated, means "hailstorm tax," is properly descriptive of the standard models. So-called "principles" of taxation were developed, and arguments on the basis of these continue to be presented in sophisticated discussions of taxes, without regard to the expenditure side of the budget.

This procedure amounts to an attempt to lay down "principles" for distributing the costs of public goods among individuals independently from any consideration of the demand for such goods. In the market for private goods under certain conditions, the prices that must be paid by individual purchasers are determined primarily by costs, and individual demands influence only the quantities that shall be taken. In this case, demand affects the total outlay on goods, but not the price-per-unit of good supplied. With public or collective goods, jointness in supply is the essential characteristic. This implies that it is impossible to provide divisible units of these goods to "purchasers" at cost-determined supply prices; individual quantity adjustment cannot take place. Cost elements can determine the supply prices confronted by the group as a unit, not those confronted by individuals. The uniformity in quantity that is made available to all individuals in the group makes necessary an apparent discrimination in "prices" charged to the various demanders, and the appropriate discrimination here can only be determined by bringing the demand side explicitly into account. The neglect of this side in deriving the so-called "principles" of taxation produces wholly arbitrary results.

I have argued in other works[3] that the arbitrariness here is reduced to the extent that all public goods and services provide "general" rather than specific benefits. If public outlay is limited to providing only those goods and services that are made available equally to all members in the community, the neoclassical models of analysis become somewhat less one-sided than initial reflection may suggest. This is especially true if specific benefit imputations among individuals are made and accepted to be reasonably descriptive. The making of such imputations incorporates the demand side into the model, but it may do so in such a manner that allows primary concentration on the allocation of costs. If, for example, it is accepted that the marginal benefits from the enjoyment of public goods and services are roughly equal for all individuals, differences in this side of the account do not affect the distribution of tax-costs, regardless of the norms that may be accepted. In such a model, all individual demands for public goods are roughly equivalent. Hence, efficiency considerations would dictate a structure of tax-prices equal for all persons. Discussion as to "principles" for distributing taxes then becomes one of the degree to which nonefficiency norms are relevant.

A different imputation of marginal benefits may be one where these are roughly proportional to some income-wealth base. In this case, efficiency considerations alone dictate proportional income-wealth taxation, at the margin, and departures from this rule could then be discussed in terms of nonefficiency versus efficiency norms. Still other possible marginal benefit imputations might be employed,

3. See my *Fiscal Theory and Political Economy* (Chapel Hill: The University of North Carolina Press, 1960), pp. 15-17.

and each would, of course, yield different "ideally efficient" distributions of marginal tax-prices.

We know, however, that the traditional approach contains few attempts to justify the empirical relevance of any of the benefit imputations required to legitimatize its methodology. Secondly, we know that the public goods and services actually supplied by governments do not fully qualify as "general" in the sense indicated. For some such goods and services, benefits, both total and marginal, are *differentially* made available to individuals and subgroups within the larger community. When this is recognized, the traditional neoclassical approach to tax principles seems to contain little that is worth preserving, and scientific advance seems to require that it be discarded.

This reaction, upon more careful consideration, seems premature. The institutional approach that Part II of this study opens up serves to rehabilitate, in a qualified sense, the neoclassical methodology in general terms, if not in its specific logic. At least in some circumstances, it may prove desirable and efficient for the choice among the institutions of taxation to be divorced from the choice among spending programs. The argument for such a partitioning of the fiscal decision process is based on the presumption that the institutions of taxation, which determine the distribution of the costs of providing public goods and services among members of the group, may be quasi-permanent or "constitutional" elements of the political-social structure whereas spending programs, which determine the distribution of the benefits of public goods and services among the members of the group, may be relatively impermanent or temporary phenomena. Whether or not this distinction is empirically relevant can only be determined by real-world events. But to the extent that it becomes so, we may discuss the individual's calculus of choice among tax instruments quite apart from any specific assumptions about the spending side.

A simplified example will both clarify the setting and suggest its limitations. Assume that a political community contains only three citizens, A, B, and C. There are three possible public spending programs in each fiscal period. One of these benefits A and B equally, but provides no benefit at all to C. A second program benefits A and C equally, but provides no benefit to B. A third program benefits B and C equally, but provides no benefits to A. Assume now that each individual considers the adoption of these three programs as being equally probable in each fiscal period. Under such circumstances as these, it seems rational for any individual in the group to discuss with his fellows the introduction of a *general* scheme for collecting taxes, quite independently of the particular benefit imputation anticipated in any specific period. Over time, the probability distribution of benefits to be enjoyed from various spending programs may be unknown, but this element of uncertainty itself is sufficient to make separate institutional choice rational. It must remain "inefficient," perhaps grossly so, in some short-run or one-period sense, for the individual who enjoys no benefits at all from particular spending programs to be subjected to tax-costs equal to those imposed on his fellows, who are direct beneficiaries. But the acceptance of the institution of taxation may, in the multiperiod setting, become "efficient" in the long-run sense provided only that the individual in question expects to get his own "fair" share in the differential benefits from public services as the tax institution remains in force over a whole unpredictable sequence of spendings choices.

15. *Income Tax Progression**

INTRODUCTION

In this chapter income-tax progression will be examined in the constitutional-institutional framework introduced in Chapter 14. Under what conditions, if at all, will the individual choose a tax structure that embodies rate progression on an income base?

This analysis may be clarified by its contrast with the traditional approach to income taxation. In the latter, progression in a rate structure is explicitly discussed in terms of externally selected ethical norms. That is to say, progression is either justified or attacked on grounds of its agreement or contradiction with a set of norms for fiscal organization that are chosen by the observer, who conceptually stands outside the whole system. Modern economists have advanced in sophistication over the English utilitarians in that they have recognized the necessity of introducing such norms. Henry Simons, who followed Adolf Wagner in this respect, openly and avowedly based his own argument for progressive income taxation on the desirability for greater income equality among persons and families, a social objective that the fiscal structure "should" be organized to promote.[1] More recently, such scholars as Paul Samuelson[2] and Richard A. Musgrave[3] have distinguished the redistributive function of the fiscal mechanism sharply from the allocative func-

---

* The central argument of this chapter was first presented in early 1964 in seminars and lectures at the University of Florida, University of California (Davis and Los Angeles), and Oklahoma State University.

1. Henry Simons, *Personal Income Taxation* (Chicago: University of Chicago Press, 1938).

2. Paul A. Samuelson, "The Pure Theory of Public Expenditure," *Review of Economics and Statistics,* XXXVI (November, 1954), 387-89.

3. Richard A. Musgrave, *The Theory of Public Finance* (New York: McGraw-Hill, 1959).

tion, and, for the former, they have suggested the necessity of introducing external ethical norms.

Progressive income taxation can be fruitfully discussed in such terms. Nevertheless, it is also true that, to the extent that value judgments enter the discussion, genuine "scientific" analysis comes to an end. It follows that if progression, or any other institution, can be discussed meaningfully without the introduction of external norms there are net methodological gains. This is not, of course, to suggest that normative discussions cannot be helpful. I suggest only that such discussions can best be postponed until analysis on a prevalue basis is fully exhausted.

What the institutional-choice approach does is to allow progression to be examined in an individualistic reference system. That is to say, we are enabled to analyze the choice calculus of the individual as he evaluates alternative tax structures, one of which is a progressive tax on income. It is not necessary to assume a position as external observer, and progression need not be discussed only in terms of its impact on a set of separate persons at different income levels. One way of putting this point is to say that, whereas orthodox analysis has considered progression largely, if not exclusively, in terms of *redistribution* among persons, the analysis here allows progression to be treated as one among several alternatives of individual choice. Both the proponents and the opponents of the neoclassical utilitarian argument in support of progression, including its modern counterparts, have overlooked the fact that interpersonal comparisons of utility need not be introduced. Progression has been discussed almost exclusively in terms of the relative tax loads imposed on Tizio and Caio. The analysis here transforms the problem into one of choice among institutions faced by Tizio alone.

What makes this difference possible? The orthodox model requires that attention be devoted to single, isolated events located precisely in time rather than to a series or sequence of events extending over time. Implicitly the standard analytical model assumes that relevant choices are among uniquely timed events. The traditional posing of the tax problem is: If the government must raise X dollars of revenue in Period t_0, how much of this sum shall be raised from Tizio and how much from Caio? Progression, proportion, regression and other terms descriptive of a rate structure are taken to refer to *comparative* rates imposed on the *separate* persons, these being, in turn, arrayed with respect to some income or wealth characteristic.

A cursory examination of real-world political process suggests that tax issues are rarely, if ever, presented in so simple a manner as the traditional discussion suggests. Tax institutions are selected independently of spending programs, but, also, choices are made among instruments that are expected to remain in being over an extended and usually intermediate number of fiscal-accounting periods. When this fact is acknowledged and when its implications are incorporated into the analysis, the question of rate structure can be treated as a problem of individual choice, and the utilitarian dilemma of interpersonal incomparability at least partially resolved. There can exist an individual choice among tax instruments, all of which may, in any one specific period, subject the taxpayer to the same charge.

Before comparison can be meaningful, however, alternatives for choice must be made roughly equivalent in quantitative impact. Familiarly, economists have employed the equal-yield assumption as a means of evaluating various taxes. Since the model to be used here implies a whole series of time periods, we may adopt the constraining assumption that the tax alternatives to the individual embody *equal present values of future tax obligations*. This provides a substitute for the equal-yield-per-period model of orthodox analysis. With this assumption of equal present values we can proceed directly to discuss the individual's choice among various tax instruments, independently of the positions of other individuals, at least initially. The following section develops the analysis under conditions of certainty. In a later section, uncertainty is introduced, with interesting consequences for the results.

INSTITUTIONAL CHOICE UNDER CERTAINTY

Consider now a political community faced with the problem of choosing a tax institution independently of public expenditure programs. To simplify the analysis, we shall introduce an assumption with regard to the spending side that will enable us to limit discussion to the tax side. The community is faced with the necessity of meeting an annual interest charge of X dollars on a deadweight public debt. We assume further that, through some collective decision rule, the distribution for the liability of meeting this debt service obligation has been determined, not for any specific period, but rather in terms of some specific assignment of present-value liabilities. Each person has assigned to him a defined share in the total community liability that the necessity of servicing the debt represents. This rather unusual assumption allows us to neglect initially the whole question of distribution of tax shares among separate persons.

In the private economy, when an individual is confronted with a fixed present-value liability, we do not normally think about his selecting or choosing an institution of payment, although we recognize, of course, that different individuals will meet such obligations differently. Some will act to discharge the obligation immediately; others will schedule regular payments over time; still others will only service the outstanding debt, leaving the principal sum unchanged. The private economy is organized so as to allow each person wide degrees of freedom in choosing privately the most preferred means of meeting an obligation of this nature. Conceptually, we could think of separate individuals meeting their own shares in a public or aggregate liability individualistically and voluntarily. Each person in our model, assigned a specific share in the liability represented in the public debt, could select his own means of payment, and different persons could be allowed to select different instruments.

We move somewhat closer to fiscal reality, however, if we require that all members of the group meet their obligation under the same institution of payment. Let us limit consideration to three fiscal alternatives: an annual tax of equal amount each year, a proportional tax on income, and a single progressive tax on income. We define these three alternatives in such a way that the reference individual, any member of the group, is presented with the same present value, this representing his own assigned share in the total community liability. These present-value liabilities must be defined with respect to an objectively-determined discount rate, which we postulate to be that rate at which the collectivity, the government, can borrow funds in the market. If, instead of this, some subjective or personal rate of discount should be used, equality in present values would simply be another way of defining the three alternatives to be equally preferred by the individual. Choice would be eliminated, which is precisely what we want to examine. In addition, the total of individual liabilities need not add to the total community liability under this sort of computation. If, however, present values are computed by some objective discount rate, equal for all persons, then equality in these values for the three separate fiscal alternatives need not imply that the individual will be indifferent among them.

Faced with the choice posed in this model, the individual will first consider possible resort to the capital market, either as a lender or as a borrower of funds. If this market works in such a way that allows the individual to lend funds or to borrow funds at the same rate at which the government borrows, the individual's own subjective discount rate will be brought into line with that rate which is employed in defining the liability. In such a case, he will remain wholly indifferent as among the three tax alternatives, regardless of his anticipations as to income and spending needs, because he can, at no net cost, convert any one time stream into any other. His own most preferred time stream of spending will not, in this case, be affected at all by the choice of the tax instrument that is imposed on all members of the group. If, however, the capital market does not operate so as to produce these results, the individual may be led, by ordinary utility-maximizing considerations, to prefer one of the three taxes to the others. If he cannot lend funds or borrow funds at the objective discount rate that is used to define the liability with which he is confronted, but must, instead, lend or borrow at different rates, he will prefer that fiscal alternative that will minimize the distortion from his own optimal time stream of spending.

It is reasonable to assume that the individual can always lend funds at the government borrowing rate; he may do so by purchasing government securities. However, private individuals cannot normally borrow at rates equal to those at which governments can borrow, for obvious reasons. Some differential over and above this rate must be paid. If this direction of difference is accepted, and if the individual expects his income to rise over time, rational choice will dictate that he "vote for" meeting his obligation through the progressive income tax, provided only that his planned or preferred stream of private spending is more uniform than that of anticipated income receipts.

A NUMERICAL EXAMPLE

Assume that the reference individual knows with certainty that he will receive $1000 in the current time period t_0, and that he will receive $2000 in the following period t_1. We limit the analysis to two periods. Assume now that a total fiscal liability, defined at the beginning of t_0, amounting to $976.19 is assigned to this individual. The discount rate is 5 per cent.

This obligation may be met by a tax of $500 in each of the two periods; by a proportional tax levied at 33.6 per cent of income received in each period; or by a single-step progressive tax on income in each period, with a rate of 50.6 per cent on all income above a $500 exemption. This third alternative is, of course, only one among many possible progressive rate structures. It is chosen here because of its numerical simplicity. The details of the situation are set out in Table 15.1.

This numerical example makes it clear that if the individual's preferred time stream of private spending is more stable than his anticipated income stream, the tax obligation can best be met through the progressive levy. This allows him to meet a disproportionate share of his liability during the period when his income receipts are high, thereby eliminating or reducing the necessity of his entering the loanable funds market to borrow at private rates of interest. In effect, the progressive tax scheme allows the individual to "borrow" from the government, at the public borrowing rate, by postponing his tax liability through time.

This model need not be nearly so restrictive or rarified as the various assumptions make it seem. The essential requirements are that desired or planned private spending be related in some way to permanent income rather than to annually measured income and that the latter be expected to increase over time. Both of these seem plausible enough, and both have been supported by empirical evidence.

As presented in this model, we have assumed that public spending in each period is limited to servicing a deadweight public debt. It is easy to see that this assumption can be replaced by one that allows public spending on almost any mix of collective goods, provided that the individual does not expect, on the average, to be benefited differentially. In other words, the analysis holds without change if the distribution of benefits from whatever public services that may be provided is expected to be determined on some essentially random basis.

FROM INDIVIDUAL TO GROUP CHOICE

The whole analysis remains highly restricted, however, in that it is applicable to the choice problem as this might be faced by the

230

single, isolated individual. To be relevant for policy discussion, the analysis must be extended to the collective outcome for the whole community of persons.

A difficult adding-up problem arises when we shift from the isolated individual decision calculus to that of a group of individuals. Assume, now, that the collectivity, as a unit, must reach agreement as to one of the three fiscal alternatives. This outcome, once selected, will be then imposed on all individual citizens. We want to examine the process through which agreement might be attained.

If we continue to assume that each person has assigned to him a fixed share in some total community liability, or else a fixed proportion of variable aggregate liability, general agreement among large numbers of people seems possible. This is because, for the majority of taxpayers, incomes will be expected to grow over time,

TABLE 15.1
(Present value of tax liability: $976.19; discount rate: 5%)

	Time Period, t_0	Time Period, t_1
Income before tax	$1,000	$2,000
Tax bill		
Under annual tax	500	500
Under proportional tax, 33.6%	336	672
Under single-step progression,		
50.6% on income over $500	253	759
Income after tax		
Under annual tax	500	1,500
Under proportional tax	664	1,328
Under progressive tax	747	1,241

and private spending patterns are, ideally, more stable than income receipts. However, it becomes clear that by continuing to assume away the basic distributional issue at this stage, we are neglecting the central and indeed the critical problem in tax choice.

Assume, therefore, that there exists no such prechoice assignment of personal fiscal liabilities, even in present-value terms. Instead, we now assume that the whole group, as a collectivity, must reach some decision on assigning the appropriate shares as well as some decision on the tax institution through which the individual tax bills are to be paid.

Regardless of the prevailing set of rules for reaching collective decisions, whether this be Wicksellian unanimity, simple majority voting, or something different, the problem quickly becomes one that is dominated by pure bargaining and the results are, of course, unpredictable. Presumably, some allocation of shares among persons will be chosen, but a great amount of investment in strategic bargaining effort may be observed to take place. Once a bargain is struck, once a "solution" as to the proportionate shares is reached, the individual calculus discussed above might come into play. Here the individual, whatever his final lot in the bargain, should rationally prefer to pay his share through the institution of progressive income taxation, given the suggested side conditions. In the process of bargaining on the assignment of shares, however, the institutions for collecting revenue take on wholly different characteristics from those that these same institutions possess in the individual calculus. It is this interdependence between the bargaining on shares in the tax bill, the distributional problem, and the efficiency problem that confounds both choices, and the analysis of choice, here. Because of this interdependence, tax institutions become means of assigning shares.

If it were possible to conceive of a separate bargaining process in which liability shares are assigned, but where the choice among institutions of payment is not settled, the distributional and the efficiency aspects could be distinguished. Interdependence almost necessarily arises, however, especially when additional constraints and side conditions are placed on the structure of the bargains or the workings of the institutions of payment. The individual who should, rationally, prefer the progressive income tax as the efficient means of meeting his own share of community liability may, also rationally, oppose this tax if a side condition is imposed to the effect that rates of tax must be *uniform over separate persons*. Through such conditions as these, the tax alternatives necessarily become counters in the bargaining game.

A NUMERICAL EXAMPLE

An extension of the earlier numerical example, summarized in Table 15.1, will clarify this somewhat complex point. Assume now a two-man community, and, as before, a two-period sequence. The first man, whom we may call A, is the one whose income prospects have been set out in Table 15.1. The second man, whom we shall call B, anticipates a somewhat lower income stream than his fellow citizen; B's income prospects, again assumed to be known with certainty, are set out in Table 15.2.

Let us, for now, assume that the distributional or share-assignment problem has been resolved and that B has a present-value liability of $748.80 as compared with A's, $976.19. Note that this figure for B is computed by imposing the same proportional rate on measured in-period income as that imposed on A under this alternative, or a rate of 33.6 per cent. As with A, B should also "prefer" to meet this obligation through the payment of a progressive tax, as Table 15.2 shows, with the suggested side conditions. If we choose the same form of this tax as that discussed with reference to A's choice, a single-step progressive structure, with a flat rate above the $500 exemption, B must pay a rate of 59.7 per cent. Note that this exceeds the comparable rate for A, which was 50.6 per cent.

TABLE 15.2
(Present value of tax liability: $748.80; discount rate: 5%)

	Time Period, t_0	Time Period, t_1
Income before tax	$600	$1,710
Tax bill		
Under annual tax	383.60	383.60
Under proportional tax, 33.6%	201.60	574.56
Under single-step progression, 59.7%		
on income above $500	59.70	712.37

The interdependence between the share-assignment problem and the institutional efficiency problem is evident in the example. It is not possible that both uniformity in rates among separate persons, *and* predetermined liability shares can be maintained over more than one tax alternative. In the example, an equalization of proportional rates, as between the two persons, implies discrimination in progressive rates that would generate the same present-value revenues. The converse also holds, of course. An equalization of progressive rates would imply some discrimination in proportional rates.

The individual or group with the higher income anticipations, A in the example, will bargain for a distributional solution that reduces his own liability. In so doing, he will find that distributional advantages can be secured through the selection of tax institutions

233

themselves under the side condition of rate uniformity. Recognizing this, A will argue in favor of the imposition of uniform annual taxes, or the institutions nearest to this alternative that seems practicable. Individual B, in the example, the person with the relatively low income prospects, will behave in the opposing fashion. He will argue for the progressive tax, under the most extreme rate structure possible. Individual A, the high-income receiver, finds that distributional and efficiency objectives come into conflict, and, in the normal case, the distributional elements assume considerably more importance. Hence, we should expect the traditional intergroup conflicts over tax institutions. The individual who expects to receive the relatively higher income is led to support the selection of fiscal institutions that are inefficient because of the nature of the political bargaining process in which he must engage.

At this point, our whole analysis seems to be back where it started. If a "social compromise" or "agreement" on tax institutions cannot be worked out without the introduction of purely distributional considerations, the tedium of analyzing the decision calculus of the single, isolated individual may appear to have been useless. To say that, if he could separate the efficiency considerations out, the individual should rationally prefer the progressive tax, really says nothing at all if such a separation is shown to be impossible when participation in group choice is introduced.

FISCAL CHOICE UNDER UNCERTAINTY

To this point in the analysis, however, the individual has been assumed to be able to predict future income receipts with certainty. The analysis is interesting here in that, when uncertainties are introduced, some of the complex interdependencies tend to disappear. In a certain world, where separate individuals and groups expect particular patterns of income over a series of time periods, the distributional elements of a choice among tax institutions can rarely be put aside. This feature is, however, modified dramatically when individual choice is assumed to take place under uncertainty in regard to future income prospects.

Again it is useful to consider a simplified example. And for present purposes, we need not consider a time sequence at all. Take an individual who faces what he estimates to be an equal probability that he will receive an income of $1,000 or $2,000 in the current period; he assigns a subjective probability of one-half to each of these prospects. We need now only to assume that his most preferred pattern of private spending is more predictable than his income receipts in order for the analysis developed to hold without qualification. Suppose that we postulate that the individual is to be subjected to a tax which carries a certainty equivalent of $100 and that he desires to maintain a private spending rate of $1,400 per period. If he selects an invariant tax, unrelated to actual income receipts, he agrees to pay the flat sum of $100 regardless of his income event. If he selects a proportional tax on measured in-period income, he has a probability of one-half of paying $132 and a probability of one-half of paying only $66. On the other hand, suppose that he chooses a single-step progressive levy, with all income above $1,000 exempted from tax. Under this fiscal alternative, he has an equal chance of paying $200 and of paying nothing at all. In the case of low-income realization in the period, his resort to the capital market is minimized under the third alternative. It seems clear that he should, rationally, opt for this scheme.

This single-period model is, of course, highly unrealistic in all respects. If we incorporate uncertainty as to income prospects into a multiperiod model, a more relevant choice situation emerges. In this case, the individual will tend to choose among tax alternatives on the basis of efficiency criteria. Distributional aspects are eliminated to the extent that the individual cannot predict the shape of the bargain that will, in fact, yield him maximum gain.

It is not reasonable to assume that the individual is uncertain as to income prospects in the near future except, of course, to a limited degree. He will tend to know with some accuracy what his income prospects are over a succession of periods subsequent to choice. But it is surely reasonable also to assume that income uncertainty increases as plans are projected forward in time. This implies that the efficiency elements in fiscal choice become relatively more important as longer and longer time horizons are introduced. It becomes possible, in this manner, to conceive of situations in which distributional considerations come to be effectively swamped by efficiency considerations in the individual's own calculus of choice among the tax alternatives. If, for example, we think of a group confronted with an aggregate fiscal liability over time (the benefits from public expenditure programs being distributed in some unpredictable fashion), with each member of the group wholly uncertain as to his own income prospects beyond some intermediate period, each individual may, quite rationally, prefer that the collectivity adopt the institution of progression with specific rates to be levied on all who may qualify as taxpayers by the designated income criteria. This agreement on the choice of a tax institution may take place despite the fact that each individual recognizes that, should he happen to receive the relatively high income, he will bear a major share of the aggregate tax load through time. In such a decision model as this, the problem of assigning shares among persons whose future income prospects are clearly identifiable cannot arise, and each person is led by utility-maximizing considerations to opt for that institution of payment that he thinks will be most "efficient" given some probability distribution of his income expectations in future periods.

INSTITUTIONAL CHOICE IN THE REAL WORLD

As we have noted, choices in the real world are not made for each period separately. Institutions are selected as if they were semipermanent. This suggests that elements of both the certainty and the uncertainty models may be present in the normal individual calculus. It is reasonable to suggest that at least some measure of the popular support for progressive income taxation in Western democratic societies has been based intuitively on some such "efficiency" calculus as that outlined in this chapter, in contrast to purely distributional motivations.

There are several features of the prevailing institutional structure that confirm this suggestion. For one thing, explicit redistribution of incomes, as such, is not normally introduced into the political commentaries on rate progression, nor, indeed, is this present to any large extent in the fiscal system as it actually operates. Instead of being employed directly as a means of transferring general purchasing power from the rich to the poor, the progressive income tax produces revenues for the financing of "general" or "collective" purposes. The result is, in many cases, net redistribution, but this remains a result, rather than an openly avowed aim except in relatively special circumstances. The sequential model of choice is confirmed by the fact that tax proposals are usually discussed, not as unique annual allocations of fiscal charges, but as quasi-permanent features of a continuing institutional structure. Temporary taxes are explicitly designated as such in the discussion.

All this is not to suggest, of course, that redistributionist arguments or objectives have been absent from the practical political discussion of tax alternatives, on the side of either the supporters or the attackers of progression. The point is rather that there may have been an undue emphasis on the redistributional elements in the choice among fiscal institutions, and perhaps especially by public finance scholars. When models that reflect the actual choice situations more carefully are used, nonredistributional aspects assume considerable importance, and progressive income taxation emerges in a somewhat different light. Egalitarian aims, explicitly avowed as ethical norms, need not be introduced to "defend" the institution of progression, or to "explain" its acceptance in modern fiscal structures.

QUALIFICATIONS

Again it must be noted that the analysis in this chapter is not intended to be an exhaustive treatment of income tax progression, even in the reference system of individual institutional choice. The purpose has been that of demonstrating the efficacy, or potential efficacy, of approaching some of the familiar institutions of the fiscal system in terms of the choices that must ultimately confront the individual taxpayer as he participates in some quasi-constitutional collective choice among several fiscal alternatives. The analysis has shown that under certain conditions progressive income taxation may be rationally preferred by the individual, and, at least to some extent, these conditions embody features of real-world institutional choice.

The required conditions may not be present in many circumstances, and the choice behavior of the individual may be predictably different from that suggested above. In the following chapter, we shall outline a set of conditions only slightly different from that postulated here and demonstrate that the individual may choose to pay his fiscal obligations through specific excise levies. Exhaustive treatment would require that many sets of possible situations of choice be examined. As an example, in the models of this chapter, income receipts have been assumed to be determined more or less externally to the individual's own decisions about earning income. This means, of course, that the models have ignored the whole issue concerning the possible effects of progression on incentives to earn taxable income, an issue that has been central to much of the traditional discussion. Alternative models could be introduced in which the individual is assumed to be able to vary the amount of taxable income earned in each period. An extreme model of this variety might allow the individual to adjust income precisely to spending plans in each period. In this case the efficiency argument in support of progression would not hold. If, however, the individual is allowed to vary his income receipts only within relatively narrow limits, and if his preferred stream of private spending is somehow independent of his measured in-period income receipts, the efficiency argument must enter his evaluation. To the extent that the individual, when confronted with institutional choice, does recognize that his own income-earning choices during future periods will be influenced by the tax alternative in existence, and that the progressive tax will introduce differential effects in this respect, the efficiency argument in support of progression is reduced in weight. Even here, however, there may be situations in which the individual will prefer the progressive tax to its alternatives. The distortions in the individual's intertemporal income-earning pattern may be more than offset by the relative improvements in his intertemporal income-spending pattern that progression may allow.

IMPLICATIONS

If the basic analysis of this and the following chapters is accepted, certain normative implications follow with respect to fiscal reforms. First of all, the advantages that may be secured from having fundamental decisions on the fiscal structure discussed, enacted, and implemented as quasi-permanent changes, whose effects are expected to endure over a long series of fiscal-accounting periods, become clear. To the extent that the individual as a potential taxpayer and as a participant in collective decisions considers the long-run implications of his choices, the purely distributional influences in these choices tend to be damped. A second, and perhaps more important, general implication that emerges from the analysis is the possible significance of social-economic mobility in affecting individual choice behavior. In a society that is descriptively characterized by the pervasiveness of the "log-cabin myth"; that is, one in which expectations of future income prospects among the young, generally, are bouyant over large subgroups, the distributional aspects of fiscal decisions tend to become secondary. By contrast, in a society that is characterized by a hierarchy of class distinctions which imply corollary income expectations, even relatively permanent decisions among fiscal alternatives may primarily involve issues of interclass or intergroup equity.

There are also important philosophical implications to be drawn from this exploratory discussion of progressive income taxation. If the efficiency-under-uncertainty argument is wholly rejected, as might appear to be the case in some scholarly discussions of progression, the nature of democratic political society itself is called into question. This is a subject about which social scientists, and especially economists, have remained strangely silent. Implicitly, as Wicksell suggested, they have been content to assume a benevolent despotism, a central decision-making authority, the "men in Washington or Whitehall," who, somehow, know what is "best" for other members of the community. This *dirigiste* vision or model of political order is useful in certain contexts, as we have suggested, but it is at odds with effective democratic process, as this latter has been traditionally interpreted. Once this simple point is recognized many of the policy aspects of modern economic analysis cease to have relevance.

In this book the collectivity is viewed as a set of individuals who seek to arrive at joint decisions for the achievement of mutually beneficial objectives. In this model or vision of political order, the whole manner of looking at most matters of economic policy must be significantly changed. Here we simply are not allowed to introduce external ethical norms to resolve issues of conflict that arise. We cannot rely on an externally-imposed objective of "equality," or upon a "social welfare function" to inform decisions about the basic fiscal structure. Somehow, and in some fashion, we must try to evolve collective agreements out of the rational calculus of men as they participate in governmental choice processes. If, in these, men are considered, and consider themselves, purely in terms of immediate and identifiable economic position or status, analysis reduces, simply and quickly, to that of coalition formation. Social and collective decisions represent solutions to zero sum games, and, as is the case with all such games, one is prompted to ask why the losers continue to play. The answer is, of course, that they enjoy playing and that the game is held to be reasonably "fair" in that losers continually expect to win in subsequent rounds of play. But purely redistributional outcomes are difficult to think about in these terms; the collectivity becomes, all too readily, a means through which the politically strong can exploit the politically weak.

239

A more encouraging, and in some respects a more realistic, vision of social process emerges from the analysis developed here. The political game is not zero sum; it is, like the economic game, positive sum. Individuals, in their capacities as participants in basic fiscal decisions, are acting without full knowledge of their own shares in the financing of general public services over time. The game has not really been played at the time the rules are chosen, and the levy of progressive income taxation may be somewhat analogous to the familiar "big winner buys the drinks" comment heard at the onset of many a parlor poker game.

16. *Specific Excise Taxation**

*INTRODUCTION

How should taxes be paid? This question has been discussed for centuries, and will continue to be discussed for centuries more. It has not been resolved, either in the formal theory of public finance or in the practical structure of modern fiscal systems. In this chapter, as in the one preceding, this old and familiar question is asked in what is essentially a novel setting. How would the individual prefer to meet his tax obligations over time if he must choose among fiscal alternatives as quasi-permanent institutions? The earlier chapter examined the standard direct tax alternatives. Here the direct tax-indirect tax problem will be analyzed, a problem that continues to occupy an important position in the literature of fiscal theory.

In recent decades, the choice between direct and indirect taxes has been discussed in terms of the now-famous excess-burden theorem, initially stated by Barone,[1] later elaborated many times, and, more recently, subjected to several criticisms. Broadly speaking, it seems correct to say, despite the acknowledged relevance of second-best arguments, most modern scholars would accept the view that,

* The analysis contained in this chapter was developed jointly with Professor Francesco Forte of Turin, Italy, in the spring of 1962, and the argument was first presented that year in a seminar at the University of Exeter, England. The analysis, in a somewhat different form, provides the basis for the paper, written jointly with Forte, "Fiscal Choice Through Time: A Case for Indirect Taxation?" *National Tax Journal,* XVII (September, 1964), 144-57, and circulated as No. 81, Studies of Government Finance Reprints, Brookings Institution, 1964. I am, of course, indebted to Professor Forte for his assistance in developing the argument, along with any other spillover effects this assistance might have had on other parts of this study.
1. E. Barone, "Studi di economia finanziaria," *Giornale degli economisti* (1912), II, 329-30, in notes.

other things equal, direct and general taxes are to be recommended over indirect and specific taxes on both equity and efficiency grounds. Employing the methodology previously applied, I shall demonstrate that this wide-spread conclusion cannot be supported. As was the case with income tax progression, the purpose of the analysis is not to defend specific commodity taxation, per se, but to use the traditional direct tax-indirect tax comparison to illustrate the efficacy of the general institutional approach to fiscal choice.

THE ONE-PERIOD ARGUMENT SUMMARIZED

Almost without exception, the direct-indirect tax comparison has proceeded on the assumption that a choice between tax instruments must be made only in a one-period setting. To my knowledge, no attempt has been made to extend the comparison to a multiperiod or long-run setting; no one has assumed, for analytical purposes, that the tax instrument chosen shall remain in effect over several income or fiscal accounting periods. The introduction of such a temporal sequence, along with the concentration on individual choice behavior, is central to the analysis that will be developed. Initially, however, it will be useful to examine briefly the standard one-period model.

Barone demonstrated that, for the individual taxpayer, a direct tax should rationally be preferred to an indirect tax of equal yield. His argument has become one of the textbook examples of indifference curve economics, and it need not be repeated here. Little showed that, strictly speaking, the Barone conclusions follow only when a lump-sum tax is compared with a specific commodity tax.[2] Friedman[3] and Rolph and Break[4] showed that the Barone theorem could be extended from the single individual to the whole community only if all of the remaining conditions necessary for Pareto-optimality should be satisfied. These criticisms, which may be summarized as those deriving from second-best arguments, need not affect the analysis to be developed here, since, initially at least, the latter does

2. I. M. D. Little, "Direct versus Indirect Taxes," *Economic Journal,* LXI (1951), 577-84.

3. Milton Friedman, "The 'Welfare' Aspects of an Income Tax and an Excise Tax," *Journal of Political Economy,* LX (1952), 25-33, reprinted in *Essays in Positive Economics* (Chicago: University of Chicago Press, 1953), pp. 100-16.

4. Earl R. Rolph and George Break, "The Welfare Aspects of Excise Taxes," *Journal of Political Economy,* LVII (1949), 46-54.

not go beyond individual choice. In the restricted one-period model, the rational person will always prefer the direct tax over the indirect tax of equal yield for the simple reason that he can in this manner enjoy the widest range of choice.

In order to relate it to the subsequent discussion, the one-period question may be put as follows: Should the utility-maximizing individual, confronted with a determined tax liability, choose to pay this liability through a lump-sum payment, a proportional tax on income, a progressive tax on income, a general tax on consumption expenditure, or a specific tax on the consumption of one commodity? In such a model, the first alternative provides the widest area of choice. The lump-sum tax will be preferred over the proportional income tax which will, in its turn, be preferred over the progressive tax which introduces an additional element of discrimination. The latter tax will, in its own turn, be preferred over the general expenditure tax. And, finally, the tax on a specific commodity becomes the least desired of the lot; it produces the largest distortion in the pattern of earning-spending behavior. These familiar conclusions hold, however, only if the individual is allowed to select among fiscal alternatives separately in each discrete period of time or if the results can somehow be generalized to apply to a sequence of time periods.

CHOICE THROUGH TIME

Let the same question be posed, only assume now that the fiscal alternative, once selected, must remain in force over a whole series of periods, $t_0, t_1, \ldots, t_n$. As was the case with the analysis of progression, it will be useful to develop initially a certainty model. Hence the individual is assumed able to predict with certainty, at t_0, what his income receipts will be in each of the periods, $t_1, t_2, \ldots, t_n$. We shall also assume that his decision, at t_0, reflects consideration of anticipated fluctuations in spending plans over time. Viewed from t_0, his preferred spending pattern over the whole time sequence is known with certainty; this pattern need not, of course, exhibit uniformity in time.

The choice calculus to be analyzed here is somewhat more complex than that required for the preceding chapter. It is useful, therefore, to establish some general principles of rational behavior for the individual before posing the fiscal decision issue specifically. For convenience, we may assume that the individual saves only in order to retire debt or to accumulate funds for future consumption spending. This is a life-cycle model of saving behavior that is similar to those suggested by several economists in recent years.[5] In such a model, the present value of the income stream, at t_0, is equal to the present value of the planned outlay or spending stream.

To avoid confusion, it is first necessary to distinguish between spending on items of consumption and actual consumption of these items. For simplicity here, assume that these acts are simultaneous. This implies that the services of all durable consumption goods are purchased or leased as consumption actually takes place. We now break down consumption spending into two provisional categories, the dividing line between which cannot be rigorously defined. The first includes those consumption services designed to meet what may be called "basic needs." The second category includes those services that are purchased with a view toward meeting "residual needs," which are, in some sense, less urgent than those in the first category. Despite the admitted arbitrariness of any dividing line here, some such order of priorities must exist for almost any individual or family unit. Some needs must be met in the normal order of affairs; others may be met only if the opportunity (in part determined by income) arises.

Orthodox rationality criteria suggest that the individual should equalize the utility per dollar spent on each consumption service in each period. This may suggest that any attempt to distinguish between "basic" and "residual" items is misleading. If income fluctuates over time, however, casual observation indicates that residual items are, in fact, purchased and consumed only in periods of relative affluence. Such behavior would, nonetheless, be irrational in a world of perfect certainty. Here the individual would, through his saving activity, attain results that would be closely similar to those attained under a stable income flow. He should, in other terms, equalize the marginal rates of substitution between any two items of consumption for all time periods, viewed from the planning moment, t_0, independently of predicted fluctuations in income receipts or in spending needs, on the assumption that price ratios remain invariant over time. If needs vary as among separate periods,

5. For a summary discussion that contains references to the other works, see M. J. Farrell, "New Theories of the Consumption Function," *Economic Journal*, LXIX (1959), 678-96.

this equalization need not, of course, imply equal consumption flows of either service in separate periods of time.[6]

Viewed from the moment, t_0, the individual will set out a pattern of saving and spending over the several periods such that, in each period, the marginal rate of substitution between any two goods, say, bread and coal, is equal to the ratio of their prices. If, as an example, we consider the two-season year as a sequence, the rational individual will plan his spending over the whole year to insure that

6. For each time period, the standard necessary conditions hold. One of these is,

$$(1) \quad \frac{MU_i}{p_i} = \frac{MU_j}{p_j}$$

, for any two goods, i and j, i $\neq$ j, in the set, i, j = 1, 2, . . . , m. Over the determined life cycle, individuals act so as to satisfy (1) in each period. If we assume that the price ratios are constant over time, necessary conditions for multiperiod "equilibrium," at the moment of planning, t_0, become,

$$(2) \quad \left(\frac{MU_i}{MU_j} \right)_{t_0} = \left(\frac{MU_i}{MU_j} \right)_{t_1} = \left(\frac{MU_i}{MU_j} \right)_{t_2} \cdots = \frac{p_i}{p_j}$$

where the subscripts outside the parentheses refer to the time periods, t_0 to t_n. No explicit discounting factor need be introduced in (2) since, by assumption, prices are not paid until consumption takes place. Hence, for periods later than t_0, marginal utilities and prices are discounted by a common factor. Note particularly that the satisfaction of (2) does not require that "tastes" remain constant over time. The equalization of the marginal rates of substitution can be achieved by widely differing "mixes" of the two items.

If we assume that the individual has no control over the income that he earns, and, further, that income payments are lagged by one period, the over-all income constraint becomes,

$$(3) \quad A_{t_0} + \frac{Y_{t_1}}{1+r} + \frac{Y_{t_2}}{(1+r)^2} + \cdots$$

$$\frac{Y_{t_n}}{(1+r)^n} = \left[\sum_{i=1}^{m} p_i q_i \right]_{t_0} +$$

$$\frac{\left[\sum_{i=1}^{m} p_i q_i \right]_{t_1}}{(1+r)} + \cdots \frac{\left[\sum_{i=1}^{m} p_i q_i \right]_{t_n}}{(1+r)^n}$$

where A_{t_0} measures initially-held assets, and p, q, and r measure the prices, quantities, and rate of discount, respectively. If the individual is allowed to vary his earnings (income) over time (3) is not, of course, the relevant constraint, and it must be replaced by a set of production constraints. The fundamentals of the analysis do not, however, require this generalization. Hence, in the discussion that follows in the text, the individual is presumed to act as if his stream of income receipts is determined exogenously to his own behavior.

245

his needs for bread and coal will be equally satisfied, in a relative sense, in each season. He will not skimp on bread during the winter merely because his needs for coal are great. Nor will he gorge himself in the summer because he need make no outlay on coal for current usage. He will, of course, save some share of his income during the summer to meet his varying need for coal over the whole sequence. The example suggests that either income or needs or both can fluctuate over a temporal sequence and that the individual must take such variations into account as he attempts to maximize the present value of expected utility.

After this digression, let us return to the problem of individual choice among fiscal alternatives. Examine now the same alternatives listed above for the one-period model, but assume a multi-period setting. How will the individual choose to pay his taxes? Or, more correctly stated, how will he "vote" in a collective decision process, elements of interdependence being temporarily neglected? As in Chapter 15, assume either that the pattern of public spending is wholly unpredictable as to benefit incidence or that such spending is committed quite independently from the individual's choice calculus.

EXCHANGE THROUGH TIME

The individual will consider his possible resort to the capital market. If this market works in such a manner as to allow the individual both to borrow and to lend at the governmental borrowing rate, the specific commodity tax remains the least desired among the fiscal alternatives listed. If the individual confronts this kind of market opportunity, no *temporal* distortion need be introduced in his spending stream under any of the tax institutions. Hence, he can simply array the various institutions in order of preference based on minimizing *pattern* distortion within each period, the setting for the one-period model. Here the one-period results are general; the lump-sum tax becomes the optimal fiscal device.

If, however, the individual cannot borrow at public rates, *temporal* distortion does become relevant. The objective of the individual is not modified. He will try, as best he can after the imposition of the tax, to maintain the desired equalities in marginal rates of substitution. Assume, now, that prior to his confrontation with tax choice, the individual attains a position of planning "equilibrium." That is to say, he has formulated a pattern of saving and spending over time that will equalize the relevant marginal rates of substitution in the different periods, always viewed only from the moment, t_0.[7] He now confronts the tax obligation, which we assume he is able to quantify in present-value terms. He will try to choose that tax instrument which introduces, on balance, the least disturbance in his planned pattern of consumption spending over time. If both income receipts and spending needs are expected to be stable, the orthodox conclusions hold. If, however, we allow for some temporal fluctuations in either income receipts or in spending, these conclusions are modified. Temporal distortion must be considered, and the one-period results no longer are general.

If spending patterns are expected to be more uniform over time than income receipts, the progressive income tax will tend to be optimal as the analysis of Chapter 15 has shown. The question to be asked at this point is whether or not the general sales tax or the specific excise tax might not be preferred, even to the progressive income tax, on similar grounds. The answer seems clearly to be negative under the conditions outlined. Either of these taxes on spending would, in the model where spending needs are more uniform in time than income receipts, introduce familiar in-period distortion that is greater than that under any of the direct tax alternatives. At the same time, these taxes would represent no improvement over the progressive tax on income in minimizing temporal distortion.

If, however, we modify the conditions and now assume that anticipated spending desires fluctuate *more* than anticipated income receipts, different results may emerge. For simplicity, assume that income is expected to be stable, but that spending is expected to fluctuate sharply from one period of time to the next. This suggests that, without some recourse to the capital market, the marginal utility of the individual's spending dollar will be expected to vary over time. If "imperfections" in the investing-borrowing market involve sizable costs, the final adjustment attainable by the individual may involve a consumption-spending sequence that allows for rather significant variation in the per period outlay on certain residual consumption items. Under this set of conditions, a specific

7. We are concerned here only with the individual's calculus at t_0. The fact that, when t_1 arrives, he may have a different set of "optimal" plans need not concern us. On this latter point, see Robert H. Strotz, "Myopia and Inconsistency in Dynamic Utility Maximization," *Review of Economic Studies,* 23 (1956), 165-80.

commodity tax, levied on a single item or set of items of residual consumption, may well minimize over-all distortion, and hence be preferred, even to the progressive income tax.

Rational behavior on the part of the individual who expects his income and his spending to fluctuate over time dictates that he adjust his consumption in time so as to "bunch" his usage of residual items during periods when the marginal utility of his spending dollar is low. He will plan to satisfy certain residual consumption requirements only during those periods when his level of spending is relatively low, or when his level of income is relatively high. This pattern of behavior need not violate any norms of rationality when it is recognized that temporal substitution among consumption services is clearly possible. Certain items of consumption are postponable, necessarily so. For example, the individual may "need" only one holiday each year. It is sensible for him to plan his holiday for a period when either income receipts are higher than usual or when his desires for remaining consumption items are lower than usual.[8]

If the individual does, in fact, tend to bunch spending on residual consumption items, an activity that is surely descriptive of real-world behavior, it seems evident that a tax on a specific commodity or service may, under the proper combination of circumstances, be the most desirable of all the fiscal alternatives posed. The familiar in-period distortion in consumption patterns may be more than offset by the advantages that this tax possesses in allowing the individual to concentrate his tax payments during those periods when the marginal utility of his spending dollar is expected to be low, and, conversely, to escape altogether tax payment during periods when the marginal utility of his spending dollar is expected to be high. The minimization of temporal distortion in the individual's spending plans which this tax instrument allows may more than offset the maximization of the in-period distortion that it also embodies.

As compared with the progressive tax levied on income receipts in each period, the tax on a single item of postponable residual consumption can allow for adjustment in tax liability for fluctuating levels of spending in addition to fluctuating levels of income receipts. To demonstrate this point by a simple example, assume that income

8. Care should be taken to distinguish postponable items of residual consumption from durable consumer goods. The durable goods-nondurable goods distinction need not concern us here, and we have assumed that all services are purchased as they are actually used. A postponable service is characterized by some nonrecurrence of "need" over time.

receipts are expected to be uniform over time; a family anticipates that, over the next decade, t_1, t_2, . . . , t_{10}, it will receive an annual income of $10,000. The decade is taken to be the relevant planning horizon. During these years, a son is expected to be attending college during t_3, t_4, t_5 and t_6. Without any adjustment in the capital market, the marginal utility of this family's spending dollar will be higher during these four years than in other years of the decade. The progressive tax would, in this example with uniform income, require the payment of the same net tax during each year. But this family, if allowed to choose, might prefer to bunch its tax payments for the whole decade in the noncollege years, t_1, t_2, t_7, . . . , t_{10}. It may do so, without recourse to the capital market either as net lender or borrower, if the tax should be imposed on some item or set of items of genuinely residual consumption spending, items that the family plans to purchase only during the noncollege years. For example, holidays in Europe may be projected for such relatively affluent periods. Despite the in-period or pattern distortion that a tax on European holiday spending would surely involve, such a tax might, over time, actually expand the range of choice open to the family in question, relative to the situation under any other tax alternative considered.

It is interesting to note that when the whole set of tax instruments considered are arrayed in some order of distortion, the general tax on all spending becomes the *least* desirable fiscal alternative. The specific tax on a single item, or set of items, of residual consumption spending allows tax liability to be bunched in periods when the predicted marginal utility of spending is low. The income tax, whether proportional or progressive, allows the liability to be spread equally over time in this example where income does not fluctuate. The general tax on spending, by comparison, would require that the family pay a higher total tax precisely during those periods when the "needs" for basic consumption items are greatest. This conclusion is perhaps noteworthy since it runs counter to the familiar argument that the general expenditure tax may be more "efficient," in some sense, than the income tax because of the removal of discrimination against saving. The contrast in results here stems from the fundamental difference in approach to fiscal choice.[9]

9. The relationship between the analysis here and the traditional "double taxation of saving" argument should be explained. This latter argument, as developed by J. S. Mill, Irving Fisher, Luigi Einaudi, and others, supports the imposition of a general expenditure tax in lieu of a general income tax on

Many other examples could be constructed by using differing assumptions about predicted fluctuations in income receipts and in spending plans over time. These need not be elaborated here since the main purpose of the analysis is showing that under *some* conditions the rational person may prefer to meet a fiscal obligation through the specific commodity tax.

The results of the analysis are strongly reinforced when we relax somewhat the rationality assumption. If moral scruples, the "Puritan ethic," influence behavior in the direction of making individuals "live within their incomes" and cause them to consider "eating up capital" or "going in debt" to be repugnant or, at best, imprudent, the marginal adjustments necessary for achieving any planned "equilibrium" pattern of spending may not take place. The marginal rates of substitution among items of spending will not be equated in separate time periods, even when viewed from a single moment. As such departures from any rationally planned equilibrium become more significant, the possible advantages of the specific commodity tax become larger.

The rationally planned pattern of spending is, of course, one normative version of the permanent-income hypothesis, either in the limited horizon, life-cycle sense, or in the unlimited Ricardian sense. To the extent that empirical findings lend support to this hypothesis, in either form, the possible advantages of the specific commodity tax in minimizing temporal distortion in spending are reduced. To the extent that the findings suggest that individuals plan spending largely on the basis of current income receipts and not on permanent income, the relative advantages of the indirect tax instrument are increased.

efficiency criteria, holding that any income tax tends to discriminate against income that is saved. This argument assumes meaning, however, only when the *distribution* of the tax load among separate persons is introduced. It is not relevant here since the analysis is limited, specifically, to the calculus of a single potential taxpayer who is placed in the position of choosing among several instruments of payment. In the life-cycle pattern of saving behavior postulated, the present value of future spending must equal the present value of income receipts. If the individual is taxed on income received in each period, including income earned as a return on saving from previous periods, the rate of tax would tend to be somewhat lower than that rate which would be required to produce an equivalent present-value tax liability under some general expenditure tax.

CERTAINTY RELAXED

To this point the individual, whose decision calculus has been analyzed, has been assumed certain as to his future income prospects, future spending needs, and the life of the fiscal alternatives considered. In any real-world setting, of course, uncertainty rather than certainty prevails. As compared with the analysis of the preceding chapter, the distinction between the certainty and the uncertainty models is less marked here, although much of the discussion there can be applied again and need not be repeated. The central point is that distributional considerations which might influence the selection among tax instruments tend to be reduced in importance as genuine uncertainty increases at the moment of fiscal choice. If the individual is uncertain as to his own income prospects over time, and also as to his own basic expenditure desires, he may accept that there are certain criteria which will, roughly and approximately, measure his unadjusted marginal utility of spending in future time periods. He may say something like the following: "If either my income is high enough or my essential spending desires low enough, I shall probably find myself purchasing a boat or a custom-tailored suit and my wife a mink cape. Such items seem now to me to be reasonably good independent measures of the marginal utility of income. Hence, if a tax is laid on the purchase of such items, I can maintain some insurance against being subjected to burdensome tax pressure when my needs for basic goods and services are unexpectedly high or my income is unexpectedly low." In one sense, the choice of the excise on residual and postponable items of consumption spending reflects the same sort of mental calculus that might support a decision to exempt certain basic consumption spending from income tax (more on this below).

In the uncertainty model, we need make no particular assumption about the workings of the capital market. With future income receipts as well as spending plans uncertain, the whole conception of an "optimal" or "equilibrium" pattern of spending over time loses much of its meaning. The individual will, more or less as a natural order of events, expect the marginal utility of his expenditure dollar to vary as among periods. If he could, with some certainty, map out a preferred stream of spending, he might find that attainable resort to the capital market would eliminate any possible differential advantage of the specific excise tax. If uncertainty exists

251

beyond some degree, however, he may find such resort to the capital market impossible.

The individual has been assumed to be motivated by straight-forward utility-maximizing considerations. A somewhat broader conception of choice allows for a more complex preference function. The first additional element involves the subjective or "felt" burden of tax payments in future time periods. At the moment of consti-tutional-institutional choice among tax instruments, the individual may be influenced by his predictions about his own reactions, in later periods, to the institution that is selected. He may realize, for example, that on each tax payment date, the income tax will impose on him a genuine "felt" burden. On the other hand, he may also recognize that, since he pays the tax along with the price of a specific commodity, such a burden may be absent under the com-modity tax. This is a fiscal illusion, and the individual in his more rational moments may recognize that he will be subject to it. But he may, deliberately, choose to impose the future taxes upon him-self in such a way as to minimize subsequent subjective burdens of payment. Or, conversely, he may recognize that the presence of illusion will cause him to act unwisely in operational fiscal choices concerned with the extension of public activities. And, for this reason, he may choose to reject the excise tax alternative.

A second possible complexity in the individual's preference function involves his attitude toward his consumption of the residual items. He may recognize that, on occasion, he is the slave of his passions, and because of this, he may choose to place obstacles on his own behavior. Sumptuary taxation can be derived from an individual calculus of choice. Nevertheless, care must be taken to distinguish this attitude from the paternalist or *dirigiste* one, through which the individual attempts to lay down standards of conduct, not for himself, but for others in the social group (more on this point below).

PROBLEMS OF AGGREGATION

Individuals are not, of course, allowed to choose separately and independently the fiscal instruments through which their financial obligations will be met. As in the earlier analysis of the progressive tax, it is necessary to shift from isolated individual choice to indi-vidual participation in group choice. The collectivity must select the tax instrument which will, when chosen, be imposed on all members of the community.

The consistency of individual decisions or preferences, one with the other, must be examined. While it may be rational for the isolated person to prefer a privately-levied tax on a specific commodity, he may not want the collectivity to impose such an indirect tax. There may exist no substantial agreement on a single commodity or service to be taxed. What one man may think of as a "luxury" good, and its purchase a reasonably good independent criterion for the marginal utility of his own spending, a second man may consider to be a basic and essential item, necessary to life, happiness, and well-being. If wide divergencies of this sort exist, the individual participant in group choice may well abandon any support for excise taxation. On the other hand, members of most political communities are culturally homogeneous to some degree. This suggests that substantial, if not total, agreement may be attainable on a relatively small set of specific commodities that might be subjected to excise levies. To the extent that the required homogeneity holds, indirect taxation may emerge from the group decision process, in which individual attitudes and choices are based, at least in part, on the sort of considerations that have been discussed here. One person, participating in group choice, may estimate his own future consumption purchases of champagne to be a good measure of his relative "welfare" in future periods of time. A second may consider his wife's purchases of perfume a somewhat better indicator. After discussion, argument, and compromise the whole group may agree that a relatively small bundle of commodities, including champagne and perfume, provides a reasonable good index for the marginal utility of future spending for each man.

Elements of paternalism cannot, of course, be eliminated from a collective choice among tax instruments. Each participant in a collective decision, be he voter, political leader, or bureaucrat, has a set of preferences, of "values" not only for himself but also regarding the behavior of others in the community. And since the outcome to be chosen must apply to all members of the group, there is no way that the individual participant can be limited to basing his choices on the considerations of his own future behavior pattern. The point to be stressed here is not the absence of paternalist elements in choice; instead, the emphasis should be on the fact that such elements need not be present to derive individual, and through

253

these, group preferences for specific commodity taxation. Alcohol may be taxed heavily in most jurisdictions because voters and political leaders think that their fellow citizens "should" be discouraged from drinking. But, also, alcohol taxes may be accepted because the potential taxpayer, himself, knows that he can escape taxation by refraining from drink. In some basic, philosophical sense, indirect taxation of specific commodities allows the potential taxpayer more ultimate choice than direct taxation precisely because it is specific. He retains an additional faculty of choice over time, so to speak, because he has available a wider range of alternatives than he would retain under direct taxation. This faculty may never be exploited; indeed, the individual will hope that he will never find it necessary to reduce his net tax payment to zero in any period. But the existence of this wider range of potential choice may be decisive in certain circumstances.

IMPLICATIONS

This chapter has not been aimed at providing a normative "defense" of specific excise taxation. The analysis has shown that there exist certain conditions under which such taxation becomes "efficient" for the rational individual taxpayer. The results may be generalized to a community of individuals only if there exists reasonable consensus on a set of commodities or services, the purchases of which provide a criterion for the marginal utility of spending in different periods of time.

At one point the similarity between the imposition of specific levies on items of residual consumption and the exemption of certain items of basic expenditure from the income tax base was noted. It will be useful to examine these two fiscal devices more carefully, since both are to be found in modern fiscal structures. Both schemes may have been introduced, and supported, at least in part, to include some recognition of fluctuating needs for basic consumption over time, and the relevance of this for defining the tax base. The exemption or deduction of such items as medical care and education from the tax base involves the acknowledgment that, during periods when expenses on these are high, income alone does not provide an adequate criterion for computing tax liabilities. Outlays for residual consumption items provide another set of independent criteria, at the "other end" of the consumption spectrum, so to speak. In either case, the taxpayer retains a somewhat greater freedom of action than he would retain under the general income tax without exemptions. The freedom of the taxpayer to adjust his own liability through a modified pattern of consumption spending is present in both cases, but there is a difference. Under the deduction scheme, the taxpayer can reduce his liability for income tax only by purchasing the specific items, say, medical services or education. Under the specific excise tax, he can reduce his fiscal liability by reducing his purchases of one or a few items, leaving him a broader range of alternatives on which to spend.

One of the interesting by-products of the analysis is the relatively low ranking that emerges for the general consumption or expenditure tax, which adjusts individual tax liabilities to total spending in each period.[10] The case that has been made out for specific excise taxation depends, strictly, on the *specificity* of the objects taxed. On the basis of an individual choice calculus, it is difficult to see how an argument for general spendings taxation could be derived. The familiar distortion in static spending patterns are, of course, smaller under the general tax than under the specific levies. However, static or in-period distortion can always be minimized with direct taxes on income which are also preferred on the temporal distortion scale.

10. The general expenditure tax is assumed here to impose a pattern of final incidence among individuals in relation to spending. This is not the place to introduce complex issues of incidence theory. However, it may be noted that, even should the final incidence of the tax not be in this pattern, the analysis traced above will hold so long as, when he considers the alternatives, the individual *thinks* that the incidence will be proportionate to spending.

17. *The Institution of Public Debt*

When should governments borrow rather than tax? This is a classic question in the theory of public finance, along with those discussed in the two preceding chapters. Can the institutional-choice approach to fiscal systems be applied to this question?

We are concerned with public debt as a fiscal institution through which a collectivity may finance public goods and services and with the individual's evaluation of this institution. Governments borrow as an alternative to taxing, and it is appropriate to consider borrowing as an addition to the revenue-raising alternatives listed at the beginning of Chapter 16. Are there any conditions that may cause the utility-maximizing individual to select, at the moment of constitutional-institutional choice, the public loan over any of the tax alternatives? Recall the characteristics of the situation that we have presumed to confront the individual with at this moment of choice. He is not choosing between debt issue and taxation for the financing of a specific public good or service in a specific time period. The individual recognizes that the fiscal instrument to be chosen will remain in force over a whole series of time periods, and that it will be employed to raise funds for a stream of public goods and services, with the precise nature, the range, and the extent of these goods and services to be determined from period to period, and with the benefits from this stream of services wholly unpredictable at the moment when the revenue-raising institution is to be selected. It is in this situation that we ask the question: Will the individual find it desirable for the collectivity to resort to debt issue?

It will be helpful to employ the same device that was introduced in Chapter 15. Assume that a given individual is assigned a specific share in some aggregate community liability and that he is able to define this share in terms of a definite present value at the moment of constitutional-institutional choice. For simplicity, we shall say that this present-value liability is set at $1,000. This liability must be recognized as such under any of the institutional alternatives that the individual confronts. Hence, the public-debt instrument, as one of these alternatives, must be defined in such a way that the individual is required to meet the obligation over a time span that is within his own planning horizon. That is to say, public debt must be considered for periods of sufficiently short maturity to insure that the individual making the choice shall recognize that he must amortize his own share in the community liability during his own planning period. If this constraint is not imposed, there would be no way of making a present-value liability under debt equivalent to those under various tax institutions. Therefore, we shall simply postulate here that the debt will, if issued, be amortized over a period of, say, ten years. In this restricted model, the individual can, through his community's resort to public debt, postpone current payment for public services for a maximum of ten years. The question becomes: Are there conditions under which he would wish to select the institution which facilitates such a postponement? Will he prefer that the government issue bonds as a means of raising revenue to finance public services for each of the first nine years? Or, will he choose to have his government rely on one or several of the standard tax instruments?

As in some of the previous models, it will be helpful to assume initially that the individual knows with certainty the pattern of his income receipts and his private spending over the relevant time period. It is not necessary to specify any particular pattern of either of these streams. When we allow the public-debt alternative to be considered, we reach quickly what appears to be an unorthodox or startling conclusion. Given such an opportunity as that posed, *the rational individual will always choose that all public goods and services be financed through public debt issue.* This result seems striking at first glance, and it seems to be so much at odds with accepted principles of fiscal practice that one searches for the fallacy that must be hidden somewhere.[1]

1. For several years this result has been discussed among economists at the University of Virginia as "Tullock's fallacy," since it owes its local origin to my colleague, Gordon Tullock. In a recently published paper, E. J. Mishan has indirectly noted the same point. See his "How to Make a

There is, however, no such fallacy lurking in the underbrush, and within the limits of the model examined here the conclusion holds. Why should the individual select the debt alternative? He will do so because this alternative is the only one that allows him full freedom of choice in adjusting his income-spending pattern over time. Public debt, as an institution, effectively allows the individual to meet his assigned liability "optimally," and it is the only revenue-raising alternative that accomplishes this, given the operation of a capital market that requires private borrowers to pay something over the government borrowing rate. As the collectivity borrows to finance currently-supplied public goods and services in each period, the individual is placed in the position of borrowing, one stage removed, at the government rate. In effect, through issuing debt, the government is borrowing for the individual. If, therefore, the individual's pattern of net income receipts or spending over time is such that he desires to postpone meeting his fiscal obligation, the public debt alternative enables him to do this at no net cost. On the other hand, if his pattern of income-spending flows is such that he chooses to discharge his obligation early during the time sequence, he can always do so by purchasing government securities and holding these until the time of debt retirement-taxation, when his accumulated assets will just offset his accumulated tax obligations. In effect, the public debt allows the individual both to borrow and to lend at government rates, and hence to remove any temporal distortion from his spending pattern.[2]

CONTINGENT LIABILITY

The analysis suggests that the isolated individual should rationally select public debt as the means for financing public goods and services. Why has this alternative not commanded more respect in the institutional structure of real-world fiscal systems? The underlying assumptions of the model require more careful consideration.

Burden of the Public Debt," *Journal of Political Economy,* LXXI (1963), 529-42, especially note 5. The point is, of course, implicit in the traditional Ricardian notion that the public loan and the extraordinary tax are fundamentally equivalent for the individual, since this argument assumes that the individual is able both to borrow and to lend at the government borrowing rate.

2. The analysis of De Viti De Marco, although itself incomplete, is suggestive of the approach to debt theory developed in this section. See Antonio De Viti De Marco, *First Principles of Public Finance,* trans. E. P. Marget (New York: Harcourt-Brace, 1935), pp. 377-98.

The individual's share in the aggregate community liability has been assumed to be preassigned in some present-value sense, at least insofar as this informs his own choices. But can such a share really be assigned in advance? The difficulties that arise here are not the same as those we have discussed previously in the analysis of progressive income taxation. The difficulties here stem from what we may call the "contingent liability" that public debt must embody under normal political circumstances.

Let us assume, as before, that, provisionally, some share in an aggregate community liability has been assigned to the reference person, and that similar shares have been parceled out to all members of the political group. Next, assume that no distributional problems explicitly arise here; the individual proceeds as if he will fully meet his own assigned share over the period in his own optimally-selected manner. On the basis of some such calculation as that outlined above, he opts for the debt alternative; others in the group agree, and all public services are initially financed by public loans. The reference person then carries out his plans as projected, meeting his fiscal obligation as these plans dictate.

Now suppose that the final accounting period arrives; all issues of debt must be retired. The individual in question has accumulated, through his purchases of bonds over the period, sufficient assets to meet precisely the share of the liability during the final period that his plans dictated. All seems well; he seems to have chosen the ideal fiscal arrangement.

All is not well; and herein lies the rub. Suppose that a second person, Mr. B, likewise made optimal spending plans when the time sequence commenced and the fiscal alternative was selected. However, suppose that B has failed, over time, to live up to such plans as he had initially laid down. The final period arrives, and he has not accumulated sufficient assets to offset the meeting of his fiscal obligation. He simply cannot "pay off debt" or "pay taxes" in this final period and discharge his assigned multiperiod liability. This failure of B to live up to his rationally-projected plans need not bother our first person, A, except to the extent that he understands that B's plight imposes a clear *contingent liability* on him. The funds have all been spent in the separate periods in financing the public goods and services. The aggregate liability for the whole collectivity must be paid, assuming that the community does not choose to default on its loan. B has, however, behaved either ir-

259

rationally or irresponsibly over the period and he cannot meet the share that he implicitly agreed to meet. Consequently, it falls to the remaining members of the political group to bear the liability that was initially assigned to B. Others will find themselves paying for B's profligacy or deceit.

Note that A himself, the individual whose calculus of choice we are considering, will behave here precisely in accordance with his plans. He will, nonetheless, be unduly burdened at the end of the period to the extent that B's behavior runs contrary to B's projected plans at the start of the time sequence. The reference person, A, will tend to recognize this contingent liability aspect that the public-debt instrument may embody. When he does so, he will tend to reject the debt alternative, and to select instead a tax institution, despite the acknowledged superiority of debt in terms of efficiency criteria in an isolated individual income-spending pattern.

No irrationality has been introduced in the analysis here. The reference individual need not fear for his own ability to meet targets that he lays down at the time of institutional choice. He will tend to reject the generalized usage of public credit not because he fears that he cannot live up to the model of behavior that he sets himself, but, instead, because he fears that some among his fellow citizens may fail to live up to their own targets of behavior. The acceptability of public debt requires then, that the individual not only predict his own rational behavior, but, also, that he can predict with reasonable certainty that all other members of the group, or at least a sufficient portion of them, will likewise behave rationally and responsibly. This requirement becomes extremely restrictive and seems likely, in most cases, to rule out general approval of the debt alternative.

Why do these same fears concerning the rational and responsible behavior of other persons not arise in the considerations among the various tax alternatives? The analysis of the preceding chapters has shown that the efficiency advantages of both progressive income taxation and specific commodity taxation may stem from the fact that these institutions allow the individual to shift his fiscal liability through time in such a way as to reduce temporal distortions in his spending pattern. Why will not irrational or irresponsible behavior on the part of others than himself here too affect the individual's own liability?

The essential difference between these tax institutions and that of public debt stems from the fact that, under any tax institution that allows for fluctuations in individual liability over time, separate persons in the group tend to offset each other. Periods when one person's income is relatively low, or private spending relatively high, may be periods when another person's income is relatively high, or private spending relatively low. If the individual assumes that over-all income and spending in the economy will remain roughly stable or rise steadily, this result is assured. Public debt, by contrast, involves no such offsetting through the fiscal structure. *All* public goods and services are financed by debt in the initial periods (in the general model considered here). Fiscal bills pile up; no one is required *currently* to pay for the stream of public services. Current-period adjustments, if they occur, must take place within the *private* accounting systems of individual citizens. The fact that rationally behaving individuals may be acting in accordance with optimal plans is not externally revealed to the observer, nor is this behavior required in any way.

The reference individual may, of course, also harbor some doubts about his own rationality in following out some predetermined plan of spending-saving. To the extent that he does so, he will reject the debt alternative, quite apart from the contingent liability effects here emphasized.

CERTAINTY RELAXED

The above analysis demonstrates that even if the individual knows with certainty his income prospects and his private spending plans over the relevant time span, and even if he is confident that he can carry out some predetermined plan of behavior, he may still reject the public debt as his most preferred general financing institution because he cannot predict that others will behave responsibly and rationally. As we have done in previous chapters, the unreal assumptions as to certain prospects must now be relaxed. Assume now that the reference individual's income prospects and/or private spending needs are uncertain and subject to some fluctuations over time. How will this change the conclusions about his attitudes toward the debt institution?

It is best to examine the individual's choice calculus on the assumption that total income in the whole community remains uniform over time or grows at some predictable rate. This allows us to concentrate on fluctuations in individual income receipts or in private spending needs independently of over-all aggregate fluctuations. As suggested earlier, with uncertainty as to receipts or outlays over time, the very notion of some optimally-planned pattern of spending through time scarcely exists. The individual's decisions will be informed largely by current or in-period comparisons of income receipts and outlays. He should be able, however, to distinguish among periods of relative affluence and relative penury, not necessarily in advance but as events materialize. In the former, he will tend to put aside some income as savings to protect his economic position contingently over possibly lean periods. In the latter, he will tend to resort to the loan market, either borrowing from himself out of accumulated savings or externally from others. Previous chapters have demonstrated how the progressive income tax on the one hand and specific commodity taxation on the other may allow the fiscal structure to facilitate the individual's temporal adjustments. The question here is whether or not public debt can accomplish similar purposes?

The answer is negative. Public debt does not provide a means of bunching fiscal liability during periods of relative affluence comparable with the other two institutions discussed. For the whole group, public debt allows for a postponing of fiscal liability through time, but in the final accounting period, when debt must be retired, some taxpayers will be affluent, some will be penurious. Not knowing to which group he may belong, our reference individual will rationally reject the debt alternative as the general financing instrument. Public debt allows such a bunching in time only in the certainty model, and only in a highly restricted form of this.

In the real world some mixture of the certainty and the uncertainty models normally is descriptive. The individual can make some reasonable predictions as to his income prospects, and he can project within limits his needs for private spending over time. There is some sense in his attempts to frame optimal saving-spending plans. The important barrier that prevents his selecting resort to public credit as the general financing device lies in the contingent liability aspect discussed with respect to the certainty model above.

PUBLIC DEBT AND INDIVIDUAL PLANNING HORIZONS

In all of the models discussed to this point, the individual has been assumed to evaluate public debt as a means of financing general public goods and services. As compared with its alternatives, debt issue has been assumed to impose comparable liabilities, computed on some present-value basis, on the individual who is making the choice among the fiscal institutions. If human beings should live eternal lives, no problem need arise. But since they do not, it was necessary to postulate that debt must be issued in such a way that amortization occurs within the planning horizon, the life span, of the individual decision maker. If this restriction is not placed on the models, there is no way in which public debt can be made genuinely comparable, in our terms of reference, with tax alternatives except through some quite arbitrary assumptions about human behavior. If individuals, despite the limitations on human life, treat their heirs as lineal extensions of their own lives, which was the assumption always made by Ricardo, no problem arises. In this case, individuals act *as if* they live forever. But individuals may not behave in such a fashion, and if they do not, public debt, which allows them to postpone fiscal liability, may provide a means of redistributing the net fiscal load intertemporally. If at the time of constitutional-institutional choice, the individual considers public debt as a means of shifting the final fiscal liability forward in time to "future generations," he will, of course, tend to select this instrument on the basis of utility-maximizing considerations.[3]

The rejection of the debt alternative in this limited-time-horizon situation must be based on the individual's acceptance of some ethical principle of intergeneration equity. If he makes plans on the basis of a limited time horizon and does not fully incorporate the interests of his descendents in his own, the individual will tend to select debt as the means of financing public goods and services unless he is deterred by some such ethical norm. Of course, if general acceptance of debt issue should become widespread, reflecting an absence of the effectiveness of this norm, the likelihood that future generations would, in fact, default on inherited debt obligations would quickly become an economic deterrent to this institution. For these and other reasons, it is appropriate that the analysis here be restricted to the model where debt is amortized within the planning horizons of the decision makers.

3. This is not the place to repeat the analysis that demonstrates that public debt does, in fact, involve a postponing or shifting forward in time of fiscal liability. On this, see my, *Public Principles of Public Debt* (Homewood: Richard D. Irwin, 1958). The discussion among scholars on this subject since 1958 is collected in James M. Ferguson, (ed.), *Public Debt and Future Generations* (Chapel Hill: The University of North Carolina Press, 1964).

Public Finance in Democratic Process

THE PUBLIC DEBT ILLUSION AND ITS CONVERSE

To this point the analysis has been limited to an evaluation of public debt as a *general* source for raising governmental revenues. It has been argued that the individual's probable rejection of this alternative stems, at least in large part, from his distrust of fellow taxpayers' ability or willingness to carry out optimal spending-saving plans. One element of this mistrust may arise out of the recognition that public debt may generate a fiscal illusion. Although fiscal liabilities are created at the moment that debt is issued, individuals may not act as if such liabilities exist. They may not fully capitalize the future taxes that the debt must embody, in service and amortization charges, and if they do not, they will not behave rationally in making plans to discharge their own shares in such aggregate liability.

The debt illusion has its converse, however, and when this is also recognized, public debt again assumes a limited but legitimate place in the acceptable array of fiscal instruments. To this point, as noted, revenue-raising alternatives, including debt, have been considered a means of raising general revenues for the financing of all public goods and services. Although the assumption was not explicitly made, the results derived are wholly appropriate only if the benefits from the provision of public goods are concentrated during the periods when the public outlays are actually made. This does not characterize all public outlay; some takes the form of capital investment which yields benefits over a whole series of time periods.

Let us now examine this sort of public outlay independently. Assume that the individual is faced with selecting the appropriate fiscal instrument or institution for financing only quasi-permanent public goods, the benefits from which will be fully realized only over the long run. As in the more general model, we assume that the individual does not know precisely the pattern of these capital projects, and he has no way of predicting whether or not he will personally benefit from such projects in particular periods of time. His task is that of selecting the fiscal means of financing public capital projects, and these only, with the actual decisions on the form and extent of these projects to be made in subsequent periods.

Here the choosing person may recognize that the temporal distortion between the receipt of benefits from public capital projects and the impact of the payment institution may tend to bias in-period decisions against such outlays under the standard taxing instruments. In other words, for projects that involve benefits which accrue over

264

time, there may exist some "asset illusion." The individual may not fully capitalize the future benefits that such quasi-permanent outlays will yield. If he does not, he will not make "proper" decisions concerning the amount of taxes to be levied or the "proper" allocation of funds within a limited revenue budget. Budgetary decisions will tend to be biased in favor of short-term and against long-term public projects.

If the individual, at the level of institutional choice, recognizes that this sort of illusion is likely to occur, he may prefer that public debt be authorized as the revenue-raising device for such projects. Here, the individual who makes in-period operational budgetary choices may suffer both a public debt illusion and an asset illusion. He may fail to capitalize both the liability that the debt side embodies and the benefit stream that the asset embodies. But these two illusions become offsetting here, and the individual may predict that more rational in-period budgetary choices will emerge under such a structure than under one that is limited to tax financing for all outlays.

Note also that if it is limited to financing only capital projects, the public debt alternative need not involve the contingent liability element to the same extent as the more general model. Operating under the debt illusion, individuals may not make adequate plans to meet fiscal liabilities when these are due. However, insofar as the projects financed are genuinely chosen so as to yield benefits over time, presumably the ability of individuals to meet postponed liabilities is enhanced by these public-service benefits, which are, in one sense, translatable into real incomes. The contingent liability element cannot be wholly eliminated, even for debt issue limited to the financing of long-term capital projects, because the accrual of benefits need not be distributionally equivalent to the optimally-projected allocation of fiscal liabilities. It should perhaps also be noted that the ethical principle against the issue of debt which embodies some transfer of net fiscal liability to future generations of taxpayers does not fully apply when debt is limited to financing genuinely long-term projects. In this case, future generations enjoy the benefits as well as inherit the liability.

The analysis suggests, therefore, that public debt issue may be chosen as an appropriate part of the over-all "constitution" of a fiscal structure, provided that limitations are imposed to insure that debt financing be restricted to projects that yield benefits over time.

"Capital budgeting" can be rationalized on the basis of the individual decision calculus here introduced. These conclusions are similar to those that were developed in the traditional or classical theory of public debt, and they have been incorporated into responsible fiscal practice. This correspondence itself, along with other instances noted in this book, tends to corroborate the efficacy of the general approach adopted.

18. *Fiscal Policy Constitutionally Considered*

INTRODUCTION

To this point, all problems concerning the possible utilization of fiscal instruments to accomplish macroeconomic objectives have been deliberately neglected. Any claim that the approach is a general one must include some reference to its ability to handle these problems. Can a normative "theory of fiscal policy" be derived from an individual choice calculus? Will an individual, at the moment when he is confronted with defining a fiscal constitution, authorize his government to employ the budget as a stabilizing, growth-inducing instrument?

Will an individual prefer that the aggregate income of the community in which he lives rise at some steady rate (or remain stable) or that it fluctuate around some long-term growth path? If he can predict his own income prospects with certainty, he need not be directly concerned with fluctuations in aggregate community income, although he may be indirectly concerned through tax-base externality. He will, however, be directly interested in aggregate income growth if his own income prospects are expected to correspond with those of the community in general. Here he will clearly prefer steady growth to unpredictable fluctuations. He may also prefer income stability to wholly predictable fluctuations if resort to the capital market is costly and private spending needs are relatively more stable than income. As the analysis of Chapter 15 indicated, the individual should select tax instruments which will mitigate the impact of his own fluctuating income prospects. Tax institutions that contain significant built-in revenue flexibility will tend to be selected. If, however, fluctuations in personal incomes are general over the whole community and not offsetting among separate persons and groups, the built-in flexibility of the tax structure will cause revenues of the government to decline sharply during periods of cyclical downswing. More appropriately stated, if aggregate community income does not grow at its average rate, governmental revenues will fall short of their projected levels, even if they do not decline absolutely. If the rule of in-period budget balance is strictly enforced, public services supply will be curtailed during such periods, and, of course, expanded sharply during booms, neglecting possible in-period tax-rate adjustments.

The question is whether or not the individual will choose to allow specific relaxation of the rule of in-period budget balance in order to facilitate a steadier flow of public service supply over time. It seems evident that he will do so. Note, however, that this departure from in-period balance is justified solely* on the grounds that it will facilitate a smoothing out of public spending over time. We have not yet examined the individual's choice calculus when he recognizes that, by allowing some departure from in-period budgetary balance, aggregate community income over time may actually be increased. Fluctuations may not take place around some long-term growth path, but, instead, may represent a "bouncing down" on occasion from a long-term growth path considered properly as a ceiling. It is this latter purpose of unbalanced budgets that the Keynesian and post-Keynesian discussion of fiscal policy is all about. It also seems clear that the individual, who is presumed here to be contemplating the design or constitution of the financial structure of his government, will tend to prefer features for this structure that will promise the highest level of community real income over time, other things equal. His motivation is found directly in the fact that his own income prospects are related, probabilistically, to aggregate community income.

FISCAL POLICY IN A CLOSED NATIONAL ECONOMY

The next question is that of determining what structural features of a budgetary policy will best accomplish this. It is necessary to make additional clarifying assumptions at this point. Assume that the individual, whose constitutional choice process we are examining, lives in an isolated, fully closed economy, with only one governmental unit. Fluctuations in aggregate money income are anticipated to occur because of changes in the demand for circulating media, and these are expected to be translated quickly into fluctuations in real income and employment on the downside because of acknowledged rigidities in the wage-price structure. Assume further that the supply of money is not directly controlled by the government, despite its money-creating powers, but is, instead, allowed to adjust passively to demands via the mechanism of a banking system. The government may, however, add directly to or subtract from the supply of money by an exercise of its money-creating power.

In such conditions as these, the rational individual should recognize that the government's budget provides one instrument that might be utilized directly to insure against downswings in community income. Some departure from the strict rule of in-period budget balance is suggested, despite the effects of in-period fiscal choice that this departure might also be predicted to produce. (These effects have been discussed in Chapter 8). The individual may, therefore, authorize or "vote for" the authorization for the government to create deficits deliberately during periods of threatened retardation in aggregate community income growth. In these conditions, *deficit creation* may be among the set of fiscal institutions judged to be efficient by the individual citizen.

Deficits, if they are allowed to occur, must be financed, and the mere authorization of deficit creation does not imply anything at all about the manner of financing them. Nevertheless, the rational response of the individual here seems clear. He will authorize the government to *create money* in order to cover deficits in its current budget accounts during periods of real income slack. *Money creation* by government along with the injection of the newly-created money into the economy via the fiscal process seems indicated. If the deficit-creating, deficit-financing institutions are successful in accomplishing the objective sought, community income will grow at a steady rate.[1] This growth in itself will require that net additions be made to aggregate purchasing power over time if final product prices are to remain stable; hence, a *net* budget deficit over time becomes desirable.[2]

1. Institutional rigidities in the economy may, of course, prevent the maintenance of both full employment and price-level stability along this growth path. Resolution of this conflict need not be discussed here. If inflation threatens, the policy institutions suggested are, of course, the reverse of those discussed.

2. The alternative institutional structure that might be designed to accomplish equivalent objectives is that one which allows strict adherence to in-period budget balance, in the sense traditionally defined, and which then allows some governmentally-created "monetary authority" to engage in

Note that nothing in the analysis here suggests that *public debt issue* be authorized as a means of financing budget deficits. Public debt is a different fiscal institution from money, despite the unexplainable and near-inconceivable refusal of many sophisticated economists to recognize the distinction. By definition, an issue of public debt must involve a *transfer* of current purchasing power (liquidity) from the lender (a member of the public who purchases the securities) to the borrower (the government) in exchange for which the borrower obligates itself to pay an interest charge during subsequent time periods. An operation of this sort is obviously undesirable when the purpose of the budget deficit is to increase the total flow of spending in the economy. Hence, the rationally chosen institutional structure will contain no provision that would allow the financing of budget deficits by debt issue, under the conditions postulated.

FISCAL POLICY IN A WHOLLY OPEN ECONOMY: THE CASE OF THE LOCAL GOVERNMENTAL UNIT

The conclusions reached above hold only in the wholly closed economy. To the extent that an economy is open, different conditions prevail and the whole analysis requires reexamination. By an "open economy" here we mean that citizens are free to purchase and to sell goods and services with citizens of other jurisdictions, and, beyond this, are free to transfer both labor and capital resources freely among separate jurisdictions. Real-world national economies normally represent some combination of the closed and open models. We shall return to discuss these mixed models at a later point. The extreme example of an open economy is that of the local community

"monetary policy." During periods of depressed community income, this authority would purchase, with new money, securities held by the public.

Careful examination reveals that this alternative structure is only superficially different from the first. Since the monetary authority must be a part of the government, its own "budget" should properly be conceived as a part of the government's budget. When this is accepted, the "monetary policy" differs from the "fiscal policy" alternative only in the fact that with the former, new money is used to purchase securities only, while in the latter, the new money is used to finance public goods supply. Viewed in this light, the fiscal policy alternative seems relatively more efficient. Other considerations may, of course, modify this tentative conclusion. Notable among these might be some consideration for the burden of outstanding public debt. The monetary policy alternative allows for some retirement *qua* monetization of this debt over time whereas the fiscal policy alternative does not.

in a larger national economy. Here not only does freedom of trade and of resource mobility exist; also, the local governmental unit does not normally possess the constitutional power to create money. It will be helpful to examine the individual's choice process when he attempts to select an optimal fiscal constitution for the local governmental unit. Will he find it desirable to include institutions that will produce a positive fiscal policy for the local governmental unit? Will provisions be made for allowing budget deficits to be created and financed during periods when the state or the municipality is characterized by relatively low levels of aggregate income?

Somewhat surprisingly, this question seems rarely to have been raised. There has been considerable discussion concerning the role of state-local governments in macroeconomic policy.[3] This discussion has been concentrated on measuring the actual impact of state-local fiscal structures on the flow of national spending over past periods. There has been almost no discussion of the normative principles which "should" guide state-local decision makers. Inferentially, the textbook or standard attitude seems to have been as follows: It would be desirable if state-local units should "co-operate" with the national government in furthering the "national interest" by explicitly adopting counter-cyclical policies. Few scholars have asked the question: What should state-local units do in this respect in furtherance of *their own interests?*[4] To rephrase this same question so that it fits our own frame or reference: Will the individual want to include in the fiscal constitution of his local governmental unit some provisions for a positive fiscal policy?

3. Although the list is by no means exhaustive, the following items may be noted: A. H. Hansen and H. Perloff, *State and Local Finance in the National Economy* (New York: Norton, 1944), especially Chapter 4; Mabel Newcomer, "State and Local Financing in Relation to Economic Fluctuations," *National Tax Journal,* VII (June, 1954), 97-109; Ansel M. Sharp, "The Counter-Cyclical Fiscal Role of State Governments During the Thirties," *National Tax Journal,* XI (June, 1958), 138-45; James A. Maxwell, "Counter-Cyclical Role of State and Local Governments," *National Tax Journal,* XI (November, 1958), 371-76; Morton A. Baratz and Helen T. Farr, "Is Municipal Finance Fiscally Perverse?" *National Tax Journal,* XII (September, 1959), 276-84.

4. This question is raised and discussed by Clarence Barber in his monograph "The Theory of Fiscal Policy as Applied to a Province," A Study Prepared for the Ontario Committee on Taxation (June, 1964), especially in Chapter 2. I am grateful to the Committee for allowing me to have access to this study. Barber's work stimulated my own interest in elaborating some of the models of this chapter, and appropriate acknowledgment should be made of this fact.

271

The answer is not so simple here as that derived with respect to the closed economy; the institutions available to the chooser are different in the two cases. For the local government, the financing of budget deficits must involve borrowing, the creation of public debt. The unit has no recourse to money creation. The fiscal structure that was shown to be optimal for the closed national economy cannot, therefore, be applied for the local unit. Will a policy of deficit creation, with deficits to be financed by debt issue, prove efficient?

Consider once again the setting in which this question is put. The individual anticipates that the income of the local community may fluctuate over time, and that his own income prospects are directly related to the levels of community income, although somewhat less so than in the previous model. If his needs for both private and public goods are expected to be more uniform over time than this income, he will tend to approve both tax devices that contain some built-in revenue flexibility and also some authorization for public debt issue. These institutions combined will facilitate a smoothing out of both private and public consumption over time.

This does not, however, get at the central question. Will a positive fiscal policy; that is to say, one that is designed to raise income levels of the community during periods of depression, seem desirable as an adjunct of local government fiscal structures? To get at this, we must inquire concerning the predicted effects of deficit creation and deficit financing in periods of locally depressed activity. Aggregate income in the community is presumed to have fallen. A budget deficit has emerged as revenues from approved tax institutions have shrunk and as spending rates have been maintained or increased. To finance the deficit, the local governmental unit has created and sold public debt instruments on the capital market. Can this combination of events be expected to generate a real income increase in the local community? The answer is clearly affirmative, and for a reason that may appear paradoxical to some scholars. The flow of spending in the local community will increase because the government here borrows funds on the national capital market. If this unit is small relative to the size of the total economy, the interest rate is not modified. The debt created is *external* to the local community; no funds are drawn away from either local consumption or investment spending. If, through some quirk, funds have been drawn from local sources, that is, if the debt is *internal,* there would be little, if any, income-creating effects of the combined operation. This seems almost to reverse the implied conclusions of much orthodox theory; the elementary textbook discussion of fiscal policy is likely to suggest or to infer that deficit financing is to be recommended as income-generating only if internal public debt is used as the financing device. By contrast, the model here suggests that deficit financing through public debt issue is efficient only to the extent that external debt is created.[5]

The combined operation tends to attract capital funds from the whole economy; these funds are expended locally by the governmental unit in purchasing public goods and services. Aggregate community income rises; unemployment is reduced. Real income of the local community over time is increased. A heritage of public debt will exist after the initial period, and this will impose a net burden of servicing this debt on taxpayers in all subsequent periods. The question becomes that of determining whether or not the current-period increase in income is sufficient to outweigh in present value the discounted value of the future tax obligations.

Consider first an extreme case in which the local community purchases the public goods supplied to local citizens exclusively from external sources. Pure examples of this sort are difficult to imagine, but one could think of a local community supplying educational services to its children by sending them bodily to other communities for schooling, paying the other communities for these services. In this case, there would be no local income multiplier effect. However, since the public services themselves represent additions to real income, the combined operation is still desirable, provided only that the decision to supply the services is an efficient one. The present value of future taxes required to service the debt that financed the services should just be equal, in some objectively quantifiable sense, to the current value of the services that are supplied. But, of course, the combined operation here would do nothing to increase local income and employment outside the particular benefit stream.

In almost all cases, there will be a local multiplier effect. The community will only in rare circumstances purchase resource in-

5. This has been recognized in a slightly different connection by Ronald I. McKinnon and Wallace E. Oates, "The Implications of International Economic Integration for Domestic Monetary, Fiscal, and Exchange Rate Policies," Memorandum No. 37, Research Center in Economic Growth, Stanford University (May, 1965).

puts exclusively from external sources. Normally, in supplying local public goods and services local citizens will be employed, local inputs will be purchased. To the extent that this takes place, some of the debt-financed spending by the local government will remain in the community and private spending in subsequent periods will increase. When this occurs, the combined deficit creation-debt financing operation will clearly be extramarginal. The present value of the future taxes required to service the debt obligation may fall far short of the current value of the public service benefits *plus* the current net additions to local income. A positive fiscal policy seems clearly to be desirable for the local governmental unit when its operations are viewed ex ante, even though this unit does not possess money-creating powers.

To this point, we have assumed that income in the local community declines without specifying what happens elsewhere in the national economy. It is perhaps evident that the analysis above holds without reservation in those situations where national aggregate income remains constant or increases at some steady rate while local community incomes vary. Suppose, however, that the over-all level of national income falls below desired levels uniformly in all areas of the economy. Will it then be desirable for a *single* local governmental unit to follow a positive fiscal policy? If the national government takes no action of its own to bring over-all national income to desired levels, there is no basis upon which a single local unit can predict the trend or growth path of national income over time. Faced with depression in its own area that is known to be matched by similar conditions elsewhere, should the local unit carry out fiscal policy?

Suppose that the central government adheres strictly to a rule of in-period budget balance, and that it undertakes no positive monetary policy. Income throughout the economy falls as a result of hoarding, and this affects all local communities uniformly. Consider then the plight of the single local government. Assume that no other community is observed to undertake fiscal policy action. What will happen if the one local unit, on its own, tries to carry out positive fiscal policy? Income in the community is below desired levels; and revenues from existing tax institutions are below those needed to finance public spending. In order to maintain public goods supplies, the local unit issues public debt. This debt will be purchased and the funds supplied by the banking system at existing rates of interest. The local community's behavior here adds a net increment to the spending stream in the economy, and, for the national economy as a whole, the full income multiplier will operate. But, for the local unit, leakages to other communities can be predicted. However, some local multiplier effect will remain, as suggested above. The fiscal policy action remains rational within certain limits.

As income in the single community rises, resources from external sources will tend to flow differentially to the area, quite apart from the ordinary leakages. These resources will compete with local resources for employment, and an unduly high level of unemployment may remain. Should the community, still acting alone, continue to add to its spending rate through deficit creation financed by debt? Beyond some point, there will be little current real income to be gained from expanding local public goods supply. However, if local income gains are sufficient, continued deficit creation is suggested, provided only that the resources which flow into the local area are somehow brought into the local tax base. In other words, if the local income generated as a result of the operation can be made the base for future tax obligations embodied in the debt that is issued, there is no reason why the single local community should not continue to carry out the fiscal policy so long as net increments to local income exceed the current value of future taxes made necessary by servicing and amortizing the debt.

FISCAL POLICY FOR THE PRIVATE CITIZEN

If the analysis of normative fiscal policy for the single governmental unit in a wholly open economy is accepted, similar conclusions should follow for the individual since his "economy" is, par excellence, wholly open. In making his earning-saving-spending plans over time, should the single person or family act so as to conduct "positive fiscal policy"?

It seems evident that he should do so. If his own income declines while the income of the whole community remains steady, he should, of course, borrow in order to stabilize spending. If this borrowing-spending generates any "private multiplier" effects on his own income, this provides an extramarginal incentive for such behavior. The difference between the individual and the local government arises solely out of the fact that the latter, being the larger, is more likely to enjoy some local multiplier effects. The point to be emphasized here is that, conceptually, there is no difference at all in the principles of rational behavior. The individual who lays out his own optimal spending-saving plans over time, and the individual who tries to lay down, constitutionally, the optimal spending-saving plans for his local governmental unit are one and the same, and behavior in each case is informed by the same criteria.

FISCAL POLICY FOR A NATIONAL GOVERNMENT IN A PARTIALLY OPEN ECONOMY

National governments possess money-creating power. This essentially distinguishes them from local governments. But they may operate in an international economic order that is substantially open, especially in that trade can move freely across national boundaries and that capital is highly mobile as ,among different nations. The model to be used in deriving a logic of fiscal policy from individual choices here must be some combination of the wholly closed and the wholly open economy models that have been examined above.

Since national governments do possess powers of money-creation, some assumptions must be made concerning the institutions that relate national currencies one to the other. It will be helpful to consider the models under each of two assumptions, freely fluctuating exchange rates and fixed exchange rates.

National Fiscal Policy under Fixed Exchange Rates in an Open International Economic Order. In specifying the conditions of this model, we may follow Mundell in assuming that the mobility of capital is such that interest rates among separate countries tend to be equalized.[6] Let us also assume that the country is small relative to the world economy.

Suppose now that a decline in the level of spending in the national economy is anticipated. Assume that the standard Keynesian conditions are present. Wages, and prices, are rigid against downward pressures. It will be useful to trace the effects of three possible sets of governmental actions designed to prevent the decline in national real income.

1. The government may create a budget deficit (or allow one

6. The models discussed are essentially the same as those examined by R. A. Mundell in his provocative paper, "Capital Mobility and Stabilization Policy under Fixed and Flexible Exchange Rates," *Canadian Journal of Economics and Political Science,* 29 (November, 1963), 475-95. See also the paper by McKinnon and Oates previously cited.

to emerge) and finance this deficit with the creation of new money. Aggregate spending is maintained at the desired level. Interest rates do not move upward or downward; hence, there is no net change in international capital flows. Prices remain steady; there is no change in the international balance of payments. It seems clear that this set of policy instruments, which is the same as those previously shown to be efficient for the wholly closed economy, remains the efficient set under this partially open model.

2. The government may attempt to accomplish the same purposes through orthodox "monetary policy," defined as the use of open-market weapons. In an attempt to stimulate internal demand, the monetary authority purchases securities. Interest rates will tend to fall; capital flows out of the country. A balance-of-payments deficit emerges, and the monetary authority may find it necessary to sell foreign exchange to restore this balance. This, in turn, offsets the initial purchase of domestic securities. Monetary policy under these conditions tends to be self-defeating.

3. Now suppose that the government, inadvisedly, decides to create a deficit, as under the first alternative, but to finance this deficit, not with money creation, but with public debt issue. Here the results are identical with those treated with respect to the fiscal policy operations of the local governmental unit in the wholly open economy. The only difference between these two cases is that the much larger national economy can expect a higher local income multiplier to be operative; potential leakages will be largely internalized. Through selling debt instruments in this model, the national government is effectively borrowing on the world capital market. It is adding directly to the national spending stream without creating new money directly. The operation becomes, in effect, equivalent to external borrowing.

If the first alternative is not possible, this third alternative may, of course, be recommended. However, when the first alternative is available, as it should be in all cases where the governmental unit does possess the power to create money, this third alternative is not efficient. It involves the creation of a future tax liability due to the necessity of servicing the debt that is created. This sort of liability simply does not exist under the first alternative since interest is not paid on money.

National Fiscal Policy under Fluctuating Exchange Rates in an Open International Economic Order. Using the same basic assumptions as before, let us now examine the same three policy combinations under a regime where exchange rates are allowed to fluctuate freely.

1. The government creates a budget deficit (or allows one to emerge) during periods of threatened declines in total spending; it finances this deficit with money creation. Aggregate spending is maintained at the desired level. No pressure is put on interest rates, and the price level does not change. There is no change in the exchange rate.

2. The government may try to accomplish the same objective with orthodox monetary policy. It directs the monetary authority to enter the open market and purchase securities. This action puts downward pressure on interest rates. Capital tends to flow out of the country; the exchange rate falls. This, in turn, generates an expansion in exports. Income and employment are maintained. This policy combination seems to be successful here whereas it was unsuccessful under a regime of fixed exchange rates.

3. Suppose now that the government creates a budget deficit and finances this deficit with the issue of public debt. The sale of securities tends to raise interest rates domestically; but this will attract capital into the country and upward pressure will be put on the exchange rate. This will, in turn, discourage exports and encourage imports. In the net, there may be little or no effect on domestic income and employment because, in equilibrium, the interest rate may not have changed and the money supply may not have increased. The fiscal policy action in this instance will fail to accomplish its desired purpose of shoring up domestic spending on goods and services.[7]

Why does fiscal policy fail here? It does so because the exchange rate effectively isolates the domestic and the foreign capital markets, and prevents the flow of foreign capital to the country that takes place under the fixed rate system, and which serves as a

---

7. As noted, this analysis follows closely that presented by Mundell, "Capital Mobility," *Canadian Journal of Economics and Political Science* He concludes that fiscal policy tends to be self-defeating in conditions of flexible exchange rates, and that monetary policy tends to be self-defeating under conditions of fixed rates. In effect, Mundell examines only alternatives II and III under each model, and he considers that fiscal policy must embody debt-financed deficits. As the analysis here indicates, if the first alternative is available, that of financing deficits with new money creation, this may be the most efficient policy combination under either fixed or flexible exchange rates.

possible base for expansions in the domestic money supply. The increased spending flow generated here by the deficit-financed purchases of public goods and services is offset by the increased foreign drainage resulting from the shift in the exchange rate.

The most interesting, and seemingly most paradoxical, conclusion stemming from the analysis of the various models here is that the efficacy of debt-financed deficits in shoring up local income is greatly enhanced when the institutions are such as to make this debt *external* in its essential respects.

CONCLUSIONS

Under a regime of flexible, as well as fixed, exchange rates, the first alternative seems to be recommended. A positive fiscal policy that incorporates the possibility of generating budget deficits during periods when total spending threatens to fall below desired levels along with the provision that these deficits should be financed with money creation can emerge from the rational constitutional-choice calculus of the individual. Similar adjustments may, of course, be included to allow for fiscal adjustments in the event of threatened or actual inflation. These have not been traced here.

It is important to note, to repeat, that the creation of public debt, as such, is never indicated for those governmental units that possess money-creating power as a part of the positive fiscal policy instruments under their control. It is clearly inefficient to create debt which requires a payment of future taxes when money can be issued without such service charges. Public debt should remain as a part of an over-all "fiscal constitution" of such governments only for issue during periods of high-level employment. For lower-level governments, as well as for private citizens, deficits must be financed by debt. In this case, a positive fiscal policy embodying debt issue may be efficient.

19. *Fiscal Nihilism and Beyond*

INTRODUCTION

This book is an attempt to develop, in a preliminary fashion, parts of a *theory of fiscal choice*. The central presumption is that individuals do make fiscal choices through their participation in political process. If the potential taxpayer-beneficiary has no part in choosing either the private goods-public goods mix or the institutions through which he pays for and enjoys public goods, there is little purpose served in any analysis of the feedback effects of such institutions on his behavior. The traditionalist moves from analysis to prescription without necessary recourse to individual preferences. He sets up criteria for fiscal reform without asking how individuals themselves make fiscal choices. Since he must presume that individuals have little or no power of ultimate choice, resort to extra-individual, external norms becomes acceptable, indeed essential, if anything at all is to be said.

This is intended to be an indictment of orthodox scholarship in public finance, but not to be an undue criticism of practicing scholars. Within the tradition, effective research has been accomplished, and the frontiers of knowledge have been pushed into continuing retreat. But what is most urgently required is precisely a shift out of this tradition, out of the mainstream. Essentially the orthodox tradition is nondemocratic, with no emotive significance intended. Decisions for the polity must be made exogenously to the individual citizen and coercively imposed upon him.

If political order is presumed to be workably democratic, individuals must be presumed to participate variously in the making of fiscal choices. They may, of course, do so quite indirectly and at times almost unconsciously, but their behavior becomes a proper

280

subject of scientific inquiry. The awesome gap in our knowledge is apparent here. We need to know much more about how individuals behave in collective decision processes, and we need to know more about the workings of those institutions that transmit and translate individual preferences into collective outcomes.

But what about norms? Where are "principles" to be found? What are the criteria for fiscal reform? Should A or B be chosen? Does the model of individualistic fiscal choice simply ignore such questions, or does it point to its own prescriptions? Is fiscal nihilism the ultimate outcome? Does the approach produce effective criticism of long-established norms while replacing these with none of its own making? The traditional objectives of equity and efficiency may be shown wanting, but they have provided a frame for discussion. What is proposed or implied in their stead?

The institutional-choice analysis has suggested a partial answer to such questions. Hopefully, such an analysis of fiscal choice processes can provide a basis for laying down criteria for reform. But what will these criteria be like? If individuals are presumed to choose for themselves, how can analysis do other than examine choice behavior and attempt to predict the outcome? To "improve" choices here must the specialist become a moralist who preaches a new choice ethic? Perhaps the answer is implied in the question. Improvements in individual choice behavior can result from positive analysis. Fiscal theorizing at this level has, as its ultimate purpose, objectives that are analogous to those that guide "consumers' research," "operations research," or "systems analysis." The ultimate choice-makers, whoever these may be, can make "better" decisions to the extent that they are made more fully informed as to the alternatives which they confront. Analysis has as its purpose the clarification of the various alternatives, the prediction of the consequences of the separate lines of action.

THE THEORY OF INCIDENCE

Properly interpreted, the whole of the theory of fiscal incidence can be incorporated in the fiscal-choice approach. Surely it is equally appropriate for the theorist to assist, ultimately, in the choice-making of individual citizens and in the presumed choice-making of some ruling authority. For the bulk of the work on incidence theory, the underlying political framework remains essentially unimportant.

The student of fiscal incidence and effects does not inquire about and is not concerned about the origin of or the selection among the alternatives that he analyzes. His task is that of predicting the comparative effects of different fiscal devices, real or imagined. He examines individual market responses to imposed fiscal phenomena, and he traces the primary, secondary, and tertiary stages of such responses to a point where final patterns of effects can be isolated.

Even within incidence theory, there remain gaps in the traditional analysis that have gone largely unnoticed because of the underlying political framework The specific objective of incidence analysis has been that of predicting the *real* effects of alternative fiscal devices, of locating the *real* pattern of final burden of taxes and benefits from public spending. Who does pay the taxes? Who does enjoy the benefits? These are important and relevant questions that should interest the fiscal decision-maker, whoever he may be. There are, however, less apparent but nonetheless significant questions that should also be asked, and, if possible, answered. Who *thinks* that he pays the taxes? Who *thinks* that he enjoys the benefits?

Incidence theory has largely ignored these latter questions. To an extent, this neglect is explained by the fact that scholars have been economists, not psychologists. And as economists they have properly concentrated on real, rather than apparent or illusory values. This apart, however, they have been uninterested in individuals' attitudes toward fiscal devices or instruments, as such. The emphasis has been, on the one hand, in predicting the allocational responses to fiscal changes, and, on the other, in determining the real pattern of final effects. The policy objectives that have been implicit in traditional scholarship, those of economic or allocational efficiency and distributional equity, have in this way exerted feedback effects on even the most positivistic elements in incidence analysis. The theorist who has operated within the orthodox allocational framework has been interested in predicting how an individual will respond in the market place when the retail price of a final product is increased due to the imposition of an excise tax. He has been unconcerned, or relatively so, about whether, in making this response, the individual attributes the price change to the tax or to any of the many other possible causal factors. The same theorist, who may have had implications for distributional equity in mind, has also been interested in imputing directly to the individual consumer a final share, in either relative or absolute terms, of the net burden that a tax embodies. How much does the individual really pay, absolutely or in proportion to some income-wealth base? Implicit here lies the presumption that the "social welfare function," the preference function for the "chooser" for the group, incorporates somehow the real pattern of incidence rather than any apparent or consciously realized pattern.

It is evident that questions about the individual's attitude toward the fisc, toward taxes and benefits, become important either in an explicitly defined ruling-class, elitist model of politics or in an individual-choice, democratic model. How conscious are taxpayers of the burdens involved in the costs of public services? How conscious are beneficiaries of the values of public goods? Such questions as these become vital in any model that presumes that individuals make their own fiscal choices, directly or indirectly. The whole problem of fiscal consciousness is relevant for fiscal choice, and, in one sense, real burdens and real benefits become important only to the extent that they are effectively translated by individuals into "felt" or "consciously realized" burdens and benefits.

If viewed in this perspective, the discussion contained in Part I of this book can be treated as an extension of incidence theory. Analysis there was aimed at predicting the effects of various fiscal instruments on individual choice behavior in political processes.

THE THEORY OF PUBLIC GOODS

Traditional public finance theory has been concerned primarily with individual choices in response to imposed fiscal conditions. In this book, we have discussed two additional levels of individual choice behavior which, combined, provide the elements of specifically *fiscal* choice. There is what we have variously called day-to-day, in-period, ordinary, operational, or budgetary fiscal choices. By these descriptive terms we have meant simply that, under any institutional setting, individuals will exercise their powers of decision and select somehow among alternative possible outcomes. Given any conceivable tax structure, and given any conceivable rule for amalgamating separate individual choices into a group decision, a specific set of public goods and services will be financed, purchased, and supplied. Apart from this level of choice, and in one sense "superior" to it, there is the stage or level where the institutional structure itself is selected. This level of choice has been the subject of attention in Part II where it has been suggested that many fiscal instruments can best be analyzed institutionally.

The operational level or stage of fiscal choice has been examined only indirectly in this whole book. The analysis of Part I was aimed at developing certain predictions about the influence of various institutions on this choice behavior of individuals, but the discussion did not contain the process of choice itself. Quite apart from the universal problem of space and time limits, there are reasons for this relative neglect. In the first place, the formal theory is quite complex, and many elements remain to be perfected. Secondly, and more importantly, the modern theory of public expenditure, which is surely the most exciting recent work in public-finance literature, can be brought within the over-all framework of this study without difficulty. Shorn of its occasional "social welfare function" overtones, which become both unnecessary and impossible in an individualistic model of political order, this modern theoretical construction may be interpreted in such a way as to allow predictions to be made about the outcomes that will tend to emerge from the complex interplay of individual preferences as these are expressed through collective decision-making processes.

In its standard formulation,[1] this theory of public goods supply is explicitly normative. It purports to lay down the necessary marginal conditions that should be met if economic resources are to be allocated optimally in the public sector. Optimality or efficiency in resource use is defined in the Paretian sense, and a single optimum point or position (any one from among an infinite number of such points or positions) is defined as one from which no change can be made without harming at least one person in the relevant group. The necessary marginal conditions that must characterize such a position are defined without reference to nonindividual norms and also without reference to the political or institutional processes that might produce such an outcome. The standard discussion stresses that such optimal outcomes cannot, in fact, be predicted to emerge from the private or independent behavior of individuals, analogous to that pressure toward optimality which does characterize behavior

1. The "classic" modern works in this theory are those of Paul A. Samuelson and R. A. Musgrave. See Samuelson, "The Pure Theory of Public Expenditure," *Review of Economics and Statistics,* XXXVI (November, 1954), 387-89; "Diagrammatic Exposition of a Theory of Public Expenditure," *Review of Economics and Statistics,* XXXVII (November, 1955), 350-55; and Musgrave, *The Theory of Public Finance.*

284

in market interactions. Individuals will rationally behave as "free riders" in trying to enjoy public goods and services; as a result they will tend to find themselves caught in a "many-person prisoners' dilemma."

Given this widely-accepted and explicitly normative version of the theory of public goods, how may it be transformed so as to enable us to predict the characteristics of the outcomes that will emerge from actual political processes? To construct this bridge between the formally correct and abstract normative theory of public goods supply (which is derived from the theoretical welfare economics that owes its origins to Vilfredo Pareto), it is necessary to go back to one of Pareto's own contemporaries, Knut Wicksell. In any over-all evaluation of the history of fiscal thought, Wicksell alone commands the heights of genius. He worked independently from Pareto, of course, and his own discussion of the "principles" for fiscal organization seem, at first glance, quite different from the formal statements of necessary marginal conditions that we associate with Paretian welfare theory. Wicksell was equally the armchair theorist, but he framed his whole discussion of fiscal choice in terms of political institutions, in terms of the processes through which individual preferences are translated into collective or group decisions.[2]

Wicksell suggested that the unanimous consent of all parties should be the criterion for decisions on fiscal matters. Although it was developed independently, it is evident that this criterion is the political counterpart of the Pareto criterion for optimality. If, from a given position, no change can be made through general agreement among all parties, the initial position may be classified as one belonging to the optimal or efficient set. On the other hand, if a change is proposed and all members of the group agree to this change, the initial position is nonoptimal. Wicksell's discussion contains specific institutional suggestions for implementing the rule of unanimity in the reaching of fiscal decisions.

In this Wicksell variant, the theory does become a theory of fiscal choice in a positive sense. If an institutional rule is imposed to the effect that all fiscal decisions, all taxing-spending decisions,

---

2. Wicksell's basic work is, *Finanztheoretische Untersuchungen* (Jena: Gustav Fischer, 1896). The major portions of this work are translated as, "A New Principle of Just Taxation," in *Classics in the Theory of Public Finance,* ed. R. A. Musgrave and A. T. Peacock (London: Macmillan, 1958), pp. 72-118.

must be made only after the unanimous agreement among all parties, the necessary conditions for optimality, defined in the Paretian sense, will characterize the outcomes that tend to emerge from the collective choice process. The only qualification that need be placed on this general proposition is that choices must be made marginally or in small steps. The theory of fiscal choice, so interpreted, does not, of course, allow us to predict *what* outcomes will tend to emerge. The Pareto surface contains an infinite number of optimal positions or points, and, at each stage of the journey toward this surface, the division of the "gains from trade" among persons will tend to restrict the size of the finally attainable set. The theory enables us only to define the characteristics of the solution, not to specify the elements contained within it. In this sense, the theory of fiscal choice is wholly analogous to the "theory of consumer's choice" which is a standard part of the economist's equipment.

While Wicksell does provide us with a bridge between the normative theory of "optimal resource allocation" and the positive predictions that may be desired in an individualistic model, the severe restrictions that his institutional constraints impose on individual behavior in collective choice must be acknowledged. Under a genuine rule of unanimity, individuals will be led to invest resources in strategic bargaining, investment which will, in the net, prove wasteful to the group as a whole. This type of individual behavior is not the same as the "free rider" sort which would characterize individual attitudes toward voluntary contributions for public goods. Under unanimity, some agreement might ultimately be reached at each stage on the way to a final outcome, but serious resource wastage might occur, the most important element of which would be measured in the costs of delaying agreement. Decision-making in groups, bargaining, is a costly process at best, and costs may become prohibitively high under a rule of unanimity, despite the acknowledged relevance of this rule, and this rule alone, for guaranteeing that action taken is, indeed, of net value for the group.

Wicksell sensed the problem here in his expressed willingness to allow for some relaxation of the institutional rule of unanimity, and in his specific proposal for a qualified legislative majority—although he left the precise size of his majority ambiguous. If the rule of unanimity is relaxed, the single participant in group choice cannot proceed on the assumption that his own agreement is required for collective decision. He will be much less inclined to invest resources in bargaining tactics. Decision-making costs are reduced dramatically. At the same time, however, any departure from the strict unanimity requirement means that inefficient or non-optimal outcomes may emerge. The final result of the collective decision process need not be Pareto optimal; the necessary marginal conditions need not be satisfied.

What is suggested is some balancing off of the two sides of the account, some comparison of the costs of inefficient or nonoptimal outcomes with the reductions in costs (benefits) that are expected to arise from the facilitation of decision making. This is essentially the comparison that Gordon Tullock and I discussed at some length in *The Calculus of Consent,* although the analysis there was not confined to fiscal choice.

Once this step is taken, the theory moves beyond the operational choice level into considerations of institutional-constitutional choice, the level or stage discussed in Part II of this book. Through some calculus of comparing costs, it becomes possible to discuss optimal rules and institutions within which choices are to be made, choices which are, themselves, predicted to produce outcomes or solutions that are not always located on the standard Pareto surface. What becomes conceptually predictable under this theory is not the characteristics of particular outcomes, but, instead, the general features of a whole probability distribution of outcomes. We shall return to a further discussion of this theory of institutional choice in a later section. Before this, however, it will be useful to return to the level of in-period budgetary choices. The discussion of the possibilities of developing positive theories of fiscal outcomes has not yet been exhausted.

FISCAL CHOICE UNDER FIXED INSTITUTIONS

At any moment in time, some political "constitution" exists that specifies the manner in which collective decisions, including fiscal decisions, shall be reached. This structure may be described in detail only by the complex rules and procedures governing the whole set of political institutions. This very complexity makes it incumbent on the theorist to abstract the essential elements of the structure, to simplify, and to construct models of political choice-making. With these models, he may then try to predict the characteristics of the outcomes that will emerge. Any realistic model will, of course, incorporate a political-decision rule that requires the assent of less than all members of the group. One such model is simple majority voting, a model that was introduced and discussed in Chapter 11. Under such an operative rule for reaching group decisions, what characteristics of final outcomes can be specified? Some analytically meaningful results can result from attempts to answer this question; the literature on the solutions to majority-rule games and on majority-coalition formation is relevant and important. Somewhat more restriction may be placed on the analysis of fiscal outcomes if additional constitutional constraints are imposed on the models. In addition to the majority-voting rule for making political choices, it is possible to fix the institution under which taxes are to be paid, through which public goods and services must be purchased. Through this dual set of institutional-constitutional restrictions, the outcomes of the fiscal choice process may be somewhat more narrowly circumscribed and the analysis made somewhat less general than in unconstrained majority-rule models. Only in Chapter 11 has this sort of theorizing been attempted in this book. The exploratory efforts there are presented more or less as lead-ins for further possible research. Both the rules for making political decisions and the institutions through which fiscal outcomes are produced are subject to wide variations, even within the framework of any existing political-fiscal order.

What results are to be expected from such theorizing? No model that allows for genuine individual choice can predict the precise outcomes that will emerge from a decision process, whether this be the private choice of a single person or the collective choice of a group of persons. The economist, the theorist of consumer's choice, cannot predict the mix of goods that a particular housewife will purchase in the market. Similarly, the fiscal theorist cannot predict the particular mix of public goods that will be chosen by a community of persons. But it may be useful to extend this comparison with the theory of consumer's choice somewhat further here. As suggested above, only under the somewhat rarified institutional assumptions imposed in the Wicksellian model can the outcome of the fiscal choice process be described by the familiar equalities among marginal rates of substitution. Under almost any remotely relevant institutional restrictions, the outcomes will tend to be nonoptimal in the Pareto sense. If the limits of theory are exhausted with the classification of particular outcomes into nonoptimal and optimal sets, there would be little purpose in the analysis of differing institutional structures. Something more than mere classification of outcomes within the nonoptimal set can be made. The various institutional combinations can be arrayed in terms of the predicted degree of "nonoptimality" of the outcomes that they are expected to produce over a whole sequence of separate decisions.

Our attention in this book is concentrated primarily on fiscal institutions, not on the institutions of political decision-making. The procedure suggested, therefore, is that of attempting to array alternative fiscal arrangements under each possible political decision structure. As an illustration, refer to the models introduced in Chapter 11. Assume the presence of simple majority voting for reaching all political decisions. The next step is that of comparing predicted outcomes under separate and alternative fiscal institutions. Compare, for example, the outcomes to be predicted under a head tax with those under a proportional income tax. Which of these series of outcomes seems to be "preferred" on efficiency criteria? The Pareto criteria can serve as the benchmarks from which possible departures are measured.

It is useful to recall that the choice of a tax institution can serve as a substitute for a decision-making institution and vice versa. Conceptually, in decisions on the appropriate quantity of a single public good, there will always exist some tax institution which will produce "optimal" outcomes, under *any and all* rules for reaching a collective decision. The more "efficient" the tax institution is in this sense, the less "inefficient" will be any given departure from unanimity in the political decision structure. This point was illustrated in some of the models developed and discussed in Chapter 11. If the tax institution should be such that each person is obligated to pay for public goods so that tax-prices equal the schedule of marginal benefits, any conceivable decision rule will yield the Pareto-optimal quantity of public goods. The fact that such a tax institution always exists conceptually does not, of course, imply that it can be determined independently of the revealed choices of individuals themselves. If an omniscient observer should be present, and if he were asked to "read" all individual preference maps, he could then describe the "optimal" structure of tax prices. Failing this, there is no means of ascertaining with any degree of accuracy the "efficient" tax structure or institution.

If the tax institution is not the "efficient" one, either because its selection cannot be made independently, or because nonefficiency criteria are also relevant, then the political decision rule can be important in determining the degree of efficiency in the outcomes that emerge. For example, if the tax rule states that all persons must pay equal taxes, then the delegation of political decision-making power to a single person produces less inefficiency than such a delegation would produce under no such tax restriction. The dictator's possible exploitation of his fellows is reduced by the requirement that he, like his fellows, must pay a share of the total tax load. Since, in the normal order of events, the tax institutions in existence will not approximate those that are "efficient," analysis must consider carefully the effects upon outcomes produced by various political decision rules. In this analysis no simple conclusions can be reached by trying to array alternative political institutions under separate fiscal arrangements. For example, suppose that the constitution dictates that all public goods shall be financed by equal taxes on all persons. It does not follow at all that the "efficient" decision rule, that of unanimity, will produce "optimal" results for any and all tax allocations. It seems obvious that unanimity in this case of equal taxes might be one of the worst of rules for reaching group decisions. There may exist some "efficient" decision rule in a regime of poll taxes, which an omniscient observer could specify, but it becomes extremely difficult to think of meaningful procedures through which such a rule could be independently discovered. For this reason, it seems preferable to consider the political decision rules as being, somehow, less subject to deliberate variation than the fiscal institutions.

The suggestion was made above that various fiscal institutions could be arrayed or ranked in terms of their predicted ability to produce "efficient" outcomes, these being defined in the standard Pareto fashion. This raises the whole question of norms once more. Is the suggested procedure not equivalent to reintroducing the economist's normative standard? If so, what has become of the model in which individuals are simply observed to choose what they will?

There is no paradox here when the proper relationship between the criteria of efficiency and individual choices is recognized. What does the economist mean by an "optimum allocation of resources"? He really means that allocation which is produced by the uninhibited interplay of private individual choices and nothing more. The extension to the supply of public goods is straightforward. An "efficient" public-goods provision is that which would tend to emerge from the "ideal" institutions of individual-collective choice. It becomes appropriate, therefore, to discuss various institutions in terms of their predicted tendencies to promote or to prevent the attainment of such outcomes. No external ethical norms concerning the actual shapes of these outcomes need be introduced at all in order that some institutions may be called "better" than others, by efficiency criteria. An analogy may be helpful. We may say that a clear windshield is "better" for driving an automobile than a dirty windshield, without any reference to where the driver wants to go. Given any route, he will drive "more efficiently" if he is able to see where he is going. Similarly, we may say that certain institutions are "better" than others, quite independently of the outcomes that will be produced. Whatever these may be, they are reached more efficiently under some institutions than under others.

The incorporation of the traditional equity norms into the individualistic model cannot be accomplished so readily. Some of these issues will be discussed in a later section. First, however, there is more to be said concerning efficiency.

THE CHOICE AMONG FISCAL INSTITUTIONS

For what purpose does the analyst array the various fiscal institutions in the procedure suggested above? Ultimately at some higher-stage or higher-level "constitutional" choice, individuals themselves must select the set of fiscal institutions, rules, and regulations, under which in-period budgetary choices shall be made. The vital distinction between fiscal choice under specified and preselected institutions and the choice among such institutions themselves cannot be overstressed, and a simple example may prove helpful even at the expense of repetition with earlier discussion. Consider a group of persons organized as a political community, and for simplicity think of the political constitution as having been fixed. But no fiscal constitution exists. The opportunity, or the necessity as the case may be, arises for some group outlay on a public good or service, say, defense against external enemies. The community, acting as a unit, must decide on how much of this public good to supply, and it must decide how the costs shall be distributed among the citizens. These two separate decisions are interdependent under any political choice rule. An individual's behavior in voting for public goods will be influenced by his predictions as to the tax allocation. As we have previously noted, it is in this setting that the "free rider" problem emerges to complicate and to confound fiscal decision-making.

One means of sharply reducing the investment in strategy and of generating directness in individual response is for the group to reach some agreement on how the tax costs shall be distributed among persons in advance of and independently of the decision on public-goods quantity. In our example, the community may approve a "fiscal constitution" even before any need or opportunity for spending on external defense is anticipated. This institutional or constitutional choice implies, of course, that some inefficiency in any final outcome as measured in public goods supply must be predicted as highly probable. In the example here, if the fiscal constitution agreed upon dictates that all public goods, including defense, must be financed from head taxes imposed equally on all citizens, the specific supply of defense in any particular period may diverge considerably from that which would be "optimal." Given sufficient investment in bargaining and discussion, some rearrangements of tax shares might be worked out that would enable the community to shift somewhat closer to the Paretian welfare surface in almost every particular case. When, however, it is recognized in advance that such rearrangements would have to be worked out for each separate public good or service supplied and in each separate time period, the costs of securing reasonably efficient outcomes may become prohibitive. Some structural adjustment in the direction of selecting tax allocations that determine individual cost shares (individual tax-prices) over a large basket of public goods and services and over a whole series of time periods may be individually and collectively rational.

Once this is recognized, the whole notion of "efficiency" is necessarily modified. An institution may well be "efficient," even though it is recognized that "inefficient" outcomes will be produced through its operation. The central question in institutional choice is that of selecting the most "efficient" institution. What scheme or rule for collecting taxes is relatively most efficient when the public goods to be supplied from the tax revenues remain wholly unspecified? As noted in Chapter 14, this shift to institutional choice seems partially to rehabilitate traditional fiscal theory and to justify a consideration of "tax principles" independently from the expenditure side of the fiscal account. Efficiency here must be discussed in terms of the probability distribution of outcomes that a tax institution is predicted to produce over a series of separate time periods and over a series of different benefit imputations.

A NEW APPROACH TO FISCAL JUSTICE

The methodology for the analysis of institutional efficiency is drawn from several sources: the modern theory of statistical inference, the theory of games, the theory of political constitutions, and, also, recent philosophical discussions of "justice."[3] This latter discussion is especially relevant since it allows us to relate the institutional choice approach to the tradtional discussion of justice or equity that has occupied so much of the fiscal literature. The methodology that embodies as its characteristic feature a sharp differentiation between the outcomes of a choice process and the rules or institutions that generate such outcomes is, of course, wholly different from the traditional approach in fiscal theory.

How will an individual choose among the alternative institutions of taxation? In an idealized position of choice here, the individual is uncertain both as to his own share of the benefits that might accrue from the spending programs that may be adopted and as to his own economic position (upon which taxes would presumably be based). In such a situation, he must try, as best he can, to choose an institution that will work tolerably well under almost any set of circumstances. The analogy with the choosing of rules for an ordinary game of poker is a close one. The individual will try to select rules that seem to be "fair." At this level of consideration, "fairness" and "efficiency" merge and come to mean the same thing. It seems also appropriate to use the word "justice" here, as Rawls has done in his discussion of ethical norms. In terms of some normative personal ethic, the individual "should" choose *as if* he is in such an idealized position, even if he is not, and the criteria for his decision can be summarized as those of "justice."

Our central concern is not, however, with the ethics of individual behavior, but rather with the prediction of behavior in institutional

3. Specifically, the reference here is to the concept of justice that is advanced in several recent papers by John Rawls. See Rawls, "Justice as Fairness," *Philosophical Review,* LXVII (April, 1958), 164-94; "Constitutional Liberty and the Concept of Justice," *Nomos VI,* ed. C. Friedrich and J. Chapman (New York: Atherton Press, 1963); and, somewhat earlier, "Two Concepts of Rules," *Philosophical Review,* LXIV (January, 1955), 3-32.

choice situations. Normally individuals will not find themselves in the idealized conditions. A person will probably have some idea as to the pattern of benefit imputations over time, and, even more probably, he will have some idea as to his own economic position in future periods. Nevertheless, it is not unreasonable to suggest that uncertainty elements in both respects loom relatively important in his decision calculus, and to the extent that they do so, it is appropriate to examine the notions of both "efficiency" and "justice" in the framework discussed here.

Theoretical welfare economics enables us to define the necessary marginal conditions that must be satisfied for an allocation of economic resources to be efficient. Straightforward extension of this analysis to "theoretical institutional economics" should enable us to define a similar set of conditions that would have to be met if an institutional arrangement or rule is to be classified as "efficient." It now seems quite possible that future developments will in fact allow for general statements of such conditions. At this time, however, we must be content with more ambiguous and less rigorous definitions. Analysis remains at the stage of examining various institutions under varying sets of assumptions, with criteria for efficiency being largely derived from introspection.

It was noted above that the criteria for "efficiency" and "justice" merge and become identical under the institutional choice approach, at least in its idealized form. This is, of course, sharply at variance with public finance orthodoxy, where these two objectives are distinct. "Equity" or "justice" has been traditionally held to require the introduction of external ethical norms. A long-standing principle of normative public finance theory has been that "equals should be treated equally," the principle that has been called one of "horizontal equity" by R. A. Musgrave.[4] Corollary to this, there has been the principle of vertical equity: "unequals should be treated unequally." But to what degree? This has remained the central issue in normative tax theory, and it has been resolved only upon the introduction of some external value scale, some "social welfare function" that is defined by the observer. Since individuals have no part in the formation of this scale, except as the observer chooses to take their preferences into account, the conceptual task of the analyst is simply that of "reading off" the solution that best achieves the indicated equity objective.

4. R. A. Musgrave, *The Theory of Public Finance* (New York: McGraw-Hill, 1959).

294

In its most modern formulation, represented in Musgrave's treatise, fiscal theory contains a paradox. The allocative function of the fiscal mechanism is sharply differentiated from the distributive function. In the former, individual choices are allowed to serve as the basic determinants of outcomes, at least in some normatively idealized sense. In the latter, however, resort to an external value scale is necessary. "Efficiency" criteria are derived from individual preferences; "equity" criteria are derived from external sources. Hence, efficiency and equity not only represent different and often conflicting objectives; they are also different philosophically, being derived ultimately from two quite distinct sets of values.

In the modified approach proposed here, these two sets of criteria become one, and both are derived from individual preferences. A fiscal institution that is efficient is also just, and vice versa, since these terms cannot be distinguished in the individual institutional choice context. The individual who is presumed to be making a choice among alternative fiscal institutions does so on the grounds of his own utility maximization. This insures that he will tend to select that institution or rule that he considers most efficient privately considered. But this institution will also tend to be that which is considered just for the simple reason that the individual cannot predict with accuracy his own position under the subsequent operation of the institution. He will be led to choose an institution that will treat him "fairly" or "justly" wherever he might find himself located.

To the extent that the individual's actual choice position is not that defined in the idealized model, the efficient fiscal instrument for him will not be that which would be observed to fulfill criteria for "justice." To the extent that the individual can predict with accuracy the future imputation of public benefits and/or his own income-wealth status, his utility maximization will lead him to select institutions that will provide differential advantages. As previously noted, and as will be discussed again below, it is the recognition that this conflict will arise which makes the importance of the conditions for institutional choice so important and points the way toward proposals for reform aimed at shifting these conditions.

THE REDISTRIBUTIVE FUNCTION

The two approaches, the orthodox or traditional one and that which has been partially developed in this book, may be compared in their treatment of the income-wealth distribution problem and its relationship to the fiscal mechanism. As suggested, the standard treatment here explicitly invokes external norms. For example, Henry Simons accepted "greater income equality" among individuals as a social objective that the fiscal system "should" be organized to promote. Modern works call on some "social welfare function" to determine the single most-desired point from among the infinite set of the Pareto welfare surface.

This resort to external norms is eschewed in the individualistic model. Is it then possible to say anything at all about the redistributive function of the fiscal mechanism? There are two separate levels of response to this question which must be kept distinct, again illustrating the relevance and importance of the two stages of fiscal choice that have been emphasized. If an individual's economic position is clearly identifiable, along with those of his fellows, and if a single one-period choice is confronted, he may, of course, choose to tax himself for the purpose of transferring income to those less fortunate than himself. In this sense, redistribution is a public good in the classical form, and there are evident externalities to be internalized by collectivizing the "consumption" of this good. Therefore, even in the purely individualistic model that is confined to single-period choice, some net redistribution would tend to be carried out by the fiscal system. The limits of this income transfer would be quite confined under normally expected circumstances, however, and this transfer would depend on the fact that individuals include the utility of others than themselves as arguments in their own utility functions.

Redistributional elements become much more important at the second or institutional level of fiscal choice. Under the idealized conditions, the individual cannot identify his own income-wealth prospects over time with accuracy. Hence the choice-maker should, raitonally, act as if he confronts a probability distribution of possible income-wealth positions, and he should select that fiscal structure that maximizes expected utility. It is easy to see that the individual might under these conditions build-in important elements of net income-wealth transfer, not because he pays any attention at all to the utility of his fellows, but simply because he wants to insure for himself a satisfactory post-fisc income level. There will surely exist some "optimal" degree of net redistribution, and this will tend to be considered in the individual's choice of a fiscal constitution under almost any political decision rule. It is to be expected, therefore, that net redistribution will characterize the operations of the fiscal constitution over time.[5] It is reasonable to suggest that this sort of calculus is helpful in "explaining" redistributional elements that are found in modern fiscal structures, perhaps even more helpful than the vaguely asserted notions of equalization presumed in the standard treatments.

DIRECTIONS FOR REFORM IN FISCAL STRUCTURE

The analysis of this book has been basically positive. The purpose has been that of predicting the effects of specific institutions upon fiscal choice and of predicting the types of institutions that might be selected. The discussion of the underlying efficiency norm was presented through its derivation from individual preferences rather than in the more usual shorthand conception which seems to imply that the criterion is independently discovered. The analysis does point toward general normative conclusions, however, and it is appropriate that some of these be outlined briefly in this section.

Given the complexities of modern budgets and the large numbers of individuals who hold membership in most governmental jurisdictions, it takes little or no theorizing to suggest that any attempt to attain efficiency in the supplying of each and every public good and service in each and every fiscal period would be economic as well as political folly. Public goods must be supplied within the context of a fiscal constitution, which is described as a quasi-permanent and quite complex set of institutions and rules that specify what tax instruments are to be employed and when and how, when public debt is to be issued, how budgets are to be made, etc. What must be sought for, realistically, in any reform, are "improvements" in this fiscal constitution. How can those elements that seem to produce inefficient results be eliminated and more efficient elements substituted?

The standard procedure is for the expert to place himself in the role of constitution-maker and to discuss the drawing up of the "ideal fiscal structure." This procedure remains possible, and the interpretation of justice-as-efficiency sketched above suggests that considerable material of interest might be developed in this fashion. Such an attempt would, however, probably be foredoomed to fail-

5. The problem of redistribution in the setting proposed here has been discussed in somewhat more detail in James M. Buchanan and Gordon Tullock, *The Calculus of Consent,* especially Chapter 13.

ure. No effectively democratic society would be disposed, nor should it be disposed, to turn over the remaking of its fiscal or political constitution to a single expert or to a body of experts.

Recognizing this, the student of the fiscal process can begin a less exciting but more productive task. He can try to suggest specific changes in the *ways in which individuals make constitutional choices* rather than changes in the choices that "should" be made. He can suggest modifications in the structure of choice itself that may lead individuals, through the political decision procedures, to choose more efficiently among alternative fiscal instruments. As noted, individuals will tend to equate efficiency with justice, properly interpreted, if they are confronted with institutional-constitutional choice in its idealized setting. It is possible in many circumstances to suggest changes which have the effects of placing individuals closer to such situations. The first requirement is that all genuinely constitutional changes (whether they be called this explicitly is largely irrelevant) should be treated by individuals as quasi-permanent or long-run changes. The most important single improvement in the fiscal system might well be the introduction of specific lags between decision and implementation along with the requirement that decisions, once made, must remain in force over some minimal period of time.

An illustrative example is provided in inheritance and estate taxation. In the standard discussion of fiscal reforms, merely to raise issues concerning this tax is to choose sides. And the choosing is not difficult. Those persons who identify themselves with favorable asset positions tend to argue persuasively against increases in and for reductions in such taxes. Those other persons who cannot or do not make this identification argue, with equal persuasiveness, that these taxes should be made confiscatory. The collective decision process becomes strictly analogous to a zero-sum game, and no reasoned discussion of an efficient or optimal scheme or asset-transfer taxation can possibly take place.

How may this state of affairs be improved? Surely not by the various experts posing as authorities and invoking time-honored principles to support their own personal preferences. The inference to be drawn is that changes in asset-transfer taxation cannot be discussed dispassionately so long as these are discussed as *current* changes. Therefore, the implication is that modifications in the structure of such taxes should, ideally, be discussed only with significant time lags between decision and action. Reasoned, and reasonable, discussion should be possible on the most efficient structure of asset-transfer taxation that would come into effect in, say, a quarter or a half-century after decision. Individuals who participate in the discussion on this basis will be unable to identify their own positions so clearly; their self-interest will be long-term. This proposal seems farfetched only because it has not been explicitly examined, although the familiar Rignano plan can be interpreted as a vague normative statement of the same idea.[6] This is presented here only as a simple and single example of the sort of reforms that might be expected to improve the choice among fiscal institutions. No exhaustive discussion of such reforms will be made here, and none is found in this book.

Time is, of course, the element that converts an interclass, intergroup decision into a reasoned one on which general agreement becomes possible. Different time lags may be appropriate for different institutions. Time has rarely been treated as a variable by economists, yet it seems evident that the temporal characteristics of a decision can have a major impact on the manner in which individual decision-makers evaluate and choose among alternatives. Everything is variable in the long run, including the individual's own economic position and the pattern of benefit imputation from public spending programs. The individual who may be quite eager to support a temporary one-year tax on new automobile purchases to finance a one-year subsidy to a world's fair in his home city, may be quite reluctant to support a permanent tax on new car purchases to finance annual world's fairs in a series of cities.

THE CONSTITUTIONAL ATTITUDE

The effective operation of democratic government, in its fiscal as well as its nonfiscal aspects, requires the adherence of its citizens to what may be called the "constitutional attitude." Given the high cost of making collective decisions, government can function properly only if a large proportion of its day-to-day operations take place within a quasi-permanent constitutional structure. Individuals, and groups, must recognize the importance of constitutional-institutional continuity, and the dependence of democratic process on firm adherence to such continuity. If this is not recognized, and

6. Cf. E. Rignano, *The Social Significance of the Inheritance Tax,* trans. W. J. Shultz (New York: Alfred A. Knopf, 1924).

if individuals come to consider governmental processes as nothing more than available means through which separate coalitions can exploit each other, democracy cannot, and should not, survive. Fiscal institutions are a part of the political constitution, broadly considered, and especially in the sense noted here. Changes in the fiscal constitution must be treated as quasi-permanent and long-lasting features of the social structure. If individuals, and groups, including politicians, come to consider seriously the possibility of manipulating basic fiscal institutions for the accomplishment of short-run-purposes, bargaining elements will quickly swamp all efficiency considerations.

In the final analysis, "justice," "efficiency," "fairness," whichever term is employed, can be expected with a reasonable degree of certainty only when individuals (or their representatives) are placed in the position of choosing for themselves, not as instant, momentary beings, but as a whole complex probability distribution of potentialities. To expect the poker player with a pat hand to agree to a new deal is to place entirely too much dependence on human ethics. The rules of the game, political or otherwise, may properly be drawn up only in advance of play, and by the players themselves. And, as play proceeds, rules should be changed to apply only to later rounds of play.

In fiscal theory, as in politics generally, scholars need to pay more attention to the working out of rules or institutions through which final outcomes emerge and less attention to the shape of these outcomes themselves although these must, of course, be relevant to an evaluation of the institutions. Improved allocations, or outcomes, can be achieved only through improvements in the institutions that generate them, and improvements in such institutions, in turn, can be achieved only if their proper role in the whole structure of democratic process is appreciated and understood. Perhaps more than their fellows, scholars themselves need to acquire a "constitutional attitude."

Index of Authors

Index of Subjects

Ability-to-pay principle, 157-58

Altruism, 198

Asymmetry, between tax and expenditure analysis, 95-96

Averaging, in personal income tax, 142

Awareness of benefits of public expenditure, 189-94

Awareness of taxes, 185, 188; of high-income taxpayers of marginal rates, 186; under indirect taxation, 186-88; under specific excise taxes, 187; distinction from estimates of taxes, 188-89

Balanced-budget rule, 103, 106; at full employment, 110-11; institutional choice of, 268

Benefits of public expenditure, directness in, 189-91; awareness of, 189-94

Bias, due to differences in capitalization, 68-70

Borrowing, use of to finance budget deficit, 99-104

Bridge, between tax and expenditure decisions, 88-97, 115-16

Budget, general fund, composition of, 82-83; unbalanced, and fiscal choice, 98-112; government, and fiscal illusion, 136. *See also* Balanced-budget rule

Budgetary ratio, in general fund financing, 76, 78-79

Burden of tax payments, 252

Capital budgeting, 266

Capital gains taxation, 142-43

Capital investment, conditions for public outlay for, 264-66

Capitalization, of taxes on wealth, 29; of taxes, and multi-period fiscal choice, 66-70; of benefits of public expenditures, 67-70; of taxes, and public debt, 132-33, 264-66

Choice calculus, of individual in selecting fiscal institutions, 214, 291-93; relevance of analysis of, 220-21; progressive income tax and, 225-40; specific excise tax and, 241-55; public debt and, 256-66; fiscal policy and, 267-79

Choice calculus, of taxpayer in voting for public goods, 12-14, 172-73, 214; under proportional income tax, 36-38; under progressive income tax, 39-43; under corporation income tax, 49-51; under general sales tax, 51-53; under specific excise tax, 53-55; when tax and expenditure decisions are separate, 91-97; effect of public debt issue on, 100-3; effect of currency creation on, 107-8; effect of uncertainty on, 108-9; effect of functional finance on, 109-10

Closed economy, fiscal policy in, 268-70

Collective choice, theory of, 3-5; relationship of individual behavior to, 173-80

Collective decision models, 144-57; of three equal persons, 145-46; of three persons with unequal evaluations of public good, 147-49; of three persons with equal evalua-

303